WRITTEN AND INTERPERSONAL COMMUNICATION

Methods for Law Enforcement

FOURTH EDITION

HARVEY WALLACE, J.D.
Deceased

CLIFF ROBERSON, L.L.M., Ph.D.
Professor Emeritus
Washburn University
Topeka, Kansas

PEARSON
Prentice
Hall

Upper Saddle River, New Jersey
Columbus, Ohio

Library of Congress Cataloging-in-Publication Data

Wallace, Harvey.
Written and interpersonal communication : methods for law enforcement / Harvey Wallace, Cliff Roberson.—4th ed.
    p. cm.
Includes index.
ISBN-13: 978-0-13-159719-8
ISBN-10: 0-13-159719-1
1. Communication in police administration. 2. Communication in law enforcement. 3. Interpersonal communication. I. Roberson, Cliff, 1937- II. Title.
HV7936.C79W35 2009
363.201'4—dc22   2007029639

Vice President and Executive Publisher: Vernon R. Anthony
Senior Acquisitions Editor: Tim Peyton
Editorial Assistant: Alicia Kelly
Project Manager: Maren L. Miller
Design Coordinator: Diane Y. Ernsberger
Cover Designer: Bryan Huber
Cover Image: Getty One
Senior Operations Supervisor: Pat Tonneman
Director of Marketing: David Gesell
Marketing Manager: Adam Kloza
Marketing Coordinator: Alicia Dysert

This book was set in Times Roman by Aptara. It was printed and bound by R.R. Donnelley & Sons Company. The cover was printed by R.R. Donnelley & Sons Company.

Pearson Education Ltd.   Pearson Education Australia Pty. Limited
Pearson Education Singapore Pte. Ltd.   Pearson Education North Asia Ltd.
Pearson Education Canada, Ltd.   Pearson Educación de Mexico, S.A. de C.V.
Pearson Education—Japan   Pearson Education Malaysia Pte. Ltd.

10 9 8 7 6
ISBN 13: 978-0-13-159719-8
ISBN 10:   0-13-159719-1

To Paul Harvey Wallace 1945–2007
"Harvey" Wallace, co-author, died on June 28, 2007.
We worked together for 16 years and wrote ten books.
He was a fellow marine and a longtime friend—I will miss him.

Contents

Preface

The success of the first three editions has provided us with the opportunity to improve the text. With differing backgrounds in the criminal justice system, we combined our experience in writing this text. I have experience as a defense attorney, and Harvey is a former prosecutor and city attorney. Our varied backgrounds provide the reader with a broad-based approach to communication in the law enforcement profession.

The main purpose of this book is to improve your communication skills, both oral and written. A secondary purpose is to improve your ability to complete the reports and forms commonly used in the criminal justice system. The best way to improve communication skills is by practicing these skills correctly. Practice alone, however, does not make perfect, only correct practice does. Throughout this text, we asked you to read background material, work through exercises, correct improper English, and refine your skills. Many instructors who have used the previous editions have requested the inclusion of actual police reports. Unfortunately, because of page limitations, including numerous actual police reports in the text was impossible. To remedy this problem, we have added a CD to the text. The CD contains police reports taken from various cases and guidelines published by various police departments for writing search warrants. The CD also contains other actual police documents and instructional material, providing the reader with more glimpses of the real world.

At the end of most chapters is a section entitled "Rules for Improvement." In these sections, we review English grammar rules and give other writing improvement tips. In several chapters, we also include checklists for the various types of communication necessary for criminal justice professionals. If you follow our recommendations and the procedures contained in this text, your oral and written communications skills both should improve. A new chapter on the art of communicating with victims and increased coverage on making speeches have been added to this edition.

We wish to thank the following reviewers for their comments: Ellen Cohn, Florida International University; Beverly Strickland, Fayetteville Technical Community College, North Carolina; Thomas Whetstone, University of Louisville, Kentucky; James E. Newman, Rio Hondo Community College, California; Kelly A. Wetzler, Remington College, Colorado; Ray Yand, ITT Technical Institute, California; Thomas J. Mason, Remington College, Arizona. A special thanks to Chief Craig Steckley, Chief of Police, Fremont, California, who was a coauthor on the first two editions. His duties and responsibilities prevented him from assisting us on this edition. Dedicated individuals like Craig help keep our country great. We would be remiss unless we expressed our appreciation to Margaret Lannamann, who corrected our grammar and rewrote our sentences on this project and several others. Thanks again, Margaret. We also express our appreciation to the law enforcement professionals and agencies who supplied material and/or comments that assisted us in preparing this text.

In this edition, we have rewritten a good portion of the material. Many of the ideas for revision came from users of the previous editions who shared their comments with us.

Register today at www.prenhall.com to access instructor resources digitally.

Online Instructor's Resources
To access supplementary materials online, instructors need to request an instructor access code. Go to **www.prenhall.com**, click the **Instructor Resource Center** link, and then click **Register Today** for an instructor access code. Within 48 hours after registering you will receive a confirming e-mail including an instructor access code. Once you have received your code, go to the site and log on for full instructions on downloading the materials you wish to use.

Corrections, suggestions for improvement, and other comments may be submitted to cliff.roberson@washburn.edu.

Cliff Roberson

CHAPTER 1

The Need for Effective Communication

LEARNING OBJECTIVES

After reading this chapter, you should understand the following concepts:

■ Why the ability to communicate effectively is critical to law enforcement officers

■ The importance of communicating with members of and groups within the community

INTRODUCTION

Man does not live by words alone, despite
the fact that sometimes he has to eat them.
— ADLAI STEVENSON

People take communication for granted. Reading this text is one form of communication. Taking a written examination on the text material is a second form. Asking a friend to go for a cup of coffee after class is a third. In all these examples, the goal is to transfer an idea from one location to another. One authority noted that 70 percent of our time is spent communicating.[1] Even with the prominence of communication in everyday functions, however, little, if any, study of communication techniques is required in high schools, colleges, and police academies. In this chapter, we provide an overview of the role of oral and written communication in a law enforcement agency, and we explain some of the dynamics of communicating with others.

We are all familiar with the old adage that "talk is cheap." Often, however, talk is absolutely worthless. We have phrases that describe this phenomenon. For example, we may engage in "idle chatter" or "jabber." Effective communications, in contrast, is like using a map. You know there is a certain route that will take you where you want to go, but you also know that dead ends and wrong turns may delay your getting to your destination. As a cardinal rule, do not assume that everything you say is clearly understood. Understand also that hearing is not the same as understanding, and without understanding there is no effective communications.

The following are barriers to effective communications:

- Language—many, at best, words are vague. For example, you ask for information regarding a case and state that you need it soon. "Soon" may mean an hour to one person and a week to another.
- Distraction—it can be external or internal. It can also be insidious. One common external distraction is noise, for example, the audible hum of an air conditioner or the ring of a cell phone. An example of internal distraction may be that your listener is hungry and cannot give you his or her undivided attention.
- False assumptions—often the receiver assumes that he or she knows everything about the subject and so does not listen with an open mind.

Communicating is essentially a mental exercise that needs to be mastered. Communicating is, at its best, a mutual service, benefitting both the sender and the receiver. Keep in mind that hearing is not necessarily understanding and talking is not necessarily communicating.

THE NEED TO STUDY REPORT WRITING

The following excerpts are from police reports, many of which were sergeant approved.

Prieto threatened that Bach was going to hers and the police were going to charged also.

They put the victim on a heart monitor and received a negative heatbeat.

Capt. Crane showed me the locatioon of the victim's location.

Rp said the victim was pronunced dead by himself at 0200 hrs today.

The rear driver's side tire was flat but I could not find an entry or exit wound through the tire.

Not only do some police officers have difficulty writing a simple sentence, but their spelling can cause laughter or professional embarrassment. Some words taken from police reports[2] follow:

Report/Interpretation

Wipelash/Whiplash	Hart/Heart
Aroda/Aorta	Pregnate/Pregnant
Trouma/Trauma	Stapping/Stabbing
Decease/Disease	

As the preceding examples indicate, report writing—and therefore spelling—is a major part of any law enforcement officer's duties. Reports are read by fellow officers, supervisors, and other professionals in the field. If you have not yet mastered the English language and spelling, now is the time to start. As a professional, you will be using them for the rest of your career.

In this text, and specifically in this chapter, we review the importance of communication in a law enforcement environment. Simply reading and understanding this material will not make you a more effective communicator. Anyone can improve his or her ability to communicate, either orally or in writing. Doing so, however, requires constant attention and hard work. In this chapter, we set forth certain basic principles that apply to all forms of communication and explain why police officers must be able to communicate appropriately in many situations.

THE IMPORTANCE OF COMMUNICATION

Communication, oral or written, is especially critical in a law enforcement agency. The mission of any police department is to apprehend law violators. Apprehension, however, is only the first step in the criminal justice system. Once a suspect has been arrested, a series of steps and occurrences follow: booking the suspect; performing follow-up investigations; submitting arrest information to local, state, and national databases; and, finally, testifying in court about the arrest. Members of police departments must also be able to communicate internally regarding procedures and policies that affect their operation. Likewise, the ability of law enforcement officers to communicate externally to groups or individuals within the community is crucial.

Communication within a Law Enforcement Environment

In this text, we emphasize report writing as the major form of communication within a police agency. All law officers, however, from rookies to law enforcement administrators, must master several types of writing skills. Arrest reports, follow-up investigation paperwork, memorandums, standard operating procedure literature, and promotion tests are a few common types of written communication involved in the day-to-day operation of a police department.

Writing is not the only form of information transfer within a law enforcement agency, however. Oral communication is equally important in many situations. Oral expression covers the entire spectrum of the communication process. It starts when officers greet one another before roll call and continues through roll call and out onto the streets. In Chapter 2, we discuss the oral communication process in more detail.

As mentioned, all officers, from the least experienced to the chief, must be proficient in the art of communication. Such proficiency includes the ability to express oneself orally or in writing. The new officer must understand how to communicate with citizens, fellow officers, and superiors. The sergeant must be able to transmit orders to subordinates and receive commands from superiors. Even the top law enforcement administrators must have effective communication skills, whether they are preparing departmental policy statements, responding to the media, or defending the department's budget to elected officials.

Clearly, communication skills are critical within a law enforcement agency. These skills include the ability to read, write, and understand what is written, as well as to orally transmit and receive information.

The communication process occurs not only within the agency, but also outside the agency. All officers must be able to communicate effectively with members of the community they serve.

Communication within the Community

Most students have no difficulty discussing classes or current events among themselves in an informal environment. Many of these same students, however, become paralyzed with fear at the thought of standing up in class to explain a theory or a position. The ability to communicate in public forums is an important aspect of law enforcement. Community support and police involvement in the community are critical aspects of any successful law enforcement program.[3] In other chapters, we address specific techniques that allow law enforcement officers to effectively transmit important information within the community. The purpose of this section is to introduce you to the concept of the community and its interaction with law enforcement.

At the local or municipal level, the chief of police is usually appointed by either the city manager or the mayor. The city manager serves at the pleasure of the mayor or the city council, which, consisting of local elected officials, reacts to pressure from the community. In most jurisdictions, the sheriff is elected by citizens of the county. Therefore, the sheriff will be interested in staying in touch with members of the community. In addition, the concept of community policing is sweeping the United States, and many agencies now want to form partnerships with local communities to battle crime. All these factors make understanding how to communicate effectively with the population of any municipality imperative for law enforcement officers.

This communication takes different forms and works on many levels. The most basic form involves one-on-one communication between an officer and a citizen. The citizen may be a victim, a witness, or a perpetrator. The dynamics of this type of communication naturally will vary depending on the citizen's status.

Another common form of communication within the community involves officers' speaking before local groups. These groups may include school organizations, service clubs, constituents of local elected officials, and college classes. In these settings, the officer provides information to the various groups.

Law enforcement officers also pass on information within the community through the local media. This form of communication reaches a large audience and in some situations is instantaneous, as in the case of a live newscast.

Many other forms of communication exist in our society. Therefore, all members of law enforcement agencies must recognize the need to perfect their skills and to be prepared to communicate on a variety of levels.

WRITTEN COMMUNICATION TECHNIQUES

This section is included to allow you to begin using these rules and techniques immediately. An understanding of the English language and basic grammar is a necessity in law enforcement. Unfortunately, administrators of colleges, universities, and police academies assume that all students can write at a basic, understandable level. Specific English grammar courses may be required in various institutions, but, like any learned ability, unless writing is practiced, the skill achieved soon lapses. This text is not a grammar or English language book. Certain basic rules, however, if learned, memorized, and used, will help police officers avoid mistakes in report writing. At the end of each chapter is a more comprehensive guide to writing. Some of the more-basic techniques are discussed next.

RULES FOR IMPROVEMENT

Rules of Capitalization

In effect, a capital, or uppercase, letter highlights a word and points out its prominence. Rather than attempting to memorize the complex rules involved in capitalization, you can become a more effective writer if you understand a few general principles underlying the capitalization of words:[4]

- The first word of any sentence or direct quotation is capitalized.
  This officer approached the suspect. The suspect stated, "I didn't do it."
- The names of specific places and regions are capitalized.

New York	Chicago	San Francisco
the North	Lake Superior	Hawaiian Islands
a city	to fly north a lake	an island

- Do not capitalize the names of seasons or compass directions.
  fall   north   southwest
- Capitalize references to family relationships when such references are used as part of a proper name.
  aunt   Aunt Mary
- Names of organizations and their members are capitalized.
  Charleston Police Department   Catholics

- Names of ethnic groups, races, and nationalities are capitalized.
  African American   Hispanic   Caucasian
- Names of days, months, and holidays are capitalized.
  Monday   June   New Year's Day
- Capitalize the title of a person when the title is used as part of a proper name. Normally titles are not capitalized when used alone.
  Dr. Whiter   Chief Brown   the chief   the doctor   victim Jones
- Capitalize the first letter of a sentence enclosed in parentheses when the parenthetical text is not part of another sentence. Do not capitalize the first letter enclosed if the parenthetical material is part of another sentence.
  The chief asked for more overtime. (He does this at every meeting.)
  Joe's rank is chief (although some persons erroneously refer to him as *colonel*).
- Capitalize the first, last, and all major words in a title.
- Capitalize a common noun or adjective forming an essential part of a proper name.
  Fourth Street   Oak Lane
- Derivatives of proper names are capitalized.
  Roman (of Rome)   Italian
- Capitalize a common noun used alone as a well-known short form of a specific proper name.
  The Capitol building in Washington, DC

Frequently Confused Words

Many words in the English language are confusing, especially those that sound alike.[5] Following are fourteen common examples.

1. *Accept* and *except*
   Accept means "to receive" or "to give approval."
   Except means "to exclude" or "to leave out an item."

2. *All right* and *alright*
   All right is correct; *alright* is incorrect.

3. *Affect* and *effect*
   Affect means "to influence."
   Effect means "to bring about" (verb) or "a result" (noun).
   We want to *affect* a major change.
   What was the principal *effect* of the Law Enforcement Administration Agency (LEAA)?

4. *Among* and *between*
   Among is used with three or more.
   Between is used with two.
   The loot was split *among* the twelve thieves.
   The loot was split *between* the two thieves.

5. *Amount* and *number*

Amount is used for things that cannot be counted.
Number is used for things that can be counted.
The *amount* of work left at the crime scene was enormous.
The *number* of dead bodies keeps increasing.

6. *Credible* and *creditable*

Credible means "believable."
Creditable means "reputable."

7. *Disinterested* and *uninterested*

Disinterested means "free from selfish motives."
Uninterested means "not interested" or "unconcerned."

8. *Eminent* and *imminent*

Eminent means "well known."
Imminent means "about to happen."

9. *Farther* and *further*

Farther is used when people are speaking of distance.
Further is used when people are referring to extent or degree.

10. *In* and *into*

In means and is used to signify a place.
Into means and signifies an action.
The document is *in* the safe.
The suspect went *into* the house.

11. *Infer* and *imply*

Infer means "to conclude."
Imply means "to suggest."
I *infer* from the report that we need additional officers.
Do you mean to *imply* that the butler did it?

12. *Its* and *it's*

Its is a possessive pronoun.
It's is a contraction of *it is.*
The food lost *its* flavor.
It's a hectic holiday schedule.

13. *Lie* and *lay*

Lie means "to be at rest or inactive."
Lay means "to place something."
Please *lie* down until you feel better.
Please *lay* the weapon on the bench.

14. *Your* and *you're*

Your means "of or relating to you."
You're is a contraction of *you are.*
Is this *your* report?
You're spending too much time in *your* patrol vehicle.

Words That Can Be Left Out[6]

Many times, superfluous words can be eliminated from people's writing. Two such examples follow.

1. *There,* unless it is the subject, can usually be left out.
Weak: There will be three officers attending the opening.
Better: Three officers will be attending the opening.

2. *That, which,* and *who* can be left out unless a misunderstanding would result.
Weak: The sergeant thinks that shorter sentences are more effective.
Better: The sergeant thinks shorter sentences are more effective.
Weak: The union agreement that we signed runs for five years.
Better: The union agreement we signed runs for five years.
Weak: Mary Smith, who is my neighbor, saw the crime.
Better: Mary Smith, my neighbor, saw the crime.

Intensives[7]

Can a person be a little dead? The answer is no. Some words should not be intensified. Adding intensive words may cause embarrassment in a courtroom. Consider the following two examples.

1. Do not overuse the word *very*.
Weak: The subject was very pregnant.
Better: The subject was pregnant.

2. Be careful with the word *definitely*.
Weak: That statement is definitely incorrect.
Better: That statement is incorrect.

Repetition

Repeating words that mean the same thing shows a lack of direction. Words should be repeated only for emphasis. Note the following five unnecessary repetitions.

1. *Each*
Weak: Each and every
Better: Each

2. *Foremost*
Weak: First and foremost
Better: Foremost

3. *Only*
Weak: One and only
Better: Only

4. *Total*
Weak: Total and complete
Better: Total

5. *Near*
Weak: Close proximity
Better: Near

Spelling[8]

Spelling is not a mysterious science that only selected individuals can master. It is a simple mechanical act. You must, however, want to learn to spell correctly. Correct spelling takes energy and concentration. With so many other important things going on in life, correct spelling is often given low priority.

Correct spelling is important for a peace officer for at least two reasons. First, it saves time and embarrassment. The patrol officer does not like having spelling mistakes in a simple report corrected by the duty sergeant. Second, sharp defense attorneys will be more than helpful at pointing out mistakes in a report during a jury trial. Rather than listing a series of commonly misspelled words that can be memorized, we provide the following six dos and don'ts of spelling for review.

1. For words ending in *e* preceded by a consonant, omit the *e* before adding a suffix that begins with a vowel.

Slope	ing	Sloping
Please	ing	Pleasing
Observe	ing	Observing

2. Except for the word *science, i* goes before *e* except after *c.*

Receive	Conceive	Perceive

3. When adding prefixes to roots, do not omit letters.

Mis	spell	Misspell
Over	rule	Overrule
Room	mate	Roommate

4. Six words end in *-ery;* the rest end in *-ary.*

Millinery	Confectionery	Stationery (paper)
Monastery	Cemetery	Distillery

5. Note every word you have to look up in the dictionary. Understand its meaning and memorize its spelling.

6. Learn how to pronounce words so that you can spell them.

No easy rules can be adopted to avoid grammatical mistakes or misspellings. Simple concentration and hard work are the keys to success in this area of writing. The reward is less time spent redrafting simple reports and multipage documents.

SUMMARY

The ability to communicate effectively is a requirement for all law enforcement officers. Police officers interact with different groups daily and must be able to communicate effectively with each. Communication plays an important role in law officers' personal and professional lives.

Communication involves both oral and written methods. Law enforcement personnel must be proficient in both forms of communication. Police officers must be able to communicate effectively within their agency and outside the agency to members of the community they serve. Both forms of communication are critical to a well-functioning law enforcement agency.

The old adage "Practice makes perfect" is especially applicable to the communication process. Law enforcement personnel should attempt to improve their communication skills daily. Learning simple rules of capitalization and other techniques that are used in written communication will make an officer a more effective member of the agency.

REVIEW QUESTIONS

1. Which form of communication, oral or written, is most important in each of the following situations? Justify your answers.
   a. To the patrol officer on a beat
   b. To the captain in charge of the Records Division
   c. To the chief
   d. To the prosecutor
   e. To the citizen who is a victim of a crime
2. Who should be responsible for correcting mistakes in a police report?
   a. The officer who makes the mistake
   b. The officer's supervisor
   c. The prosecutor who tries the case
3. If you were advising a rookie on the importance of grammar and spelling and could state only one rule, what would it be?

PRACTICAL APPLICATIONS

1. If you discovered a grammatical mistake in your sergeant's report, how would you handle the situation in the following cases?
   a. If the sergeant was your supervisor
   b. If the sergeant was a peer
   c. If you supervised the sergeant
2. Review a classmate's notes from another class. Do these notes give you a clear picture of what occurred in the class? List your reasons and ask the classmate whether he or she agrees with you.
3. Circle the correctly spelled word in each of the following rows.

abandon	abandan	abondon	abonden
abaord	abord	aboard	aboarde
absenca	absence	absenc	absance
backward	bardward	backard	backword
bialliff	bailliff	bailiff	balift
barbiturate	barbutrate	bardutirade	barbiturete
cafeteria	cafteria	cafetiria	cafetiria
calcalute	calcaulate	calcarute	calculate
calendar	callander	calander	callender
damage	demage	damege	dameage

4. Rewrite the following sentences as needed.
   a. The amount of dead bodies found at the scene kept increasing.

   _____

   b. We had four dollars between the three of us.

   _____

   c. The officer excepted the package from the mail carrier.

   _____

   d. His conduct was designed to effect the voting patterns of hispanics.

   _____

   e. Its a cold day in june when the snow is still on the ground.

   _____

5. Define and explain the following words, concepts, or terms.
   a. communications

   _____

   b. intensives

   _____

   c. external communications

   _____

   d. report writing

   _____

6. The following paragraph was taken from a police report. Make it a better paragraph.

   This officer responded to the location of the parking lot of Von's and upon arrival oberserved two male subjects facing each other as if they wanted to fight. This officer exited the police vehicle and upon doing so subject Wolson turned and ran eastbound through the alley. At this time this officer responded to subject Hamm who was standing at the location and this officer yelled at subject Wolson to freeze and to return to this officer.

   _____
   _____
   _____
   _____
   _____
   _____
   _____

ENDNOTES

1. David K. Beryl, *The Process of Communications* (New York: Holt, Rinehart & Winston, 1960), 12.
2. Source: Sgt. Pie, "Police Stories Unabashed . . . and Unedited," *The Kopout* (November/December 1991): 10.
3. John Gnagey and Ronald Henson, "Community Surveys Help Determine Police Strategies," *Police Chief* (March 1995): 25.
4. See Arthur H. Bell and Roger J. Wyse, *The One-Minute Business Writer* (Homewood, Ill.: Dow Jones–Irwin, 1987), 128; Donna

Gorrell, *A Writer's Handbook from A to Z* (Boston: Allyn & Bacon, 1994); and Diana Hacker, *Rules for Writers,* 4th ed. (Boston: Bedford/St. Martin's, 2000), 34.

5. *The New York Times Everyday Reader's Dictionary of Misunderstood, Misused, and Mispronounced Words,* ed. Laurence Urdang (New York: Weathervane Books, 1992), 184.

6. See Laura Brill, *Business Writing Quick & Easy,* 2d ed. (New York: American Management Association, 1981), 12.

7. William Zinsser, *Writing to Learn* (New York: Harper & Row, 1988), 81.

8. Bell and Wyse, *The One-Minute Business Writer,* 131.

CHAPTER 2

Oral versus Written Communication

LEARNING OBJECTIVES

After reading this chapter, you should understand the following concepts:

■ The process of communication

■ The different types of channels and directions of communication

■ The basic elements of writing

INTRODUCTION

Every word that you write in your report, you must be able to justify in a court of law.
— VETERAN PROSECUTOR TO A ROOKIE COP

The preceding quotation is one that every officer should remember when he or she picks up a pen or sits down at a computer to fill out a police report. A police officer must be able to explain why the report was written as filed, justify any omissions, and testify from the contents of the report in a court of law. Testifying in court combines both written and oral communication skills. Testifying, however, is only a small part of a law enforcement officer's duties. A professional must master written and oral communication skills to effectively carry out the diverse duties that are encountered by officers in any modern police agency.

A document published by the U.S. Navy states that communicating is essentially a mental maze to be mastered. To improve it we must become more aware of the proper paths to take and the dead ends to avoid. Poor communications is a waste of everyone's time and energy and, in reality, there is no excuse for it. According to the Navy document, barriers to effective communication can exist only in an atmosphere of apathy and, with common sense, can usually be dealt with successfully.[1]

Oral communication skills are necessary to talk with members of the general public, request assistance from other officers, advise suspects of their *Miranda* rights, and inform supervisors that certain actions have occurred. In addition, oral skills are needed for officers to understand and transmit statements made by citizens, suspects, and superiors.

Written communication skills are required for law officers to fill out various police reports, draft narrative summaries, and understand written policy directives.[2] Written reports are the basis for recalling past events, and police officers rely on them daily when they testify in court. The ability to write in a clear and concise manner does not come naturally. Like any activity, it must be practiced until it is mastered. Once mastered, this skill must continually be used or it will become unfocused and useless. A professional athlete spends hours each day honing the skills necessary to participate in a sport. Police officers, however, may spend less than 10 percent of any shift writing reports about their activity.

All police officers, from rookies to chiefs, must be able to speak, listen, write, and understand. The ability to effectively communicate orally does not eliminate the need for writing. Conversely, effective writing does not eradicate the requirement for good oral communication skills. These skills are intertwined and dependent on each other. Effective police officers acquire, maintain, and continually sharpen both skills. Oral communication is the foundation on which written skills are built.

Communication Defined

The communication process is both a simple and a complex series of events. So that you can properly understand this process, the term *communication* must be defined. The definition of "communication" has concerned scholars since the time of ancient Greece. The authors of one text stated that at least 94 definitions of *communication* exist.[3]

English literary critic and author I. A. Richards in 1928 offered one of the first—and in some ways still the best—definitions of communication as a discrete aspect of human enterprise:

> Communication takes place when one mind so acts upon its environment that another mind is influenced, and in that other mind an experience occurs which is like the experience in the first mind, and is caused in part by that experience.

While Richards's definition is both general and rough, its application to nearly all kinds of communication—including those between humans and animals—separated the contents of messages from the processes in human affairs by which these messages are transmitted.[4]

Regardless of which definition you choose, it encompasses the following three elements:

1. It is a process, not an isolated event.
2. It involves at least two persons.
3. Its primary purpose is the exchange of information.

Communication can thus be defined as "a process involving several steps, among two or more persons, for the primary purpose of exchanging information." In the following sections, we discuss this process and explain the different directions or channels through which information is processed.

A communication is susceptible to considerable modification and mediation. Entropy distorts, whereas negative entropy and redundancy clarify. As each of these types of modification and mediation occurs differently in the communication process, the chances of the communication being received and correctly understood vary.

Entropy and Negative Entropy

Entropy originally was considered as a noise source by Claude Shannon, but was later associated with the principle of entropy derived from physics, which has been imposed on the communication model. In most communication entropy is analogous to audio or visual static—that is, to outside influences that diminish the integrity of the communication and, possibly, distort the message for the receiver. Negative entropy occurs in instances in which messages, although incomplete or blurred, are nevertheless received intact. It occurs because of the ability of the receiver either to fill in missing details or to recognize, despite distortion or a paucity of information, both the intent and content of the communication.

Redundancy

Redundancy is the repetition of elements within a message. It prevents the failure of communication of information and is considered to be the greatest antidote to entropy. Most written and spoken statements, for example, are roughly half-redundant. For example, if 50 percent of the words of an article were to be taken away at random, an intelligible message would still remain. Similarly, if we hear only half the words of a radio news commentator, we usually understand the broadcast. Redundancy occurs in most human activities. Because it helps to overcome the various forms of entropy that turn intelligible messages into unintelligible ones, it is an indispensable element for effective communication.

How the Process Occurs

In this section, we examine how the process of communication takes place and explain the three elements of the communication process.

Communication Is a Process, Not an Isolated Event

Some authorities believe as many as seven distinct steps compose the communication process.[5] For simplicity, however, we will break down the flow of information into five basic steps. Communication requires (1) transmitting an idea, (2) sending the idea through a medium, (3) receiving the message, (4) understanding the idea, and (5) providing feedback to the message sender. If a failure occurs during any of these five steps, the communication process becomes flawed, and information will not flow in a smooth, accurate manner.

Transmitting an idea   This step implies the formation of one or several thoughts and the desire to express these ideas. Every day, people have thoughts that are better left unsaid, but they act on these thoughts anyway—even though expressing these thoughts, or the reason for certain actions, to another person might be inappropriate.

For example, a fellow officer might have a bad body odor. In such a situation, another officer might express his or her feelings, either in a joking manner or otherwise: "Boy, I can tell you love garlic on your bread; I can still smell it this morning. Why didn't you bring me some?" This kind of message, coupled with the act of moving away from your partner, is an expression that has been transmitted and acted on.

In contrast, you might simply move away and not express any offense if the person is unknown to you or you are uncomfortable communicating sensitive thoughts or ideas. Therefore, for communication to occur, an idea must be formed and an intentional act must take place to transmit that idea to another person.

Sending the idea through a medium   Once a message is formed, it must be sent. There are many ways to transmit ideas: orally, in writing, or by action. Everyone understands the difference between an oral reprimand and a written reprimand that is made a permanent part of an officer's personnel file. The same information can be conveyed by either medium; however, a written reprimand is considered more grave than an oral reprimand. By the same token, written memorandums are more formal and more serious than oral directions are. Even spoken communications have many variations, and the tone of voice may have a dramatic impact. "I would like you to leave" can be a soft-spoken, friendly request, or it can be shouted and delivered as an order. Thus, the *medium*—the method by which an idea is transmitted—will determine how it is received and acted on.

Receiving the message   Drafting a memorandum or standard operating procedure (SOP) without distributing it to department personnel does not accomplish anything. In addition, the memorandum or SOP must be understood by the parties it affects. Thus, receipt of the message is a critical step in the communication process. It is the reverse of message transmission in that the message must be received and acted on for it to be effective.

Understanding the idea   Transmitting a message is useless unless someone comprehends its content. Because this step occurs prior to receipt of any feedback, the sender should attempt to place him- or herself in the receiving party's position and frame the message so that the essence of the idea is communicated. Therefore, it is critical that the message be clear and easily understood by the receiving party.

Providing feedback to the message sender   Providing feedback is the last step in the communication process, the point at which the communication loop is closed. By this, we mean that the sender receives data indicating that the message was understood or needs clarification.

Let us now return to the example of a departmental SOP document. Normally, many such documents are circulated in draft form for review and comment. Individuals in the affected divisions of the department comment on the impact of the SOP on their operations and suggest any changes that would improve their operations or would assist in carrying out the objective of the SOP. The division officer responsible for submitting the final draft of the document to the chief for signature then makes any necessary changes to the SOP, on the basis of the comments from the other divisions. This process is an example of providing feedback in a formal setting.

Feedback may also occur orally—such as when one partner tells another, "I don't understand what you want me to do"—or by actions, such as a quizzical look or a shrug. No matter what form feedback takes, its purpose is to acknowledge the receipt of the message, to clarify the content of the message, or to indicate some response to the message. Feedback is discussed in more detail subsequently in this chapter.

Communication Involves at Least Two Persons

Communication does not occur in a vacuum. The desire or motivation to express ideas, thoughts, and feelings is based on the need for expression from one person to another. Many people talk to themselves at times, whether with an expletive when they hit their thumb with a hammer or with a simple question to themselves, such as, "How could I have been so stupid?" The purpose of these statements, however, is not to convey information to another person; rather, they are rhetorical or reactive types of utterances. The purpose of communication is the expression or transmission of data. Communication is not limited to one-on-one situations, however. Law officers communicate to individuals, to groups, and, in some cases, to the general public. A patrol officer may face all these situations during a single day.

The officer may start the day in roll-call training by asking the patrol sergeant about the condition of a new stop sign at an intersection on the officer's beat. This questioning involves one-on-one communication. Later, during the shift, the officer may address a crowd of citizens at the scene of an accident, requesting that they move out of the way of the emergency vehicle. This request is communication with a group. Finally, the officer may describe the accident for Action News on television. This discussion is communication with the general public. All these examples reinforce the principle that communication involves the transmission of data to someone else.

The Primary Purpose of Communication Is the Exchange of Information

Most of the time, people do not act without an objective. Although patrol officers may engage in small talk to pass the early morning hours on a stakeout, even this type of communication serves a need: to pass the time and keep each officer alert, to form or maintain a professional association or friendship, or to serve another purpose.

The exchange of information also occurs both formally and informally. For example, on a formal level, the information may be a new departmental directive regarding the use of force that each officer must sign after he or she has read it, or the information might be a roll-call briefing on the modus operandi of a serial rapist. At an informal level, two officers may discuss, over a cup of coffee, which type of handgun is the best weapon to carry while off duty.

Channels and Directions

Channels and directions of communication deal with the flow or movement of information from the sender to the recipient. *Channels of information* refer to the methods or avenues by which information flows from one party to another, and *direction of information* indicates the way in which communication flows.

Channels

Two communication channels are used in any organization: formal and informal.

Formal channels   The traditional route or method of communication in any police organization usually follows the chain of command. This type of communication channel is typified by formal orders, directives, and written memorandums. These forms of communication provide a sense of order and security to a police organization. Excessive or exclusive use of formal communications within a law enforcement agency, however, has several disadvantages. First, strict adherence to formal channels of communication is a time- and personnel-consuming effort. The memorandums must be carefully drafted, endorsed through the chain of command, and forwarded to the addressee pursuant to departmental policy. The second major drawback of formal channels of communication is the effect they have on the free flow of information. By nature, their rigidity restricts spontaneous ideas and thought. Third, formal routes usually require a written record, which may further restrict the flow of information because many people hesitate to put their thoughts or ideas in writing. A fourth disadvantage is the inability of this form of communication to respond rapidly to changing situations. As mentioned, formal channels are naturally rigid, and any change or modification must be reviewed within these same channels. If new situations arise, the modification process may not be able to keep pace with the need for change.

Considering all these disadvantages, the need for formal channels of communication might be questioned. Nonetheless, formal channels also provide certain advantages to any organization and to law enforcement agencies specifically. First, formal communication ensures uniformity—all officers within the department receive the same information. This factor is critical when new directives are formulated or when information concerning certain crimes needs to be passed to all officers on patrol. Second, formal communication is usually clearer and more concise than is informal communication, so less confusion arises regarding the purpose or content of the message. Finally, formal communication establishes a paper trail for purposes of court hearings.

Formal communication channels are a fact of life in any large organization. With law enforcement's emphasis on court hearings and testimony, the need for this type of communication is critical.

Informal channels   As mentioned previously, total reliance on formal communication channels can be detrimental to the effective operation of a police department. Informal channels—that is, the grapevine, or departmental gossip—are the unofficial routes of communication within a law enforcement agency. These channels do not appear on any organizational chart, and they may not be officially sanctioned by the department. Nevertheless, they, too, are a fact of life. A police department is a notorious rumor mill regarding what goes on within the department. But informal channels of communication do more than serve as a conduit for idle gossip—they provide a needed link within the organization.

Most formal communication channels flow from the top of an organization to the bottom. Few police departments provide for formal communication across the organization. Informal communication channels provide this necessary linkage.

Informal channels are used within a department in a number of situations. One of the most common is the interaction between detectives and patrol officers. At times, detectives approach patrol officers to ask for clarification of an initial report. Conversely, a patrol officer may remember something about a crime scene that was not recorded and go to the detective assigned to the case to discuss the matter and determine whether a follow-up report detailing the additional fact should be submitted to the detective's sergeant.

Another instance in which informal channels are used is when time is a critical factor. The formal channel would require the information to go up the chain of command and come back down to the intended recipient. This process is time consuming. By using informal channels, the officer can cut across lines of authority and responsibility to pass on the information quickly.

Informal communication channels are also used in situations in which two sections or divisions need to cooperate on a case or with regard to a series of crimes. Robbery and homicide divisions may find themselves in this situation when a robbery victim is killed. The robbery division might have information that would assist the homicide detective in solving the crime.

Because informal channels of communication provide an alternative method of receiving information, senior law enforcement officials should not attempt to extinguish them. Rather, they should allow them to exist in a form that enhances the effectiveness of the organization. In fact, some scholars have suggested that formal and informal channels of communication be blended into one communications network that is responsive to the departmental goals.[6]

Summary   Formal and informal channels of communication provide the means or avenues for the movement of information within a police department. These are the highways and back roads on which information moves from one point to another. The formal channels are similar to highways—they are well known, clearly marked, and occasionally congested with traffic. The informal channels are sometimes known only to the locals—they twist and turn and often encounter detours and other roadblocks.

Directions

Although channels of communication explain how information moves in an organization, they do not explain the different directions in which information travels. Information may travel in any number of directions within an organization, but the most common movements are upward, downward, and horizontal.[7] In the remaining portion of this section, we examine the directions of communication flow within a law enforcement agency.

The most obvious directions of information flow in any organization are upward and downward. This is traditionally the chain of command, and it coincides with the formal channels of communication.

Downward communication   *Downward communication* is information that travels from managers or supervisors to subordinates. Downward communication is usually classified into three broad categories: (1) orders, (2) procedures, and (3) personnel information.

Orders are downward communications that relate to a specific job assignment or performance. An example is the patrol listing that assigns officers to various beats, shifts, and work days. Orders are specific and usually related to a short time period. They are directed at individual officers rather than at the whole department.

Procedures are downward communications directed to a broad subject. For example, departmental *SOPs (standing, or standard, operating procedures)* are information that flows from the top to the bottom of an organization along the formal channels of communication. SOPs are intended to exist for an indefinite period and apply to all personnel, or to certain classes of personnel, within the department.

Personnel information is a broad area of communication that covers the entire spectrum of personnel issues, from performance evaluations to authorization of overtime or leave time. In many instances, this type of information has a substantial impact on the morale of the department. This type of downward communication has a direct impact on the personal lives of officers and their families.

Upward communication   The three types of downward communication are critical to management's ability to direct the department. The second direction of communication, upward communication, however, is just as important to the healthy functioning of a law enforcement agency. *Upward communication* is information from subordinates that travels from the bottom of the department to its managers. This type of communication may be divided into three major categories: (1) performance communication, (2) information, and (3) clarification.

Performance communication is information that travels upward to police managers from subordinates to keep the managers informed about their subordinates' performance. This information could be statistics gathered by the patrol sergeant on the number of arrests made during each shift or complaints by individual officers about working conditions. This form of upward communication may go through either formal channels or informal channels, but it is more likely to take place through formal channels, in the form of reports on the performance of certain divisions or sections.

Information is a form of upward communication that is usually in response to a request from supervisors. For example, a draft of an SOP for record filing is distributed to certain patrol sergeants by the lieutenant of records. Accompanying this draft is a request that the documents be reviewed from a patrol perspective and any comments for possible changes to the draft sent back. This type of upward communication usually flows through the formal channels of a department because it is a type of formalized feedback.

Clarification is the final form of upward communication. As its name implies, it is a request from subordinates for managers to make a previous downward communication more understandable. Similar to the upward flow of information, clarification usually occurs within the formal channels of a law enforcement department. For example, an upward request for clarification could deal with a new directive on the number of leave days officers are authorized during official holidays. Does the holiday count against an officer's leave if it falls on a normal day off? Or, must the officer work even if he or she has requested vacation? Unfortunately, many police agencies' personnel directives are unclear, and officers or their immediate supervisors will request either an oral interpretation or written guidance to explain the broad policy statement in the directive.

Upward communication serves a critical function in a law enforcement agency. It provides police supervisors with a form of feedback that can assist them in performing their duties.

Horizontal communication   The third and final direction that communications may take is horizontal. *Horizontal communication* is the flow of information among officers at the same organizational level. This type of communication provides a necessary link between officers and divisions within the department. Horizontal communication may be classified into three categories: (1) coordination, (2) social issues, and (3) problem solving.

Horizontal coordination communication is an attempt by several parties to ensure the proper order or relationship between various law enforcement functions. Persons engaged in this type of communication are concerned with the proper performance of various tasks. For example, the robbery detail needs to coordinate with the patrol units in the area when planning to stake out a store that they believe may be hit in the near future.

Social issues are also critical in any police organization. Horizontal communication is used by individual officers as a way to have contact with their peers and friends in the department. This form of communication may run the spectrum from an invitation to have a beer after the shift to the imposition of social expectations on fellow officers by passing the word that Officer X was seen at a local bar and had to be driven home by a friend.

The final form of horizontal communication—*problem solving*—concerns the ability of peers to discuss and solve common problems. All people are reluctant to reinvent the wheel. If someone has already devised a solution that works, for the most part people will readily adopt such an approach. Peace officers are no different. An officer who is confronted with a problem will discuss the issue with peers in an effort to determine whether someone else has faced the issue and how they solved it.

Summary

The channels and directions that communication takes are important in understanding how information moves from the sender to the receiver. Formal channels of communication are the easiest to recognize because they traditionally follow the chain of command. Informal channels of communication, however, provide a necessary link within any organization. Communications may move in any number of directions, the most common being downward, upward, and horizontal. This network of information within an organization provides the glue that holds it together in good times and bad.

In this section, we discussed the concept of communication and defined this term. We examined how communication is processed and reviewed how it travels from one person or place to another. Understanding communication, however, is just the beginning of understanding communication in a police agency. Another aspect of communication is the written word.

COMMUNICATIONS AND COURTESY

Displaying courtesy to citizens is an important part of any law enforcement officer's duties. People express themselves in a number of ways, and the way officers express themselves to citizens is an extremely important aspect of the law enforcement profession. Seven simple guidelines follow that address the most common applications of courtesy and communication in law enforcement:[8]

1. *Introductions.* Whenever practical, all officers should identify themselves by title and name on first contact with a citizen. Furthermore, the simple use of common greetings such as "Good morning" or "Good afternoon" can go a long way toward setting the tone of any encounter.

2. *Tone of voice.* Speech is the primary communication tool used by law enforcement officers. Officers should always be aware of their tone of voice and use it to their advantage. The voice should never betray anger, contempt, sarcasm, or other inflections that are likely to provoke opposition.

3. *Forms of address.* Officers should not address citizens by their first names unless the circumstances clearly make doing so appropriate.

4. *Body language.* Although officers must often assume stances that are required to preserve safety during encounters with the public, care must be taken to avoid mannerisms that needlessly provoke negative reactions from citizens. Resting a hand on the butt of a weapon is one example of such behavior.

5. *Profanity.* The use of profanity is never appropriate.

6. *Demeaning remarks.* Any form of address that ridicules a citizen or expresses contempt is never appropriate.

7. *Explaining what law officers do.* The most simple form of courtesy and communication is explaining what you as a law officer are doing and why.

ORAL COMMUNICATION

Talking and listening are skills you learn at an early age. As you progress through school, these skills are sharpened under pain of failing classes. After formal schooling ends, the police academy is behind you, and you are a sworn officer on the street, you will find yourself in a subculture that has its own formal language, customs, and traditions. Not only must officers communicate within their immediate professional circle, but all law enforcement officers must interact with various groups outside the police department. This interaction requires the ability to communicate with others on many levels.

WRITTEN COMMUNICATION

Voltaire used to read to his cook everything he wrote. If she could not understand it, he would rewrite it.[9] If one of the world's most famous philosophers could rewrite his works in an effort to make them more understandable, so can any law enforcement officer.[10]

One of the main problems with written communication is the lack of instant feedback. Oral communication is interactive and allows for almost instantaneous correction by using feedback to clarify any misunderstanding. Written communication does not provide this mechanism. If a report, memorandum, or directive is ambiguous, that fact must be transmitted to the writer after the document has been placed in circulation. Because of this lack of instantaneous feedback, written communication requires more effort than oral communication does.

Records and record keeping occupy a critical place in any law enforcement agency. Without the ability to communicate in writing, any police department would be crippled. Arrest reports, follow-up reports, departmental directives, and budget documents are just a few examples of necessary written statements that are present in any police agency—large or small.

Writing Defined

The term *writing* has many definitions. In this text, we deal with a specialized form of writing—report writing for law enforcement professionals. On the basis of the scope of this text, *writing* may be defined as "a method of recording and communicating ideas by means of a system of visual marks." This definition has three basic elements:

1. *A recording of ideas.* Writing is lasting. It is a permanent form of communication. The spoken word is gone from our senses as soon as it ends, whereas writing is a permanent record of our thoughts and ideas. It may be reviewed ten days or ten years after it is transmitted.

2. *A method of communication.* In the preceding section, we explained the process of communication. One of the distinctions between oral communication and written communication is the lack of instant feedback that allows the person transmitting the data to correct, refine, or focus the information into a more understandable format.

3. *A system of visual marks.* Writing used to be confined to printed or cursive matter. If a person's printing or handwriting was illegible, other people had to struggle to interpret it. The fact that the person was using known and accepted words, however, helped them decipher the meaning of the printed or written message. In this day of computers, certain symbols have taken on meanings. For instance, the symbol *C:* has an accepted meaning for almost anyone who uses computers. Similarly, *.* carries a distinct meaning. In police work, numbers are just as important. Depending on the jurisdiction, a certain collection of numbers connotes a crime. *P.C. 459* indicates a burglary in California. These numbers are usually shorthand for the criminal statute defining the crime. For example, in *California Penal Code,* § 459, the elements of burglary are listed. Each jurisdiction has its own set of numbers that are recognizable to its police officers. These numbers may be shorthand for crimes, may be specialized codes used over the radio, or may represent other law enforcement–related activities that have by custom or practice become known by a string of numbers.

Writing police reports is no easy task. Nor can any single test deal with the many forms and procedures used by the various law enforcement agencies in the United States or the world. A few simple guidelines, however, may help any law enforcement officer when he or she begins to draft police reports.

RULES FOR IMPROVEMENT

Correct Word Usage

In English, the word *cleave* can mean "to cut in half" or "to hold two halves together." The word *set* has 126 meanings as a verb, 58 as a noun, and 10 as a participial adjective.[11] As a result, incorrect word usage is a common problem in written communications. Following are rules for the correct usage of 16 commonly used words.

1. When to use *a* and when to use *an*

   When the first letter of the next word is a vowel, use *an*—*a* car, *an* arm, *a* boat, *an* eye.

   When the first letter of an abbreviation is pronounced as a vowel, use *an*—*an* FBI agent, *an* IBM employee, *a* CSU employee.

2. When to use *appendices* and when to use *appendixes*

   In modern usage, either is correct.

3. When to use *compare to* and when to use *compare with*

   Compare to should be used to liken one thing to another.
   She *compares* Houston *to* Los Angeles. [Meaning that she sees them as similar]
   Compare with should be used to discuss the relative merits of two things.
   Los Angeles, when *compared with* San Francisco, is flat.

4. When to use *connote* and when to use *denote*

   Denote means "to convey information."
   Connote means "to imply additional aspects that follow from what is denoted."
   The coat I am wearing as I approached the house might *denote* that I am warm but *connote* that I have a new coat.

5. When to use *discreet* and when to use *discrete*

   Use *discreet* when you mean "circumspect," "careful," or "showing good judgment."
   Use *discrete* to mean "unattached" or "unrelated."
   The police officer promised to be *discreet* when asking questions of the neighbors.
   The officer's report was composed of five *discrete* parts.

6. When to use *drunk driving* and when to use *drunken driving*

   Drunken is the usual and preferred form when the word appears adjectively before a noun.
   The *drunken* driver was arrested.
   [*Note*: Not all style arbiters agree on this usage.]

7. When to use *Earth* and when to use *earth*

   When the word is used to refer to a planet, use *Earth*.
   When the word is used in more general terms, use *earth*.
   The *Earth* is a planet in our solar system.
   The weapon was fired into the *earth*.

8. When to use *especially* and when to use *specially*

   Specially means "for a specific purpose or occasion." If you can substitute the word *particularly,* then use *especially*.

Potential Trouble Spots

Following are five rules that will help you avoid typical problems in writing.

1. All sentences must have a subject—except imperatives, in which the subject *you* is understood.

   Have a collection of books. [No sentence; no subject]
   Have a good patrol. [Complete sentence; *you* is implied]

2. Do not repeat the subject of a sentence.

   The *police officer he* approached the car.

3. Do not repeat an object or an adverb in an adjective clause.

   The police station *where I work there* is near my apartment.

4. Use *at, on, in,* and *by* to show time and place.

   Will you be *at* the station?
   Will you meet me *on* Broad Street?
   We will meet again *in* December.
   The roll call begins *at* 7:20 A.M. (*not* The roll call begins *on* 7:20 A.M.)

5. Use an *-ed* or *-d* ending to express the past tense of regular verbs.

   During the weekend, the chief retir*ed* from the department.

Better-Writing Drill

Law enforcement officers are often required to use nouns and adjectives to describe a suspect, a witness, or a victim's nationality. The following chart lists the name of a country or region and the corresponding noun and adjective for that country. Look at the country name and attempt to spell the noun and adjective for that country correctly.

Country or Region	Noun	Adjective
Afghanistan	Afghan(s)	Afghan
Argentina	Argentine(s)	Argentine
Australia	Australian(s)	Australian
Belgium	Belgian(s)	Belgian
Brazil	Brazilian(s)	Brazilian
Canada	Canadian(s)	Canadian
Colombia	Colombian(s)	Colombian
Cuba	Cuban(s)	Cuban
Denmark	Dane(s)	Danish
Haiti	Haitian(s)	Haitian
Laos	Lao or Laotian(s)	Lao or Laotian
Mexico	Mexican(s)	Mexican
Spain	Spaniard(s)	Spanish
Thailand	Thailander	Thai
Vietnam	Vietnamese	Vietnamese

COMPOUND WORDS

A compound word, with or without a hyphen, conveys an idea that is not as clearly or quickly conveyed by the separate words. Word forms constantly undergo modification. Two-word forms often acquire the hyphen first and are printed as one word later. Not infrequently, however, the transition is from the two- to the one-word form, bypassing the hyphenated stage. The following sections present examples of compound words and some guidelines for their formation.

Solid Compounds

1. One-word compounds.

antiunion	newsprint	rulemaking
backpay	nighttime	runoff
biweekly	engineroom	nonunion
evenhanded	nonworking	bookseller
checkoff	interstate	pickup
subregion	checkout	intrastate

2. Suffixes in compound words.
The following italicized suffixes are usually nonhyphenated, but a hyphen is used with proper names and to avoid tripling a consonant.

give*away*	movie*goer*	
show*down*	kilo*gram*	
twenty*fold*	man*hood*	
spoon*ful*	life*like*	
inner*most*		
cut*off*	area*wide*	clock*wise*
but		
Florida-*like*	bell-*like*	

3. Prefixes in compound words.

a. Prefixes written solid

amoral	electromagnet	midsummer	pseudonym	
aftercare	antedate	forefinger	multicolor	semiannual
antitrust	stepfather	biannual	supermarket	inbound

b. Prefixes with capitalized words. Use a hyphen with capitalized words unless the combined form has acquired independent meaning.

ante-Norman	inter-American
anti-Semitic	mid-April
non-Government	trans-Canadian
but	
nongovernmental	transatlantic

Hyphen Omitted in Compound Words

1. When the meaning is clear and readability is not aided.

a 401(k) provision   civil rights case

civil service examination   due process law
flood control study   fringe benefit plan

2. When the last element of a predicate adjective is a present or past participle.

The area was used for drug dealing.   The area is drought stricken.
The effects were far reaching.   The boy is freckle faced.

3. When the first element of a two-word modifier is an adverb ending in *ly* or the first two elements of a three-word modifier are adverbs.

eagerly awaited moment   wholly owned subsidiary but
ever-normal granary   ever-rising earnings
unusually high strung supervisor   longer than usual lunch period
still-lingering doubt   well-kept office
still-new car   well-known lawyer

SUMMARY

As much as 70 percent of people's time is spent communicating with others. Communication is a process involving several steps, among two or more persons, for the primary purpose of exchanging information. This process requires sending an idea, receiving the idea, understanding the idea, and providing feedback to the message sender.

Information moves through various channels and in various directions. In most police departments, formal communication channels follow the chain of command and have several advantages and disadvantages. Informal communication channels also exist in all law enforcement agencies. These informal channels should be used to upgrade the flow of information within the department.

Written communication is more difficult to master than oral communication because of the lack of instant feedback when written communication is used. Police reports form the basis for future action in the criminal justice system. Prosecutors rely on them when issuing criminal complaints. Officers will refer to them to refresh their memories when testifying in court. Probation officers may review them when deciding what form of punishment the accused should receive.

There is no simple method by which a police officer becomes an experienced writer. Practice, hard work, and attention to detail are the key ingredients of a successfully drafted police report.

KEY TERMS

Channels of information The methods or avenues by which information flows from one party to another

Clarification A request from subordinates for managers to make a previous downward communication more understandable

Communication A process involving several steps, among two or more persons, for the primary purpose of exchanging information

Direction of information The way in which communication flows

Downward communication Information that travels from managers or supervisors to subordinates

Horizontal communication The flow of information among officers at the same organizational level

Horizontal coordination communication An attempt by several parties to ensure the proper order or relationship between various law enforcement functions

Information A form of upward communication that is usually in response to a request from supervisors

Medium The method by which an idea is transmitted (e.g., telephone, written orders, or e-mail)

Orders Downward communications that relate to a specific job assignment or performance

Performance communication Information that travels upward to police managers from subordinates to keep the managers informed about their subordinates' performance

Personnel information A broad area of communication that covers the entire spectrum of personnel issues, from performance evaluations to authorization of overtime or leave time

Problem solving Horizontal communications designed to solve current problems within the department

Procedures Downward communications directed to a broad subject

Social issues Horizontal communications that concern social aspects or events (e.g., using an e-mail to invite a fellow officer to go to the ball game with you)

SOPs (standing, or standard, operating procedures) Information that flows from the top to the bottom of an organization along the formal channels of communication. SOPs are intended to exist for an indefinite period and apply to all personnel, or to certain classes of personnel, within the department. They are set procedures to be used when certain events or circumstances occur. For example, most police departments have an SOP for the investigation of a shooting by a police officer

Upward communication Information that travels from subordinates to managers

Writing A method of recording and communicating ideas by means of a system of visual marks

REVIEW QUESTIONS

1. What is more important—oral or written communication? Why? Justify your answer.
2. If you could use only one channel of information in an agency, which would it be? Why?
3. On the basis of your reading to this point, what is the purpose of a written report? How is it different from an oral report?
4. Why is improving your communication skills important?
5. What are the chief differences between oral communication and written communication?

PRACTICAL APPLICATIONS

1. The most effective way to improve your writing is to do freewriting exercises regularly, at least twice a week. These exercises are sometimes called "babbling" exercises. The idea is to write for at least ten minutes without stopping. Never look back, and do not stop to correct spelling or to think about what you are doing. The only re-

quirement in the exercise is to never stop writing until the time has expired. During this semester, do one freewriting exercise regarding any subject before each class. At the end of the semester, compare your earlier free-writing exercises with your later examples. You should notice an improvement in your writing ability.

2. Punctuate the following sentence.
   Woman without her man is a savage.[12]
   Compare your punctuation with that of your classmates. Does punctuation change the meaning of the sentence?

3. Circle the correctly spelled word in each of the following rows.

abutement	abuttment	abutment	abuttement
accessible	acessible	acessibile	accessibile
beligerent	beligeront	belligerent	beligorent
bactera	bacteria	bacterria	baterria
cartilage	cortilage	cartolige	cartilag
conscientious	consceintious	consceintous	conscentous
dupilicate	duplicat	duplicate	duplecate
evaise	evasive	eavaise	evsiave
gurdian	guardian	guardin	gaurdian
homice	homicide	homcide	homcidi

4. Rewrite the following sentences as needed.
   a. He saw the bank rounding the corner.
   _____

   b. The officer found marijuana outside the car wrapped in paper.
   _____

   c. Went to the crime scene and lost his gun.
   _____

   d. He ran quick.
   _____

   e. Drinking coffee often keeps me and him awake.
   _____

5. Define and explain the following words or terms.
   a. performance communication
   _____

   b. upward communication
   _____

   c. horizontal communication
   _____

   d. direction of information
   _____

   e. channels of information
   _____

6. The following paragraph was taken from a police report. Make it a better paragraph.

   At this point, this officer asked subject Hamm what transpired and the subject simply did not answer this officer. It should be noted that at this time Officer Smith arrived and the scence and while this officer was briefing Officer Smith the subjects were once again facing each other and at this time this officer heard subject Hamm state "Okay you still want to fitgh. At this time the officer stepped among the subjects and drawed his baton from the baton ring and ordering the subjects to go to the rear of the vehicle."

_____
_____
_____
_____
_____
_____
_____
_____

ENDNOTES

1. See U.S. Navy Publication, _Don't Talk: Communicate_ (Washington, DC: GPO, 1980).
2. Michael T. D'Aulizio and Kathy M. Sheehan, "Instituting Quality Control Measures for Police Reports," _The Police Chief_ (October 1992): 129.
3. Harry W. More and W. Fred Wegener, _Effective Police Supervision_ (Cincinnati, Ohio: Anderson, 1990), 38.
4. See Colin Cherry, _On Human Communication_ (Boston: The MIT Press, 1978).
5. See R. C. Huseman, _Interpersonal Communication: A Guide for Staff Development_ (Athens, Ga.: Institute of Government, University of Georgia, August 1974).
6. Bernard Beryls and Gary A. Steiner, _Human Behavior: An Inventory of Scientific Findings_ (New York: Harcourt, Brace & World, 1964), 370.
7. See Anthony Davis, _Inside Bureaucracy_ (Boston: Little, Brown, 1967), 235–47.
8. Thomas J. Lange, "Cultivating the Practice of Courtesy," _The Police Chief_ (January 1989): 35.
9. Voltaire (1694–1778) was a famous French writer and philosopher. He traveled throughout Europe and penned numerous treaties, poems, and articles. Considered one of the most prolific writers of that period, he wrote memorable passages distinguished by elegance, perspicuity, and wit. One of his most famous essays was "The Henriad" (1728).
10. We (both authors) were marine officers, and our superiors drilled into us in basic school to KISS (Keep it simple) when formulating or writing orders.
11. Bill Bryson, _Bryson's Dictionary of Troublesome Words_ (New York: Broadway Books, 2002), 139.
12. One English professor directed her students to punctuate this sentence correctly. One male student wrote this: "Woman, without her man, is a savage." A female student wrote this: "Woman! Without her, man is a savage."

CHAPTER 3

The Communication Process

LEARNING OBJECTIVES

After reading this chapter, you should understand the following concepts:

■ How the Johari window model of communication works

■ The model Schramm developed to explain the communication process

■ How Lasswell viewed communication

■ The difference between individual communication and group communication

INTRODUCTION

No records system can be effective without clearly communicated policies, directives, and procedures. Nor can any police agency or officer carry out a mission or survive without clear communications. Furthermore, communication involves more than shouting, "Halt; police officer!" or ordering a patrol officer to respond to an emergency call.

In this chapter, we examine the basic parameters of interpersonal communication and organizational communication in a law enforcement agency. In succeeding chapters, we review special situations involving communication issues. In Chapter 2, we indicated that the communication process can be both a simple and a complex series of events. *Communication* was defined as "a process involving several steps, among two or more persons, for the primary purpose of exchanging information." The dynamics of communication, or how we react to information, is an important aspect of the communication cycle. Thus, in the next section, we review the interaction between a person who sends a message and the way in which the receiver processes that information.

THE JOHARI WINDOW

In the preceding section, we pointed out how important effective communication is in a law enforcement agency in general, and to a police officer, as a member of that organization, specifically. In this section, we examine one model that law enforcement officers can use to evaluate their communication skills. One of the simplest and most common communication models within law enforcement is the *Johari window*.

The Four Regions of Knowledge

Joseph Luft and Harry Ingham created a communication model and named it after themselves. They combined their names and called the model the *Johari window*.[1] This model has four regions, or areas, that represent basic areas of knowledge or information held by the manager and others. The Johari window is illustrated in Figure 3.1.

FIGURE 3.1 The Johari Window

	Known to self	Not known to self
Known to others	Free area I	Blind area II
Not known to others	Hidden area III	Unknown area IV

The four panes, or windows, represent relevant information about the manager's ability to interact with other persons effectively. The Johari window has two basic aspects of communication: exposure and feedback. The *exposure* aspect concerns the ability of the police administrator to express feelings and ideas in an open method. This aspect basically represents the manager's ability to transmit information. The *feedback* aspect involves the ability of the administrator to receive information from others.

The Johari window panes are distinct regions that encompass the following characteristics:

Area I: The area I pane is known as the *free area,* or *arena.* It represents the portion of a manager's communication ability that allows him or her to freely share and receive information with and from others. This ability is the key to a successful interpersonal relationship in an organization.[2] Therefore, the larger this pane, or region, is in relationship to the other panes, the more effective the manager is in dealing with superiors and subordinates.

Area II: The area II pane is known as the *blind area,* or *blind spot.* Everyone has heard or used the saying "I was blindsided!" This area represents information known by others—superiors, peers, or subordinates—that is not known to the administrator. In many bureaucracies, individuals believe that knowledge or information is power. In some ways, this belief is true. Police officers cannot make a valid decision if information is hidden from them. The larger this pane, the more information is being withheld from the manager.

Area III: The area III pane is known as the *hidden area,* or the *facade.* This area represents how much information an officer keeps private. Everyone makes conscious or unconscious decisions to withhold certain information from others. This information may relate to personal habits or professional knowledge. When an officer withholds information, area I—the free area, or arena—is prevented from expanding. Although withholding a portion of ourselves from others is normal and healthy, a problem arises when an individual withholds information to the extent that it prevents a free, honest interchange of knowledge.

Area IV: The area IV pane is called the *unknown area.* This area represents the amount of information that is unknown to both the manager and his or her superiors, and to his or her subordinates. As the free area, or arena, grows through effective communication, the unknown area shrinks.

These four areas expand or contract depending on the type of interpersonal communication patterns the manager adopts.

The Four Basic Types of Communication Patterns

The Johari window establishes four basic types of communication patterns in relation to the process of exposure and feedback. So that you can understand how the Johari model functions, let us briefly examine each of these types.

Type A
The officer who uses the type A communication pattern provides little feedback or exposure. The person who is typified by this communication style does not communicate with subordinates or superiors. This type of individual withdraws from the decision-making

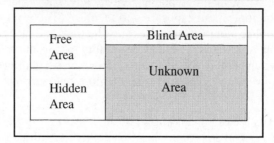

FIGURE 3.2 Type A Communication Pattern

process and is not willing to take a risk by making a decision. He or she is more concerned with self-protection than with functioning effectively. The unknown area is the dominating factor with this type of manager, while the free area, or arena, is correspondingly smaller (Figure 3.2).

Type B
An officer who uses the type B communication pattern does not transmit information to superiors, subordinates, or peers, but will accept some interaction and feedback from them. This type of individual does not trust fellow officers but must receive information from them as a survival technique. This type of person constantly asks for opinions or thoughts but is hesitant to reciprocate by telling others what he or she believes or feels. The model for this type of officer has a large hidden area, or facade (Figure 3.3).

Type C
The officer who uses the type C communication pattern is characterized by continual self-expression and refusal to accept feedback from others. In this situation, the model shows an increase in exposure with a corresponding decrease in feedback. Individuals in this category have egos so large that they believe they have all the correct answers and strive to emphasize their authority and dominance over other officers. Friends and colleagues soon come to believe that these individuals do not value the opinions of others or will tolerate only feedback that confirms their own

FIGURE 3.3 Type B Communication Pattern

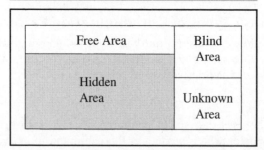

FIGURE 3.4 Type C Communication Pattern

Free Area	Blind Area
Hidden Area	Unknown Area

beliefs or position. The Johari window for this type of officer is characterized by a large blind spot (Figure 3.4).

Type D

An officer who uses the type D communication pattern is the kind of individual who shows outstanding leadership. He or she emphasizes open lines of communication and accepts feedback from superiors and subordinates alike. Unfortunately, many police officers are not accustomed to dealing with this type of person and may distrust such communication techniques at first. The model for this type of officer has a large free area, or arena (Figure 3.5).

From the preceding discussion, you can probably ascertain that the most effective type of law enforcement officer is type D. This officer's relationships are characterized by trust, open lines of communication, and candor with superiors, peers, and subordinates. Open lines of communication result in high-quality work from all the parties who interact with this type of police administrator.

The Johari window is an abstract concept that illustrates certain principles regarding the quality and style of interpersonal relationships. Its principles can be applied to any relationship; however, it is particularly applicable to law enforcement agencies. By studying and understanding the dynamics of the Johari window, you can enhance your ability to become an effective law enforcement officer.

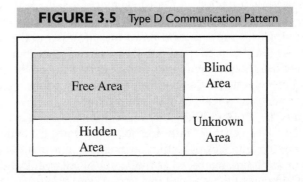

FIGURE 3.5 Type D Communication Pattern

OTHER COMMUNICATION MODELS

Several other models deal with the dynamics of communication. All these models or theories seek to explain how the communication process works. Each model has its advocates; however, you should understand that advocates of different respected theories merely examine the same process from different perspectives. Schramm and Lasswell were two of the early pioneers in the field of communications. Both these leaders established communication models that are still viable.

Schramm's Model

Wilbur Schramm (1907–1987) introduced a model that illustrated the importance of interpersonal communication.[3] He is considered by many people to be the father of the study of communications, and he played a critical role in the development of this research.[4] Schramm was the first academic professional to identify himself as a communications scholar, he created the first academic degree in communications, and he trained the first generation of communications scholars. He founded research institutes at the University of Iowa, the University of Illinois, and Stanford University, and he published numerous texts and articles dealing with the dynamics of communications.

From 1948 to 1977, Schramm produced almost a book a year dealing with the study of communications,[5] in addition to the articles, conference papers, and high-quality academic reports that he turned out during this period. Schramm also wrote several influential texts, including *Mass Media and National Development*.[6] This book was an international best-seller, studied by people throughout the world. Schramm established a model of communication that attempts to explain the problems inherent in human communication. His model evolved in stages. It proceeded from a relatively simple individual form of communication to a complex model involving interaction between two parties.

In the first stage of Schramm's model, a source sends a message through an encoder; the message is received by a decoder and transmitted to its designation. The *source* is the mind of the person starting the communication process. The *encoder* is the process by which ideas are converted to symbols for transmission to another person. The *decoder* is the process by which symbols are received and converted into ideas by the person receiving the information. The *signal* is symbols that are produced and transmitted.

Schramm slowly modified his first-stage model to include the concept that only the information that is shared in the respective parties' fields of experience is actually communicated. This is the only portion of the information that is communicated because it is the only shared portion of the signal that both parties understand. Schramm's contribution to communications theory included the concept that each person has a field of experience that controls both the encoding and decoding of information and determines the meaning of this information.

In the third stage of the model, communication is viewed as an interaction in which both parties actively encode, interpret, decode, transmit, and receive signals. This model includes the feedback of continuously shared information (Figure 3.6).

Schramm will be remembered as the father of communications and a remarkable scholar who formalized the study of this important discipline.

FIGURE 3.6 Schramm's Final Model

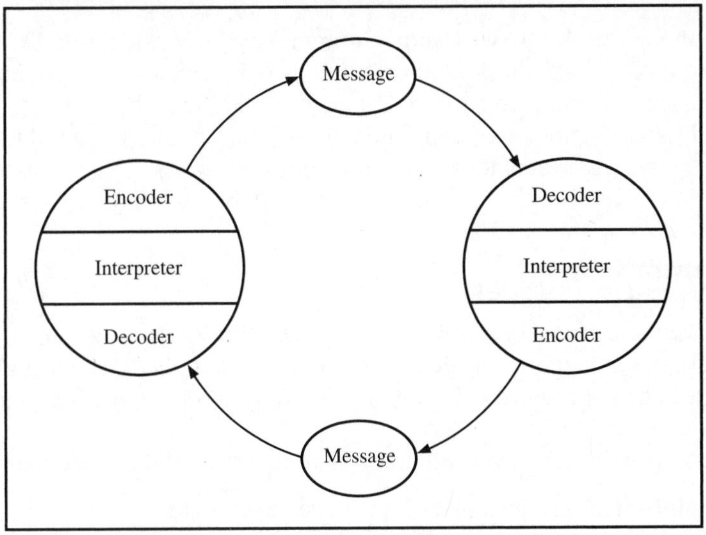

While Schramm was developing his theories, another leader in the field was perfecting a different perspective on communications. Harold Lasswell studied propaganda and created the *content analysis* method of communications research.

Lasswell's Model

Harold Lasswell (1902–1978) published more than six million words during his lifetime. The theme of his doctoral dissertation, "Propaganda Techniques in the World War," was the effect of propaganda on people during World War I.[7] Lasswell defined *propaganda* as "the management of collective attitudes by the manipulation of significant symbols." He did not consider propaganda good or bad; to him, that determination depended on the sender's and receiver's viewpoints and the truthfulness of the messages.[8]

Harold Lasswell is best known for one sentence: "Who says what in which channel to whom with what effects?" In one of his early classic works, Lasswell identified five common variables in the communication process.[9] These variables are the building blocks for his well-known sentence. He stated that one way to analyze the act of communication is to answer the following questions:

Who? When scholars analyze the *who* component, they look at factors that initiate and guide the act of communication. This is called *control analysis.*

Says what? Scholars who examine this aspect of the communications process engage in *content analysis.*

In which channel? Scholars who look at the method or ways information travels engage in *data analysis.* They look at radio, press, film, and other channels of communication.

To whom? Scholars who investigate the persons reached by the media engage in *audience analysis.*

With what effects? Scholars who are concerned about the impact of the information on audiences study *effect analysis.*

Although both Lasswell and Schramm were in Washington, D.C., during the war years of 1942 to 1945, they did not meet until 1954, at Stanford. Like Schramm, Lasswell was a prolific scholar. He authored or coauthored more than 300 articles and 52 books. Harold Lasswell pioneered content analysis methods and invented the qualitative and quantitative measurement of communications messages. He also introduced psychoanalytic theory into political science. Lasswell will be remembered as one of the giants in the study of communication.

Mathematical Model

One schematic model of a communications system emerged in the late 1940s, based on the work of mathematician Claude Shannon. The simplicity of his model, its clarity, and its surface generality proved attractive to many students of communication in a number of disciplines.

As originally conceived, Shannon's model contained five elements:

- An information source, which produces a message
- A transmitter, which operates on the message to create a signal that can be sent through a channel
- A channel, which is the medium over which the signal, carrying the information that comprises the message, is sent
- A receiver, which transforms the signal back into the message intended for delivery
- A destination, which can be a person or a machine, for whom or which the message is intended

When these elements are arranged in linear order, communications travel along this path, to be changed by the transmitter, and to be reconstituted into intelligible language by the receiver. In time, the five elements of the model were renamed to specify components for other types of communication transmitted in various manners. The information source was split into its components (both source and message) to provide a wider range of applicability. The six elements of the revised model are (1) a source, (2) an encoder, (3) a message, (4) a channel, (5) a decoder, and (6) a receiver. For some communication systems, the components are as simple as (1) a person on a telephone, (2) the mouthpiece of the telephone, (3) the words spoken, (4) the electrical impulses (5) the earpiece of another telephone, and (6) the mind of the listener. In other communication systems, the components normally are more difficult to isolate; for example, the communication of the emotions of writer Ernest Hemingway in writing to an audience who may receive the communication long after the writer's death.[10]

GROUP VERSUS INDIVIDUAL COMMUNICATION

To this point, we have been discussing the communication cycle without distinguishing whether the process involves a one-on-one relationship or a situation among more than two people. Most of the information that has been presented applies to an interpersonal relationship—that is, a relationship between two persons. Such a relationship might involve a sergeant's talking to a patrol officer or a lieutenant's responding to a question from a captain. Many of the communication principles described in this chapter, however, also apply to group communication. For example, feedback may occur at roll call when a patrol officer asks the shift sergeant to clarify the description of a rape suspect. Therefore, let us define *interpersonal communication* as "the sharing of information between two persons." In addition, let us define *group communication* as "interaction among three or more individuals, in a face-to-face situation, who have a common need that is satisfied by the exchange of information."

Group Size

The term *group* has been defined as "a number of persons gathered or classified together."[11] The definition of *group communication* does not set limits on the ultimate size of the group. Practical considerations inherent in the definition, however, do define a maximum number of people who can interact effectively. For instance, individuals attending a professional sporting event may have a commonality of interest, but they may not have an opportunity to become involved in a face-to-face situation in which they can exchange information that satisfies a common need. If you compare the group of 100,000 people who attended the Super Bowl with a group of five fans planning a tailgate party before the game, you can easily see that group size can be a factor in determining the ability of individuals to communicate with one another.

Numerous scholars have examined the dynamics of group communications.[12] The results of various research studies have indicated that between three and 20 people is a natural size for purposes of defining group interactions.[13] Once the group size exceeds 20 people, the ability of individual members to influence one another diminishes. The nature of the gathering then takes on more of the characteristics of a mass meeting or conference, in which one person may influence the group but the ability of individual members within the group to influence one another is limited. Because group size has a direct bearing on the nature and type of communication involved, we limit our discussion of communication to groups that do not exceed 20 individuals.

Once the size of the group involved in the communication process has been determined, group interaction must be addressed.

Group Interaction

Leading scholars, such as Fisher,[14] generally accept that group interaction consists of four phases: (1) the orientation phase, (2) the conflict phase, (3) the emergence phase, and (4) the reinforcement phase.

In the *orientation phase,* group members attempt to get to know one another and discover the problems that face the group. This orientation may occur as strangers meet in a group for the first time. Alternatively, it may transpire with people who know one another and attend periodic meetings, such as roll call before the beginning of patrol shifts. In the roll-call situation, group members already know one another, and the orientation is aimed at common problems facing the group. These problems could range from new shift hours to planning a social gathering after the shift.

The second phase, the *conflict phase,* involves disagreement among the group members. This phase is characterized by an atmosphere of polarization and controversy. For instance, patrol officers may be sharply divided concerning the benefits of the new shift hours or have strong feelings about the location of the social gathering.

During the *emergence phase* of group interaction, more emphasis is placed on positive statements. This phase allows dissenting members to save face by moving toward the majority's position. Officers who oppose the new shift hours may begin to find other benefits that were not previously discussed. In a similar vein, the location for the social gathering may be determined to be a third alternative that is acceptable to all members.

The final phase is the *reinforcement phase.* This phase is the period when group members comment on the positive aspects of the group and its problem-solving ability.

In the preceding discussion, we focused on the dynamics that normally occur in a problem-solving group; however, such interaction in one form or another will usually be present in most groups.[15] A police officer may determine which phase a group is in by listening to the types of comments being made by group members, then using this information to express personal views in the most effective manner. Group interaction is an important aspect of any organization. Law enforcement officers need to understand these group dynamics to carry out their duties effectively.

Communication Patterns

Anyone who has observed a group of people discussing a topic has observed that not everyone in the group spends the same amount of time talking. Information flows according to status or power. In general, persons with high status or actual or perceived power send and receive more messages than do other members of the group.[16] These persons serve as the hub for group communications. They will receive and send more messages than any other group member.

Once a group has been established, certain communication dynamics begin to emerge. A *communications network* is the pattern of information that flows among members of a group. After a group has been in existence and functioning for a period, certain members will repeatedly talk with other members. Such communication forms a network through which information flows within the group.

Another communication dynamic that occurs in group communication concerns the centrality of communication. *Centrality of communication* is the degree of centralization of the message flow and decision making. In a more centralized group's communication pattern, information is funneled to one or two persons with high status or power, who then transmit the same message to other group members.

The classic studies of Leavitt and Bavelas[17] established that more-decentralized communication networks are faster at solving complex problems, whereas centralized networks are more efficient in dealing with less complex issues. Efficiency in problem solving, however, should not be the only factor the officer considers. The results of studies indicate that members of decentralized communication networks experience a greater degree of satisfaction with their participation in the group.[18]

Communication patterns within a group are an important part of the communication process. An intelligent police officer will take the time to understand these patterns and ensure that they are used to the advantage of the department.

The group and individual communication cycle is a dynamic and changing environment. Careful study and persistence will allow you to communicate effectively and, thus, become a leader within the department.

RULES FOR IMPROVEMENT

Use of the First Person

Use of the first person means referring to yourself as *I* rather than *this officer.* In the past, many police officers were taught to use the third person rather than the first person. The first person is recommended because it is clearer and more direct. Following are two examples.

This officer arrested the suspect.

I arrested the suspect.

This officer saw the victim sitting in the street.

I saw the victim sitting in the street.

Use of the Active Voice

Sentences may be written in either the active voice or the passive voice. Clear writing generally requires use of the active voice. To determine whether the active voice or the passive voice is used, apply the following test.

Locate the subject and the verb of the sentence. (*Remember:* The subject tells *who* and the verb tells *what was done.*) If the subject performed the action, the sentence is written in the active voice. If the subject did not perform the action, the sentence is written in the passive voice.

Active: The accused fired the gun.

Passive: The gun was fired by the accused.

Active: The accused did not fire the gun.

Passive: The gun was not fired by the accused.

Active: The suspect drove the car.

Passive: The car was driven by the suspect.

Use of the passive voice may be appropriate if the doer of the action is unknown.

Someone fired the gun three times.

Better: The gun was fired three times.

[Individual who fired the gun was unknown]

The passive voice may also be appropriate if you want to call attention to the receiver of the action rather than the doer.

The victim was hit by the accused.

Finally, the passive voice is also used to prevent embarrassment of the doer.

The training was canceled because Sergeant Williams failed to order the proper equipment.

Better: The training was canceled because the proper equipment was not ordered.

Correct Usage of Pronouns

A *pronoun* is a word used in place of a noun.

Noun	Pronoun
Joe	He
Joe and Jill	They
Jill	She
the gun	It

Pronouns should refer to only one person or object. The most common mistake people make when they use pronouns is the creation of unclear pronoun references. For instance, "When I nod my head, hit it" is a classic example of an unclear pronoun reference. In case of doubt, do not use the pronoun. For example, "When I nod my head, hit the nail."

Poor pronoun references can also be observed in the following sentences.

The suspect told the police officer he had made a mistake.

The officer read the suspect the *Miranda* warnings, which he understood.

The suspect was seen by the apartment manager while he was in the elevator.

To whom does *he* refer?

Correct Word Usage

1. When to use *fewer* and when to use *less*

   My local supermarket has a sign over its express lane that states, "This lane reserved for customers with 15 items or less." I tried to explain to the manager of this national chain that the statement is incorrect. He told me that he was a former English teacher and that nothing was wrong with his sign. His belief is erroneous.

   Less applies to quantity and *fewer* applies to number.

   Less is often used with singular nouns, and *fewer* with plural nouns.

   Customers with *less* than a gallon of ice cream and *fewer* than ten items may use this checkout lane.

2. When to use *former* and when to use *latter*

   Former refers to the first of two things.

   Latter refers to the second of two things.

   Both words should be avoided because they require the reader to recall an earlier reference.

3. When to use *indict* and when to use *indite*

   Indict means "to lay a formal charge."

   Indite means "to set down in writing."

4. When to use *intense* and when to use *intensive*

   Intense should be used to describe things that are heavy, extreme, or occur to a high degree.

   Intensive implies a concentrated focus, such as an *intensive search* of the vehicle.

5. When to use *its* and when to use *it's*

   Its is a possessive form of *it.*

   It's is a contraction of *it is.*

   It's a lawful search. [*It is* a lawful search.]

SUMMARY

Communication plays an important role in people's personal and professional lives. As much as 70 percent of work time is spent communicating with others. Communication is a process involving several steps, among two or more persons, for the primary purpose of exchanging information. This process requires sending an idea, receiving the idea, understanding the idea, and providing feedback to the message sender.

The Johari window is a communication model that allows police officers to examine their ability to communicate with subordinates and superiors effectively. The window is divided into four panes that represent basic areas of knowledge. The Johari window establishes four basic types of communication patterns: individuals who use communication pattern type A provide little feedback or exposure, those who use type B do not transmit information to others, those who use type C constantly express opinions but refuse to accept feedback from others, and those who use type D allow open lines of communication and accept feedback from all parties.

Schramm and Lasswell are considered to be early pioneers in the field of communications. They also established models of communication. These models further explain this complex interchange of information.

Although most of the principles of the communication process apply to both groups and individuals, certain interpersonal dynamics occur in a group setting. The police officer should understand these interactions to be able to communicate in any situation.

KEY TERMS

Centrality of communication   The degree of centralization of the message flow and decision making

Communications network   The pattern of information that flows among members of a group

Decoder   The process by which symbols are received and converted into ideas by the person receiving the information

Encoder   The process by which ideas are converted to symbols for transmission to another person

Group   A number of persons gathered or classified together

Group communication   Interaction among three or more individuals, in a face-to-face situation, who have a common need that is satisfied by the exchange of information

Interpersonal communication   The sharing of information between two persons

Propaganda   The management of collective attitudes by the manipulation of significant symbols

Signal   Symbols that are produced and transmitted

Source   The mind of the person starting the communication process

REVIEW QUESTIONS

1. Describe the concept behind the Johari window. What is the purpose of this concept?
2. How can use of the Johari window make you a better communicator?
3. Because police officers work in a quasi-military organization whose members follow orders, why should they understand the concepts pertaining to group communication?

PRACTICAL APPLICATIONS

1. Ask another student to write a five-sentence statement. This person should then orally repeat the statement to the next person. The person who receives the message should repeat it to another person and so on until the oral message ends up back at the first person. Ask the first person to repeat the oral message and read the original written message.

2. Listen to another person and see whether you can repeat everything the person says to you during a three-minute conversation.

3. Are there any physical barriers to effective listening in your classroom? What are they? Can you do anything to improve the situation?

4. Identify each statement that is written in the third person and change it to the first person:
   a. This officer pulled his gun and pointed it at the suspect.
   b. This arresting officer pulled his gun and pointed it at the suspect.
   c. This investigating officer questioned each victim.
   d. This traffic officer stopped the driver of the stolen vehicle.

5. Which of the following sentences are written in the active voice? Change those written in the passive voice to the active voice.
   a. The car was stolen by the accused.
   b. The house was broken into by Joe.
   c. The case was tried by the new deputy attorney.
   d. The police officer read the suspect his rights.
   e. A confession was given by the accused.

6. Improve the following sentences by correcting any faulty pronoun references.
   a. Angered by the language, Jerry told Jim that he would have to leave.
   b. After the robber took the gun from the purse, he threw it into the river.
   c. Joe told Jim that he would soon be a police officer.
   d. The chief told the police officer that he was in good health.
   e. If the preface of a book bores me, I do not read it.

7. Circle the correctly spelled word in each of the following rows.

handerchief	handkerchief	handkrchief	handkercheif
hereditary	hearditary	herditarty	harditary
narcoitic	narocotic	narcotic	narccotic
loitering	liotering	loiterring	liotering
maintennance	maintenance	maintanence	maintenonce
objecteively	objecteviley	ojectivily	objectively
obstrcuted	obstructted	obstrucked	obstructed
qualification	qualifcation	qualificattion	quailification
sobatage	sobotage	sabatage	sabotage
subponena	subpoena	subpeona	subpeono

8. Rewrite the following sentences as needed.
   a. The car was driven by the offender from the robbery.

   _____

   b. The subjects gun was fired at the victim by the offender.

   _____

c. This officer arrived at the scene and arrested the victim's assaulter.

d. The wanted person was observed by a citizen while he was in a school.

e. Who and why aren't you going?

9. Define and explain the following words or terms.
   a. encoder

   b. signal

   c. Johari window

   d. Schramm's model

   e. Lasswell's model

10. The following paragraph was taken from a police report. Make it a better paragraph.

It should be noted that while both offenders were facing each other this officer observed the condition of both faces. Subject Wolson's face had a small cut below the right eye which appeared as if subject Wolson had been hit by subject Hamm. Subject Hamm had a back eye that could have been caused by subject Wolson. This officer asked each subject what had happened and each subject claimed that the other subject had hit him. At this point, this officer suspected that the two subjects had been fitghtin amoung themselves.

ENDNOTES

1. The following material is adapted from Joseph Luft, *Group Processes: An Introduction to Group Dynamics* (Palo Alto, Calif.: Mayfield, 1970), and Joseph Luft, *Of Human Interaction* (Palo Alto, Calif.: National Press Books, 1969).

2. J. Hall, "Interpersonal Style and the Communication Dilemma: Management Implications of the Johari Awareness Model," *Human Relations* 27, no. 4 (April 1974): 381.

3. Wilbur Schramm, "How Communications Works," in *The Process and Effects of Mass Communications,* ed. Wilbur Schramm (Urbana, Ill.: University of Illinois Press, 1955).

4. Everett M. Rogers, *A History of Communication Study* (New York: Free Press, 1994).

5. Emile McAnany, "Wilbur Schramm, 1907–1987: Roots of the Past, Seeds of the Present," *Journal of Communication* 38, no. 4 (1988): 109–22.

6. Wilbur Schramm, *Mass Media and National Development* (Stanford, Calif.: Stanford University Press, 1964).

7. Harold Lasswell, *Propaganda Techniques in the World War* (New York: Knopf, 1927; New York: Peter Smith, 1938; Cambridge, Mass.: The MIT Press, 1971).

8. Everett M. Rogers, *A History of Communication Study* (New York: Free Press, 1994).

9. Harold Lasswell, "The Structure and Function of Communication in Society," in *The New Communication of Ideas,* ed. L. Bryson (New York: Harper & Brothers, 1948).

10. C. E. Shannon, "A Mathematical Theory of Communication," *Bell System Technical Journal* 27 (July, October 1948): 379–423, 623–656.

11. *Webster's New World Dictionary* (New York: Warner Books, 1990), 262.

12. See Michael Burgoon, Judee K. Heston, and James McCroskey, *Small Group Communication: A Functional Approach* (New York: Holt, Rinehart & Winston, 1974), 2–3.

13. See Robert Ardrey, *The Social Contract* (New York: Atheneum, 1970), 368, in which Ardrey theorized that the size range for a natural group is 11 or 12 and Marvin E.

Shaw, *Group Dynamics* (New York: McGraw-Hill, 1971), in which Shaw asserted that the maximum number of persons is 20.

14. B. Aubrey Fisher, "Decision Emergence: Phase in Group Decision-Making," *Speech Monographs* 37 (1970): 53–66.

15. Mark W. Field, "The Abilene Paradox," *Law and Order* (March 1995): 89.

16. Barry E. Collins and Harold Guetzkow, *A Social Psychology of Group Processes for Decision-Making* (New York: Wiley, 1964), 170–77.

17. See H. J. Leavitt, "Some Effects of Certain Communication Patterns on Group Performance," *Journal of Abnormal and Social Psychology* 465 (1951): 38–50; and Alex Bavelas, "Communication Patterns in Task-Oriented Groups," *Journal of the Acoustical Society of America* 22 (1950): 725–30.

18. Leavitt, "Some Effects of Certain Communication Patterns on Group Performance," 38–50.

CHAPTER 4

Improvement of Communication

LEARNING OBJECTIVES

After reading this chapter, you should understand the following concepts:

■ The various types of barriers to communication

■ How to overcome each type of communication barrier

■ How to become an effective listener

■ The different types of feedback and when using them is most effective

INTRODUCTION

In this chapter, we look at how to improve communication. The barriers to communication and the various types of feedback are discussed. Understanding both the barriers to communication and the concept of feedback is critical to the communication process.

BARRIERS TO COMMUNICATION

No matter how brilliant and invaluable your idea, it is worthless unless you can share it with others. For this reason, effective communication is crucial at every level of an organization. However, the ability to communicate effectively does not come easily to many people, and it is a skill that requires practice.
—Barbara Stennes, president and owner of Resources Unlimited,
Des Moines, Iowa

Barriers are influencing factors which impede or breakdown the continuous communications loop. They block, distort, or alter the information. By identifying the barriers and applying countermeasures, team members can effectively communicate.
—U.S. Coast Guard Training Manual,
Effective Communications, 2004, p. 15

In previous chapters, we examined how information flows from one person to another. On the surface, sending and receiving information appears to be an easy task, one that anyone could successfully accomplish. As everyone knows, however, numerous pitfalls await individuals who try to express themselves clearly on a personal level. These pitfalls, or barriers, become more troublesome when people attempt to communicate in a professional or working environment.[1] In this section, we examine the various barriers to effective communication in a law enforcement setting. Barriers to communication often arise when one party is concerned about personal or professional status.[2] The four basic categories, or types, of obstacles to effective communication are as follows: (1) emotional barriers, (2) physical barriers, (3) semantic barriers, and (4) ineffective listening. Each of these barriers can cause either the sender or the receiver to fail to communicate effectively.

Emotional Barriers

When a bear roars, he is not listening. Barriers are those obstacles that stand in the way of a successful negotiation. Barriers are obstacles to effective communications. Most barriers stem from simple communications issues between the parties.
—Anonymous

Emotional barriers may be present in either the sender or the receiver. People base their encoding or transmitting of information on their personal experiences and expectations. An officer who expects to be rejected or laughed at for making a suggestion or comment will not send his message. The need to preserve our self-esteem is universal.

Individuals with low self-esteem use certain patterns when attempting to communicate.[3] Some use *tag questions* at the end of a sentence—for example, "This is an interesting case; *isn't it?*" Other people with low self-esteem use qualifiers or disclaimers in everyday speech. Qualifiers include "sort of" and "perhaps"; disclaimers include such statements as "I really don't think this is a good idea." When we hedge or qualify language, it becomes less clear and our true intent is often hidden. An officer with low self-esteem may not be forthcoming with opinions about the cause of an accident or who committed a crime. In general, low self-esteem translates into the inability to make an assertive statement. Other emotional barriers that cause communications to break down range from simple depression to complex psychological problems.

In an effort to address emotional problems within law enforcement departments, administrators of some agencies have developed peer support systems.[4] These programs are designed to implement small interventions before the situation develops into an emotional crisis for an officer. Peer support involves officers' working with one another to solve problems. In many departments, peer support is also used with other professional help when an officer has been involved in a shooting or another critical incident.

Physical Barriers

Physical barriers are the aspects of an environment that make communication more difficult. These barriers include a rigid chain of command that requires the officer to report to a supervisor instead of informing a peer about information obtained regarding a crime. Equipment malfunctions, such as a faulty radio or computer, are another source of physical barriers to effective communication. Even such a simple factor as the distance between officers conducting a search of a wooded area is a type of physical barrier. Any obstruction that slows or impedes the free flow of information is a physical barrier to communication.

Semantic Barriers

> *The difference between the right word and the almost right word is the difference between lightning and the lightning bug.*
> —MARK TWAIN

> *Classic English language signs found in countries around the world:*
> *"Order your summers suit. Because is big rush we will execute customers in strict rotation."*
> *(At a Hong Kong tailor shop)*
> *"A new swimming pool is rapidly taking shape since the contractors have thrown in the bulk of their workers." (In an East African newspaper)*
> *"Teeth extracted by the latest methodists." (Advertisement of a Hong Kong dentist)*
> —KATHLEEN M. SWEET, UNIVERSITY OF CONNECTICUT

Semantics can pose another form of communication barrier. Strictly speaking, *semantics* is the study of the development and meaning of words. *Semantic problems,* however, can be defined as "the inability to agree on the meaning of certain terms, with a resulting loss in the ability to communicate clearly."[5] When Officer Jones states, "He is a real juvenile delinquent," other officers may come to several conclusions regarding what Officer Jones means. One officer may interpret the statement to mean that the suspect is a minor with repeated convictions in the juvenile justice system. A second officer may believe that Officer Jones is opining that the suspect, although younger than age 18 years, is simply acting out and is not a hard-core criminal. A third officer may mistake the focus of the comment and believe that Officer Jones is discussing a fellow officer who acts immaturely.

Ineffective Listening

The first indication I had that my education had a hole in it occurred in the Marine Corps. A kindly colonel gave me a bit of advice. "Lieutenant," he said, "you need to learn how to listen." "What?" I replied. Obviously it was going to take more than his counsel to get the point across.
—ED BRODOW, AUTHOR OF *NEGOTIATION BOOT CAMP,*
WWW.BRODOW.COM

The final barrier to effective communication is *ineffective listening*—failure to hear or receive what the other party is transmitting.[6] As a group, people—including police officers and administrators—are poor listeners. Numerous reasons exist for this deficiency. In addition, other factors cause a person to be inattentive in any given situation. First, the subject under discussion may be boring or irrelevant to the listener's interests. Second, the topic of the conversation may be too complex or too simple for the listener. Finally, the listener may be preoccupied with personal problems.

The general cause of ineffective listening is habit, which can be traced to the individual's earliest development. The pattern of being a talker rather than a listener is learned during childhood. As children, when we cry or tell our parents we are hurt, we receive attention. This pattern continues during the early school years, when students are encouraged to assert themselves. Schools tend to produce good talkers but poor listeners because the emphasis is on self-assertion. Talking is a form of potential power, a way to control others, to change their ideas, to shape their reality. All people use language in this manner, whether they are a presidential candidate trying to gain popular support, a student attempting to get a grade change, or a six-year-old child trying to obtain a parental favor. Talking is a basic emotional need. To be heard is to be recognized by others. Through words, people can relieve tension or punish others for their acts.

Four general variables are related to listening. First, the listener must have the ability, on the basis of experience, education, and oral proficiency, to absorb what is heard. Second, the speaker's ability to transmit the message effectively affects the listener's attention span. Third, the message being transmitted must be of interest to the listener. Fourth, the environment in which communication occurs affects the listener's ability to receive the information.

Certain factors cause people to tune out certain messages. An effective listener guards against the following barriers:

- *Uninteresting topic*—The officer may not be interested in what the speaker is saying. The officer may already be aware of the problem or issue that is being discussed.
- *Critique of the speaker*—There may be a bias against the speaker because of the speaker's manner of expression.
- *Emotional involvement*—In some situations, the officer may be excited, and stress will interfere with the communication process.
- *Failure to adjust to distractions*—Officers must listen to many people within a short period. A police officer may interview a victim, interrogate a suspect, and

receive instructions from the sergeant all within an hour. The administrator may receive information from a subordinate, sit in a meeting with the chief, and attend a community relations luncheon within the same time period. The effective listener must be able to adjust to new situations quickly and screen out distractions to receive the information that is transmitted.

- *Emotionally laden words*—Regardless of context, certain words may be offensive. The officer's reaction to these words may interfere with his or her ability to listen critically, free from bias.

Effective listening requires an environment and training that are conducive to concentration. An officer must constantly attempt to improve his or her listening skills.

Three steps in the listening process are important to police officers. First, the officer should try to avoid developing a preconceived notion of the speaker or the message. The officer must scrutinize the speaker's motives, viewpoint, and accuracy but should not draw any conclusions until after listening attentively to the speaker. The officer should not try to anticipate what the speaker will say, because doing so will influence the manner in which the officer interprets the speaker's message. In effect, people will hear what they expect and want to hear if they anticipate the message.

Second, the officer may work in a city or state in which many language systems are used. Ethnic groups abound in many jurisdictions, and each uses the English language differently. Officers must be certain that they and the speakers are speaking and interpreting the same language.

Finally, as a listener, the officer must make an effort to retain the message for later use. At a minimum, the officer must be able to retain the message until its substance is recorded in a written report.

The value of effective listening in police work is twofold: (1) It enhances the investigative function, and (2) it improves relations with individuals, both within the department and with members of the public who come into contact with police officers. Put simply, poor listening increases the difficulty of functioning in a law enforcement environment.

Barriers to effective communication prevent people from transmitting information clearly and rapidly. At the same time, these barriers may prevent the other party from receiving the intended message. One method to ensure that the intended message has been received is through the use of feedback. In the next section, we examine this important aspect of communication.

Listening Speed

The words *listening* and *hearing* do not have the same meaning. Hearing is only the first step in the communication process. Hearing occurs when your ears physically pick up sound waves, which are then transmitted to the brain. Listening is the next part of the communication process and, to be successful, must be an active process. In other words, you need to be an active participant in the communication process. For active listening, listeners must evaluate the message before they respond. Therefore, the listener should be actively working (thinking) while the speaker is talking. Because a person's thought speed is much faster than his or her speaking speed, the lag between the two processes can result in daydreaming. The listener must concentrate to overcome this hazard in an attempt to become an active listener.

TEN KEYS TO EFFECTIVE LISTENING

These keys are a positive guideline to better listening. In fact, they're at the heart of developing better listening habits that could last a lifetime.

10 Keys to Effective Listening	The Bad Listener	The Good Listener
1. Find areas of interest	Tunes out dry subjects	Opportunitizes; asks "what's in it for me?"
2. Judge content, not delivery	Tunes out if delivery is poor	Judges content, skips over delivery errors
3. Hold your fire	Tends to enter into argument	Doesn't judge until comprehension complete
4. Listen for ideas	Listens for facts	Listens for central themes
5. Be flexible	Takes intensive notes using only one system	Takes fewer notes. Uses 4-5 different systems, depending on speaker
6. Work at listening	Shows no energy output. Fakes attention.	Works hard, exhibits active body state
7. Resist distractions	Is easily distracted	Fights or avoids distractions, tolerates bad habits, knows how to concentrate
8. Exercise your mind	Resists difficult expository material; seeks light, recreational material	Uses heavier material as exercise for the mind
9. Keep your mind open	Reacts to emotional words	Interprets color words; does not get hung upon them
10. Capitalize on fact *thought* is faster than *speech*	Tends to daydream with slow speakers	Challenges, anticipates, mentally summarizes, weighs the evidence, listens between the lines to tone of voice

Source: Advising Center, Cuesta College, San Luis Obispo County Community College District, California

In short, a person with good listening skills actively performs the following tasks:

- Concentrates on the speaker
- Interprets the speaker's words
- Evaluates their meaning
- Responds effectively[7]

FEEDBACK

> *Tell me and I forget. Teach me and I remember.*
> *Involve me and I learn.*
> —BENJAMIN FRANKLIN

Sending and receiving a message does not end the communication cycle. Every law enforcement officer must also ensure that the receiving party understands the transmitted information. At this point, feedback enters the picture. Without feedback, officers talk or transmit into a black hole that absorbs all the information and does not give any indication that it was received, was understood, or will be acted on. Communicating without feedback is similar to ordering a product and not including a return address. You realize something is wrong only after the fact, when the product fails to arrive.

Understanding the Types of Feedback

Norbert Wiener, a cybernetics scholar, defined *feedback* as "the property of being able to adjust future conduct by past performance. Feedback may be as simple as that of the common reflex or it may be a higher order feedback, in which past experience is used not only to regulate specific movements, but also whole policies of behavior."[8] Although at first this definition may seem to be technical, it can be reworded more simply as "the process that allows persons transmitting information to correct and adjust messages to adapt to the receiver." This definition clearly indicates that feedback is not a single act, but a series of acts that allows the sender to understand that the other person has received the information. Just as feedback is not a single act, more than one type of feedback exists.

Direct Feedback
In the most simple feedback message, the receiver consciously and intentionally constructs feedback that is sent directly back to the message transmitter. "Sergeant, I don't understand what you want me to do" is an example of direct feedback that a patrol officer might use to indicate that the sergeant's message is unclear. This type of feedback is also known as *purposive feedback*.[9]

Indirect Feedback
Indirect feedback is a more subtle form of feedback. As its name implies, it is not information that is intentionally sent to the transmitter. It may take many forms; for example, actions by the receiver may indicate the message is not interesting. Not making eye contact, shifting the body, or yawning may indicate that the message is not one the receiver has any interest in understanding or acting on. This type of feedback is known as *nonpurposive feedback*.[10]

Positive Feedback
Positive feedback indicates that the receiver is happy or pleased with the message received. This type of feedback may be unspoken—a smile or a nod—or spoken—"Thanks for your advice on this project, Lieutenant." This type of feedback indicates that the person not only has received the message, but also approves of the content.

Negative Feedback
Negative feedback is the flip side of positive feedback. It informs the transmitter that the receiver does not agree with the content of the message.

Both positive feedback and negative feedback are important in the communication process. Positive feedback encourages the transmitter to continue to send messages, and negative feedback informs the transmitter that certain information does not please the receiver.

Immediate Feedback
Immediate feedback usually occurs in a face-to-face meeting. It may be spoken or unspoken, but it is of great value in immediately understanding whether the message has been clearly understood. Immediate feedback, however, may not be wise or

productive on some occasions, even in a face-to-face personal setting. If the situation is emotional or tense, immediate feedback may not be understood or acted on. In some of these situations, delayed feedback may be the appropriate form of interaction.

Delayed Feedback

Delayed feedback may occur when departmental memorandums are circulated. In these situations, officers may respond orally or in writing, indicating their feelings about a directive or memorandum. One of the problems with using delayed feedback is that it does not inform the sender that the message was received and understood immediately. The sender must wait until the feedback is received to confirm the validity of the information.

The preceding discussion indicates that various forms of feedback exist. These forms, however, may merge to allow feedback in a combination of ways. For example, you might receive direct, negative, or delayed feedback—or any combination thereof—on a particular message. The various types of feedback form a basis for understanding in the communication process. In the next section, we examine how feedback is received by the sender.

Receiving Feedback

Receiving feedback involves the process of effective listening; however, receiving feedback involves more than simply being an effective listener. To initiate the process of receiving feedback, the officer must make an open attempt to encourage such action. Citizens hesitate to ask a law enforcement officer to clarify a message. A number of reasons exist for this hesitancy: fear of rejection, an angry officer, belief that the officer will fail to act on the feedback, and clear indications from the officer that no feedback is wanted are a few of the more common factors. All these reasons can be traced to the actions or perceptions of the law enforcement officer.

The police officer must take the first step in the process. The officer should ensure that others understand that he or she is open to honest comments on any information the officer transmits. Effective leaders do not just state that they believe in these principles; more important, their actions support this belief. Cops on the street are great judges of character, and they can tell a phony—whether it is a con artist bilking senior citizens out of their life savings or a superior officer who mouths "communication principles" and then ignores them.

The decision to encourage feedback involves taking a risk. At some time in any police officer's career, he or she will probably receive information that is not pleasing or is threatening to the ego. An effective listener must be a risk taker. This does not mean attempting to stop an armed robbery single-handedly; it means accepting the principle that gains in efficiency in operating the division can occur only if someone is open and willing to change.

Receiving feedback is not an easy process. It requires constant attention and an honest desire to improve the ability to communicate. The rewards, however, are immeasurable. The individual who accepts feedback becomes a more effective officer.

Giving Feedback

The receipt of feedback is only a portion of the feedback process. Equally important, a police officer must understand how to give feedback. Any law enforcement officer

---

A POLICE DEPARTMENT RECEIVES FEEDBACK FROM THE COMMUNITY

Citizens of Clearwater, Florida, are considered "customers" of the police department, and, as any manager of a well-run organization knows, what your customers think of your business is important. With this in mind, the police department management developed a "customer satisfaction" survey so that officers could better serve the citizens' needs.

Traditional survey methods, such as telephone calls, letters, and so forth, are inadequate for revealing a department's effectiveness. Most people call or write only if they are extremely happy or unhappy with the way the department responds to their specific complaint. The middle ground and overall judgment are lost.

The Clearwater Police Department and the Clearwater City Managers' Office developed an 11-page survey with 32 questions designed to obtain feedback in two main areas: (1) the feelings and concerns of the respondents about their neighborhoods, and (2) the respondents' feelings about the performance of the police department and its employees.

Police management uses the survey to get feedback on public concerns and opinions of the department in general. The survey also enables the public to grade the department on the way it looks and the efficiency of its operations. The survey has opened avenues of communication that have traditionally been closed and is an asset to the department.[11]

---

must be a problem solver, which requires not only being receptive to receiving feedback, but also being able to give feedback effectively.

Giving feedback requires sensitivity to the person who is to receive the information. Following are some general guidelines any manager should use when he or she is giving feedback.

- *The person who is receiving the feedback must trust the officer.* Giving feedback must not be part of a power game or an attempt to play one party against another. The party receiving the feedback must be able to accept the information at face value to act on it. This involves the establishment of a trusting relationship or, at the least, acknowledgment that the information being transmitted is for the purposes stated and that the officer has no hidden agenda.

- *Feedback should be timely.* Telling a citizen that you did not understand his or her report two weeks after it was submitted is not effective. Feedback must be given and received by the other party in sufficient time for him or her to react to the information.

- *Feedback must be given in an understanding, sensitive manner.* If an officer humiliates private citizens by telling them that they cannot express themselves and are therefore stupid, other citizens will not readily accept comments from that officer in the future. Conversely, if the officer points out the positive aspects of citizens' statements or reports and indicates that although they are good, some points can still be improved on, the citizens will not be so hesitant to ask for or receive feedback from the officer in the future.

- *Feedback must be factual.* The police officer must ensure that comments made to citizens are fact based. Simply saying "I don't understand your statement" does not give the citizen receiving the feedback any details or facts on which to act. But saying "Your statement indicates the attack occurred at night. I need to know what time during the evening the attack occurred" will ensure that the citizen understands the area that needs to be improved.

- *The process of giving feedback should be consistent.* The law enforcement officer must daily provide timely, accurate, and sensitive feedback to subordinates, superiors, and citizens. Once this pattern is established, it should become an accepted part of the officer's style.

Giving feedback is an essential part of becoming and remaining an effective police officer. Feedback improves relationships among subordinates, superiors, and citizens, and it allows increased cooperation among all the parties involved in the process.

Using Feedback

Giving and receiving feedback is useless unless the police officer is willing to use it and is capable of doing so. The term *using feedback* describes how the superior responds to feedback or acts when he or she is giving feedback. As stated previously, feedback is part of the communication process and may involve simply clarifying transmitted information. Feedback, however, can also result in changed relationships between the law enforcement manager and superiors as well as subordinates. This change in relationship can result from either a modified perception by others about the manager or a change in the manager's actions as a result of the feedback process.

In the preceding sections, we examined the techniques involved in clarifying information that is sent from one party to another. In this section, we briefly review how officers may change their behavior when they are sending or receiving feedback. Behavior modification is one of the most difficult tasks anyone can undertake; however, the reward for the police officer will be a more effective law enforcement agency.

Feedback should never be given when an officer is angry. This rule poses a dilemma because feedback should be timely. If the officer waits to cool off, the window of opportunity for giving effective feedback may have passed. Therefore, the police officer must learn to integrate emotions and feelings with intellect and reason. Responding with anger is perfectly normal in some situations. The critical issue is to accept the emotion and review the cause of it. The officer should work toward an expanded vocabulary to become more expressive of feelings without resorting to raising the voice.

When receiving feedback, managers should paraphrase the information in their own words. Doing so allows officers to state how they interpret the other person's ideas and feelings. Police officers should practice *parasupporting*. This is a technique in which an officer not only paraphrases the other person's comments, but also carries these ideas further by providing examples or other data that the officer believes will help to illustrate and clarify the ideas.[12]

Using feedback effectively is critical to improving relations within a law enforcement department. Feedback is the glue that holds the communications cycle together. The feedback process is not something that comes naturally; however, with practice it will enhance police officers' interpersonal relationships and allow them to become more effective officers.

RULES FOR IMPROVEMENT

Effective Listening Exercises

Effective Listening Exercise 1

If the officer arrives at the scene of a crime and is approached by a tall male with a beard, with his hair in a ponytail, and wearing dirty clothes, what type of preconceived notions may the officer have?

1. A street bum, who did not see anything
2. A long-haired hippie, probably on dope
3. An undercover detective, who can assist in the investigation

Effective Listening Exercise 2

On arriving at the scene of a crime, the officer is approached by a person speaking a foreign language that the officer cannot understand. What should the officer do?

Effective Listening Exercise 3

Many times officers will be in situations that prevent them from writing down information immediately. Suggest some ways in which officers can remember a description of a suspect until they can write it down.

Misplaced Modifiers

As noted previously, clear writing requires that modifiers not be separated from the words they modify. Accordingly, modifiers should be placed as close as possible to the words they modify. This is especially true of words such as *almost, just, merely,* and *only.*

Examples

Wrong: The accused bought a gun from a man in Texas with a broken firing pin.
Better: The accused bought a gun with a broken firing pin from a man in Texas.
Wrong: The accused only shot one victim.
Better: The accused shot only one victim.
Wrong: The briefcase was found in the hall doorway partly opened.
Better: The partly opened briefcase was found in the hall doorway.

Squinting Modifiers

Squinting modifiers are modifiers that seem to modify both the word they follow and the word they precede. Accordingly, the sentence has two possible meanings. Modifiers should clearly modify only one word or phrase.

Examples

Wrong: The accused decided at that instant to fire his gun.
Better: At that instant, the accused decided to fire his gun.
Wrong: The accused had planned with his friend to rob the bank.
Better: The accused and his friend had planned to rob the bank.

Dangling Modifiers

One morning I shot an elephant in my pajamas. How he got in my pajamas I'll never know.
—GROUCHO MARX

Local Woman Hospitalized by Accident
—HEADLINE IN A COLORADO NEWSPAPER

A *dangling modifier* is a word or a group of words that does not refer clearly or logically to any other word in the sentence. Place modifiers in a position so that they clearly and directly refer to a word or a phrase in the sentence.

Examples

Wrong: Before arresting him, the suspect was informed of his rights.

Better: The suspect was informed of his rights before he was arrested.

Wrong: To hide the evidence of the crime, the body was burned.

Better: He burned the body to hide the evidence of the crime.

Wrong: Completely exhausted, I saw the man collapse to the floor.

Better: I saw the completely exhausted man collapse to the floor.

Faulty Parallelism

Parallelism results when two or more grammatically equivalent sentence elements are joined. Accordingly, *faulty parallelism* results when dissimilar elements are joined. Clear writing requires parallelism.

Examples

Wrong: The officer drew a deep breath and his eyes closed. (Active/Passive)

Better: The officer drew a deep breath and closed his eyes. (Active/Active)

Wrong: The overproduction of goods and having easy money policies both contributed to the Depression. [Note: The verb phrase having easy money is not parallel to the noun phrase the overproduction of goods.]

Better: The overproduction of goods and easy money policies contributed to the Depression.

SUMMARY

Several barriers to communication exist. They range from emotional feelings to physical obstacles that prevent the free flow of information. Although not a barrier per se, the failure to listen can disrupt the flow of data from one party to another. Effective listening is a technique that anyone can learn.

Feedback is the process that allows persons transmitting messages to adapt to the receiver. Various forms of feedback exist, all of which may be combined or merged to present data to the person transmitting the message. Receiving feedback and giving feedback are processes that enhance police officers' ability to effectively communicate with others.

KEY TERMS

Emotional barriers   Barriers that are emotional in nature and lessen the effectiveness of the communication (e.g., an officer with low self-esteem may have an emotional barrier to transmitting information to his commanding officer)

Feedback   The process that allows persons transmitting information to correct and adjust messages to adapt to the receiver

Ineffective listening   Failure to hear or receive what the other party is transmitting

Physical barriers   The aspects of an environment that make communication more difficult

Semantic problems   The inability to agree on the meaning of certain terms, with a resulting loss in the ability to communicate clearly

Semantics   The study of the development and meaning of words

REVIEW QUESTIONS

1. Of the barriers to communication discussed in this chapter, which is the easiest to overcome? Justify your answer.
2. What is the most common type of feedback?
3. What is the importance of feedback?
4. How are listening and speaking interconnected?
5. What can people do to improve their listening skills?

PRACTICAL APPLICATIONS

1. Rewrite the following sentences to eliminate misplaced, squinting, or dangling modifiers.
   a. Without asking to be repaid, the officer almost gave us all the money we needed.
   b. The door that he opened quickly closed.
   c. The rains that the crops had needed badly damaged the roads.
   d. Situated in San Francisco, tourists will enjoy Fisherman's Wharf.
   e. When in Houston, the heat and humidity may be a discomfort to visitors.
   f. To see Washington at its best, a walking tour is recommended.
2. Rewrite the following sentences to correct errors, if any, in parallelism.
   a. The police officer should be neat and cleaner.
   b. Running is better exercise than to walk.
   c. Acting wisely is more difficult than to think wise.
   d. The burglar was obviously inexperienced and not well educated.
   e. The police want respect and to be liked.
3. Circle the correctly spelled word in each of the following rows.
   strangaluton   strungulation   strangulation   strangulaton
   seducetion   seduction   secdiction   sudection

sowage	sowege	sewoge	sewage
sargeant	sargaent	sergeant	sargent
secretery	secretary	secratery	secretory
prohebited	prohibeted	prohibited	prehibited
prosepective	prospective	prospecteve	prosspective
promisory	promissery	promisery	promissory
proistitution	prostution	prostitution	prostutition
pursuade	persuade	purseade	pursuede

4. Rewrite the following sentences as needed.
   a. He ate fast because she had already ate.

   _____

   b. The food smelled awfully.

   _____

   c. His mood changed sudden.

   _____

   d. The offender was heavy armed.

   _____

   e. He admitted that he was mistake.

   _____

5. Define and explain the following words or terms.
   a. feedback

   _____

   b. semantics

   _____

   c. emotional barriers to communication

   _____

   d. physical barriers to communication

   _____

   e. parallelism

   _____

6. The following paragraph was taken from a police report. Make it a better paragraph.

   This officer caused the subjects to be transported to the city police department where he was placed in a detention cell. The subjects were arrested and booked under the suspision of distrubing the peace. No further action was taken by this officer except writing this report.

   _____
   _____
   _____
   _____
   _____
   _____
   _____
   _____
   _____
   _____

ENDNOTES

1. See Carl R. Rogers and F. J. Roethlisberger's classic article, "Barriers and Gateways to Communication," *Harvard Business Review* (November–December 1991): 105–11, for an excellent discussion of barriers to communication.

2. Mervin Kohn, *Dynamic Managing* (Menlo Park, Calif.: Cummings, 1977).

3. Mervin D. Lynch, "Stylistic Analysis," in *Method of Research in Communications,* ed. Philip Emmert and William D. Brooks (New York: Houghton Miffin, 1970), 315–42.

4. James Janik, "Who Needs Peer Support?" *The Police Chief* (January 1995): 38.

5. Barbara Marquand, "How Are We Doing?" *Law and Order* (December 1994): 41.

6. This section is adapted from "Effective Listening," International Association of Chiefs of Police Training Key Series, no. 290 (Alexandria, Va., n.d.).

7. Channing L. Bete Co., Inc., "How to Improve Your Listening Skills," *The Leader Reader* (Urbana-Champaign: University of Illinois, 1987).

8. Norbert Wiener, *Cybernetics* (New York: Wiley, 1948), 33.

9. John Keltner, *Interpersonal Communications: Elements and Structures* (Belmont, Calif.: Wadsworth, 1970), 92.

10. Ibid., 92.

11. Source: Adapted from Douglas L. Griffith, "Citizen Feedback Line," *Law and Order* (December 1993): 37.

12. John Stewart and Gary D'Angelo, "Responsive Listening," in *Messages: A Reader in Human Communication,* ed. Jean M. Civilly (New York: Random House, 1977), 191, 192.

CHAPTER 5

Special Communications Issues

LEARNING OBJECTIVES

After reading this chapter, you should understand the following concepts:

■ Why understanding other cultures is desirable

■ How officers in some law enforcement agencies are learning Spanish

■ How to communicate with a person who has a hearing impairment

INTRODUCTION

In previous chapters, we examined the communication process and its impact on criminal justice personnel. The principles described in those chapters apply to the operations of any police department as well as many other government entities and private businesses. In this chapter, we review communications issues that are especially important to members of law enforcement departments. The focus of this chapter is on the communication skills needed by the officer on the street, whether that person is a patrol officer working traffic detail or a homicide investigator. By the nature of its mission, a law enforcement agency has unique issues that are not found in any other organization. No other bureaucracy in the free world holds the power of life and death over other human beings. The duties and requirements of police officers are distinct from those of any other professional. With these different job requirements comes the need for special communication skills in a variety of situations.

Communicating with persons from other cultures or encountering an individual speaking a foreign language is becoming more common during a routine patrol. Cities, counties, and states in the United States are becoming more populated, and the

For years, visitors to China have delighted in the strange English translations that appear on the nation's signs. They range from the offensive ("Deformed Man," outside toilets for the handicapped) to the sublime ("Show Mercy to the Slender Grass," on park lawns). The sign police conduct spot checks "to see if the signs are right," says Beijing Vice Mayor Ji Lin. These signs point out the problems of translating other languages into English. An officer should be aware that individuals may not be expressing themselves clearly. (Photo by Professor Ron Wasserstein.)

number of different cultures within any given area is increasing. In many major cities, some areas are completely occupied by specific groups of people from different cultures. An officer must be prepared to communicate effectively in this environment.[1] Similarly, as persons with hearing impairments continue to enter the mainstream, they need the assistance of law enforcement personnel. The person with a hearing impairment is one of the most misunderstood individuals in modern society. Therefore, law officers need to know how to effectively communicate with these individuals as well.

COMMUNICATION WITH PEOPLE FROM OTHER CULTURES

Communicating effectively with individuals from other cultures is an area in law enforcement that is still evolving. The United States is a melting pot for other races and cultures. With the increase of Southeast Asian refugees and the increasing Hispanic population, the problem of communicating with persons who do not speak English as a primary language is critical within the law enforcement community.[2]

Survival Spanish[3]

Hispanics are the fastest growing minority group in the United States. Therefore, development of a course called "Survival Spanish for Police Officers" began in mid-1986 at Sam Houston State University, in a cooperative effort between the police academy and a faculty member of the university's Spanish department. A cross-cultural training component of *Survival Spanish* grew from a minor part of the language component when people realized that cultural barriers were just as important as the language barrier and had to be addressed in more detail.

Despite an awareness that minority populations continue to expand in the United States, the ability to communicate with them will continue to be a problem for officers in most law enforcement agencies. Heads of various departments are attempting to solve this problem in a number of ways. In some departments, bilingual officers are being hired and offered additional compensation for their services; in other departments, lists of qualified interpreters are being maintained. Finally, in many agencies, cultural awareness programs are included in roll-call training.

Methods of Responding to Language Differences

An officer who arrives at the scene of a crime and is confronted by a non-English-speaking citizen must attempt to gather information from that person. In some cases, not only must this information be gathered quickly, but it must be accurate. The citizen may be a victim of a crime or a witness who can provide a description of the suspect. The most obvious people to turn to for assistance are family members or neighbors who are bilingual. By using these individuals as on-the-scene interpreters, the officer can obtain the initial information quickly. The officer should ensure that not only the witness's name, but also the translator's name and address, is recorded. In follow-up investigations, the services of trained translators are normally used. In some cities, the courts, prosecutors, and police agencies maintain lists of interpreters to call on if the need arises. For example, in the main Los Angeles County courthouse, interpreters are available for 78 languages.

SPANISH LANGUAGE COMPONENT (EIGHT HOURS)

Curriculum: Instruction begins with a crash course in Spanish pronunciation that emphasizes eliminating problems with the most troublesome sounds for Anglos learning Spanish. As an aid to pronunciation, a list of the fifty most common Spanish names is used for practice. The gain is twofold: not only are officers given an opportunity to work with single-word units (names), but they also quickly perfect the pronunciation of the names they will encounter on the street. The class then learns to read the *Miranda* warning in Spanish, thus moving on to entire-sentence units. This lesson increases the officers' confidence and level of comfort with unfamiliar Spanish sounds.

The core of the day consists of four one-hour classes that include 39 "survival" commands, questions, warnings, and exchanges. Some of the items included are "Sit down," "Shut up," "I'm a police officer," "Stop," "Get out of the car," and "Put the weapon down." The Spanish equivalents are taught as purely rote items to be mastered quickly through a variety of language techniques.

The last session of the day is devoted to simulations and role playing. During this session, officers act out a variety of scenarios, using their newly acquired abilities.

CROSS-CULTURAL TRAINING COMPONENT (EIGHT HOURS)

Curriculum: The cross-cultural training component of Survival Spanish is a multifaceted treatment of the Hispanic community in the United States and the relationship of this community to law enforcement and the criminal justice system. Population trends, racial characteristics, Roman law versus English law, and alien documentation are studied. Numerous subtle but important cultural barriers are explored, including deception, eye contact, differing concepts of time and direction, the Hispanic surname system, personal space and touching, and the use of the body as a personal "bank." More in-depth presentations and discussions cover such topics as machismo, Hispanic women (vis-à-vis spousal abuse, domestic disturbances, rape, and incest), Hispanics and vehicular law (bribes, driving without a license or insurance, speeding, and hit-and-run incidents), and Anglo–Hispanic stereotypes. In addition, a cross-cultural simulation exercise designed especially for police officers dramatizes the problem of cultural barriers.[4]

Naturally, inherent problems exist with using family members or neighbors as interpreters. They may have difficulty with English, and some terms may be outside their knowledge or vocabulary. In addition, they may be biased and want to help the victim or witness, to the detriment of others. Because of these issues, department administrators try to use bilingual officers. These officers can speak and write in both English and another language. In many cases, they not only speak a second language, but also are members of that ethnic group and are familiar with the history, traditions, and customs of the culture.

In many departments, additional compensation is offered to bilingual officers. Such officers respond to situations in which their language skill is needed, and they provide an independent interpretation without the complication of friendship or bias.

老人、儿童上扶梯时
需有家人陪同

When old man's child go up hand ladder
temporary need the family to accompany

Another Chinese sign that was incorrectly translated. Individuals whose first language is not English have similar difficulties communicating with police officers and other government officials. (Photo by Professor Ron Wasserstein.)

In many departments, roll-call training that emphasizes the cultures of minorities within the department's jurisdiction is encouraged. Such training is another method by which officers may learn basic phrases of a different language. As another incentive in some agencies, officers will be reimbursed if they take and pass conversational language courses that enable them to interact with minority groups.

Other Multicultural Issues[5]

There are two eternal truths about human beings:

- *People differ from one another.*
- *People are similar to one another.*

STATEMENT IN A 1996 NATIONAL VICTIM
ASSISTANCE ACADEMY TRAINING PROGRAM.

The term *culture* can be applied to various population categories, but it is normally associated with race and ethnicity. Diversity of race and ethnicity both enriches and obstructs a law enforcement officer's involvement and interaction with other persons, groups, and cultures.

Officers should remember that most minorities have developed a sharp sense for detecting condescension, manipulation, and insincerity. There is no substitute for compassion as the foundation, and sincerity as its expression, in carrying out law enforcement services equally and fairly.

Although feeling the same amount of compassion for all victims is not possible, law enforcement officers must provide the same compassionate service to every victim. For example, the plight of undocumented residents or illegal aliens involves complex issues of personal prejudice and international policies. Many of these persons suffer financial exploitation and other criminal victimization once they enter the United States. Officers must make an effort to understand these persons' situations and not let personal opinions affect interaction with these individuals when such individuals are victimized.

The first contact minorities have with law enforcement officers will either confirm or dispel suspicion as to how they will be treated. Proper pronunciation of a person's surname is an excellent way to begin contact with a person. Surnames have histories and meanings that allow for conversation beyond the introduction. Likewise, when working with immigrant, refugee, or native populations, an officer will find it helpful to learn a few words of greeting from that culture. This willingness to go beyond what is comfortable and usual conveys the officer's intent to communicate.

Listening is fundamental to human relationships. The principles and manner of listening, however, differ among cultures. For example, Asians and Pacific Islanders deflect direct eye contact during conversation as a sign of patient listening and deference. These groups therefore consider staring to be impolite and confrontational. In contrast, people in many Western cultures value direct eye contact as a sign of sympathy or respect. Looking elsewhere is seen as disinterest or evasiveness. Misunderstanding in the communication process can occur if some allowance is not made for these differences.

Multicultural issues must be understood by all law enforcement officers. Understanding that "different" does not mean "criminal" will assist officers attempting to communicate in an environment that continues to become more and more diverse.

COMMUNICATION WITH PERSONS WITH HEARING IMPAIRMENTS

More than 21 million Americans have some degree of hearing impairment. A serious problem ensues when a law enforcement officer encounters a person who is completely deaf because the ability to communicate with such individuals is limited. Many persons with hearing impairments use movements of their hands, body, and face as a way to communicate. This is known as *signing*.[6] American Sign Language, also known as *Ameslan,* is the sign language used by some people who are deaf in America (Figure 5.1). Many colleges and universities across the United States offer Ameslan as a course to satisfy the foreign language requirement for graduation.

Basic Principles

The interpersonal and communication skills of a police officer who has contact with a person who is deaf will be drawn on to their fullest extent. The most important rule for dealing with a person who is deaf is never to assume he or she understands what is being communicated until positive feedback is received, either through signing or other actions.

FIGURE 5.1   Basic Sign Language Chart

Use of the following phrases and their American Sign Language counterparts should enable the police officer to establish a sound working relationship with the deaf victim, suspect, or witness. After initial communication has been made, the officer can write his questions and comments or, when available and appropriate, an interpreter can be used.

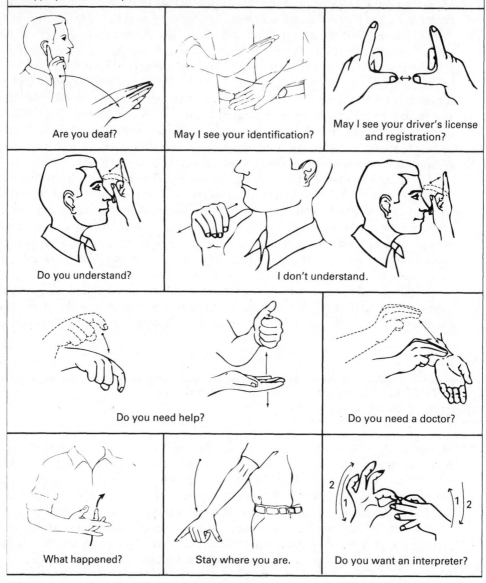

SOURCE: "The Deaf and the Police," International Association of Chiefs of Police, Alexandria, Va., Training Key Series no. 244.

Other basic principles that officers should use when dealing with individuals who are deaf include the following:

- *Recognize that the person is deaf.* When persons who are deaf are approached by an officer, most will usually indicate their condition by pointing to their ears or shaking their head. The person who is deaf may attempt to speak, but many times the officer will not be able to understand what the person is saying. The officer should understand that this is a sign of the individual's disability and not the result of alcohol or drugs.

- *Understand the disability.* Because many people who are deaf rely on written communication, they may reach for a pen and paper when they are stopped by an officer. In some situations, such an action might be viewed as reaching for a weapon. The officer should be alert to this possibility and not interpret the action as threatening.

- *Attempt to establish communication through any available means.* Ideally, the officer would understand Ameslan and be able to communicate with the person who is deaf. Usually this is not the case and the officer must use the next most acceptable method of communication: written notes. The officer's written notes should be clear, concise, and legible. [*Note:* Contrary to popular belief, most people who are deaf do not read lips.]

The officer who comes into contact with a person who is deaf should treat that individual the same as any other person with a disability; respect, patience, and understanding will go a long way toward opening communication lines.[7] Many officers work a number of years before coming into contact with a person who is deaf; however, when they do, they must understand the disability and act accordingly.

The Americans with Disabilities Act (ADA) requires organizations to take all reasonable steps to accommodate persons who have disabilities. This Act is complex and is not discussed in depth in this book. Some public safety agencies, however, have been sued for failing to provide adequate sign language interpreters for persons with hearing impairments. Therefore, this issue is another example of special communications that have an impact on officers.

Police officers, administrators, and agencies face unique communication issues in the modern world. These issues range from dealing with individuals from different cultures and those who speak different languages to communicating with persons who are deaf. By understanding these issues and addressing them in a training environment, law enforcement personnel will be better able to effectively carry out their mission of protecting the public.

COMMUNICATION WITH PERSONS WITH MENTAL ISSUES

It is estimated that three out of every 100 people have mental problems. Accordingly, the chances of a police officer coming in contact with a person who has a mental disability are very high. The ADA prohibits state and local governments from discriminating against an individual with a disability. This includes mental disabilities.

Mental Retardation or Mental Illness?

Individuals with mental retardation have limited ability to learn. The degree of limitation varies. Most people with mental retardation live independently and are useful members of society. Individuals classified with severe mental retardation are institutionalized. The majority of people with mild mental retardation are only mildly retarded, which makes it difficult to discern that they are retarded. Many people with mental retardation want to be considered normal and therefore they attempt to hide or mask the retardation, especially when dealing with authorities.

Mental illness affects a person's thought processes, moods, and emotions. Mental retardation generally occurs before a person reaches adulthood, but mental illness can occur at any time in a person's life. Mental illness has nothing to do with intelligence. People with mental illness may have average, below-average, or above-average intelligence.

Detection of Mental Problems

There is often no way to determine whether a person has mental retardation. Certain traits are frequently exhibited by a person who is mentally retarded, but a person exhibiting these traits is not necessarily mentally retarded. Those traits are:

- Limited vocabulary or a speech impairment
- Difficulty in understanding or answering questions
- A short attention span
- Acts inappropriately with peers or the opposite sex
- Is easily influenced by and eager to please others
- Is easily frustrated
- Has difficulty with some of the following tasks:
  - giving accurate directions
  - making change
  - using the telephone or telephone book
  - telling time
  - reading or writing

Contact with the Person

The mentally disabled person may

- not want his or her disability noticed
- not understand rights
- not understand routine questions
- not understand simple commands
- be overwhelmed by the presence of a police officer
- act very upset at being detained and try to run away
- say what he or she thinks the officer wants to hear
- have difficulty in describing facts or details of an event

- be the last to leave the scene and the first to get caught if involved in the criminal activity
- be confused about who is responsible for the crime and "confess" even though innocent

Communication Tactics

There are no hard and fast rules for communicating with a person with either mental retardation or mental illness. The following tactics are recommended:

- Speak directly to the person.
- Keep your sentences short.
- Use simple language.
- Speak slowly and clearly.
- Divide complicated instructions or information into smaller parts.
- If possible, use pictures, symbols, and actions to help convey meaning.
- Be patient:
  - Take time in giving or asking for information.
  - Avoid confusing questions about reasons for behavior.
  - Repeat questions more than once or ask a question in a different way.
- Use firm and calm persistence if the person doesn't comply or acts aggressive.
- When questioning the individual don't ask questions in a way that solicits a certain answer (i.e., don't ask leading questions).
- Try to avoid the use of questions that can be answered with "yes" or "no." Use open-ended questions such as, "Tell me what happened."

Common Sense

Most people who have such issues or problems do not like to be called "retarded" or "crazy." Do not assume that individuals with such problems are totally incapable of understanding or communicating. Treat them as adults, not as children. When communicating with persons with mental issues, give them the same respect you would give any other citizen.[8]

COMMUNICATION WITH INDIVIDUALS UNDER THE INFLUENCE

For the law enforcement officer confronting a person who is intoxicated or "under the influence of alcoholic beverages or drugs . . . one thing remains certain: . . . the potential for real danger is inevitably present."
—GERALD GARNER, CHIEF OF THE GREELEY, COLORADO POLICE DEPARTMENT[9]

Gerald Garner states that the safe and humane handling of a person under the influence can prove a serious challenge for the most experienced, skilled, and compassionate officer. When attempting to communicate with such individuals, the individual often will exploit your vulnerabilities by personally directing obscene, threatening, or belittling comments toward you. Often, attempting to communicate with individuals in this condition is not only a waste of time, but dangerous because of their unpredictability. As a general rule, if the person you are trying to communicate with is under the influence, stop trying to communicate and take certain defensive steps. Garner recommends the following procedures when dealing with intoxicated persons:

- Recognize that the demeanor and actions of the person can change quickly.
- Always get a backup.
- Handcuff and search the person if you have taken him or her into custody.
- Never ridicule or needlessly antagonize the person.
- Take nothing for granted and watch for self-destructive behavior.
- Continuously monitor the physical condition and actions of the person.

RULES FOR IMPROVEMENT

Use of the Colon

A colon is used primarily to call attention to the words that follow it.[10] A colon should be used after an independent clause to direct attention to a list or a quotation. The colon is used after the salutation in a formal letter, between a title and a subtitle, and to indicate hours and minutes. A colon is also used between independent clauses if the second summarizes or explains the first.

Do *not* use a colon between a verb and its object. For example, a colon should not have been used in the following sentence.

Police officers are: educated, intelligent, and well paid.

Likewise, do not use a colon between a preposition and its object. For instance, the colon in the next sentence should be deleted.

The officer's training consists of: twelve weeks of academy and six months of on-the-job training.

Finally, do not use a colon after *such as, including,* and *for example.*

Correct Word Choice

In language, clarity is everything.
—Confucius

"You should say what you mean," the March Hare went on.
"I do," Alice hastily replied; "at least—at least I mean what I say—that's the same thing, you know."
"Not the same thing a bit!" said the Hatter.
"Why, you might as well say that 'I see what I eat' is the same thing as 'I eat what I see!'"
—Lewis Carroll, *Alice in Wonderland*

Clear writing includes the use of correct words. As a general rule, do not use legal, technical, slang, or unfamiliar words. An additional characteristic of clear writing is conciseness. All unnecessary words should be left out. Details necessary in a report, however, should not be left out. The overuse of certain words, such as *stated* and *advised*, also detracts from clear and concise writing.

Examples

Wrong: He commenced the investigation.

Better: He started the investigation.

Wrong: The prosecutor failed to ascertain the facts necessary to prove the crime.

Better: The prosecutor failed to provide the necessary facts to prove the crime.

Wrong: The aforesaid investigation was closed.

Better: The investigation was closed.

Wrong: The victim was very pregnant.

Better: The victim was pregnant.

Wrong: He was not very often on time.

Better: He was usually late.

Wrong: There are many police officers in the city of Houston.

Better: The city of Houston has many police officers.

Better-Writing Drill

Are your reports clearly written? Consult the following checklist for clear writing.

- I used the first person.
- I used the active voice.
- I correctly used modifiers.
- My pronoun references are correct.
- I used parallelism.
- My report contains common words.
- I did not use unnecessary words.

SUMMARY

Police officers and administrators face unique communication issues as law enforcement officers. The mission of law enforcement is such that these issues are rarely encountered by any other group of professionals. Officers must be aware of these special situations and strive to communicate effectively when they encounter them. Communicating with minorities and persons who are deaf poses special communication needs. By becoming more sensitive to these persons' needs and backgrounds, officers will be able to communicate with them more effectively.

KEY TERMS

Ameslan   American Sign Language, the sign language used by some persons who have hearing impairments

Signing   Movement of the hands, body, and face as a way to communicate

Survival Spanish   A course developed for police officers that includes a Spanish language component and a cross-cultural training component

REVIEW QUESTIONS

1. Is requiring police officers to learn a second language while attending roll-call training a realistic expectation? Justify your answer and present any alternatives you can think of.
2. Should officers be required to learn sign language? Why?
3. Some individuals argue that because people from other nations live in the United States, they should speak English. If you accept this principle, officers should not need to know how to communicate with persons from other cultures. Do you agree or disagree with this position? Why?

PRACTICAL APPLICATIONS

1. Review and practice Ameslan for three days. Attempt to carry on a conversation with other students by using this sign language. Draft a report on your experiences and what you learned.
2. Correct or improve the following sentences.
    a. The police officer ran on foot after the suspect.
    b. The officer recognized him as being one Robert White.
    c. The investigation report contained information which is considered as confidential in nature.
    d. The victim was found lying in a position on her back.
    e. The accused entered the stolen vehicle and started it up.
    f. The officer opened the shotgun to see whether or not it was loaded.
    g. The room in which the crime occurred did not appear to have anything out of place. It appeared very neat.
    h. Officer would you be of assistance to me?
3. Circle the correctly spelled word in each of the following rows.

purversion	purvirsion	perversion	pervirsion
procecute	prosecute	procidute	porsecute
pneumatic	penumatic	penumatec	pnematic
pusionous	poisonous	pousuinous	poisionous
prisumptive	presumteve	presumptive	presumpative
sophesticated	sophisticated	suphisticated	suphistcated
specific	spific	spefeci	specifice
spacuious	spacous	spaciouse	spacious

stationarry	stationury	stationerry	stationary
stering	sterring	steering	steeing

4. Rewrite the following sentences as needed.
   a. The victim was very dead.

   _____

   b. The car was really on fire.

   _____

   c. This officer dismounted from his vehicle.

   _____

   d. He was not very often on time.

   _____

   e. The female officer was very pregnant.

   _____

5. Define and explain the following words or terms.
   a. signing

   _____

   b. Ameslan

   _____

   c. Survival Spanish

   _____

6. The following paragraph was taken from a police report. Make it a better paragraph.

   This officer asked Mrs. Smith if she had seen or noticed any actions that had taken place at this location at which time she responded by stating no and that she was not going to say anything else. It should be noted that Mrs. Smith appeared to be drinking and smelled like she had been drinking beer. The witness gave her name and telephone number to this officer and was released. Her name and address is appended to this report.

   _____

   _____

   _____

   _____

   _____

   _____

   _____

   _____

   _____

ENDNOTES

1. For an excellent article on cultural awareness, see Stephen M. Hennessy, "Achieving Cultural Competence," *The Police Chief* 60 (August 1993): 46.

2. Spanish is not the only language that officers will encounter. For a discussion of law enforcement agencies' experiences with Chinese, see C. Fredric Anderson and Henriette

Liu Levy, "A Guide to Chinese Names," *FBI Law Enforcement Bulletin* 61, no. 3 (March 1992): 10.

3. Gene B. Blair and Sam L. Slick, "Survival Spanish: Needed Training for Police," *The Police Chief* 57 (January 1990): 42–47.

4. Survival Spanish is not just a theory. Several law enforcement agencies, including the Huntsville and Austin Police Departments, as well as the Georgia State Police Academy, have benefited from this type of training.

5. Brian K. Ogawa, *Focus on the Future: A Prosecutor's Guide for Victim Assistance* (Washington, D.C.: National Victim Center, 1994), 21–34.

6. See Jeri F. Traub, "The Hearing Impaired Individual: Suspect or Victim," in *Law Enforcement and Social Welfare: The Emergency Response,* ed. John A. Brown, Peter C. Unsinger, and Harry W. More (Springfield, Charles C. Thomas, 1989), 241–79.

7. Robert D. Jones, "Law Enforcement and the Deaf Community," *FBI Law Enforcement Bulletin* (November 1993): 24–31.

8. The information in this section was taken from materials provided by The Arc (a national, tax-exempt, nonprofit organization of and for people with intellectual and developmental disabilities) and the Disability Rights Section, Civil Rights Division, U.S. Department of Justice.

9. Gerald Garner, "Handling People under the Influence," *Police Magazine* (December 2006): 48.

10. Diana Hacker, *Rules for Writers,* 4th ed. (New York: Bedford/St. Martin's, 2000), 296.

CHAPTER 6

Communicating in Public

LEARNING OBJECTIVES

After reading this chapter, you should understand the following concepts:

- How to draft a speech

- How to present a speech

- The different types of mass media and their objectives

- How to conduct an interview with the media

- The rules that apply to media access to crime scenes

INTRODUCTION

This is not the end. It is not even the beginning of the end. But it is, perhaps, the end of the beginning.
—SIR WINSTON CHURCHILL

Who can forget the morning of April 23, 2007? That Monday morning, 32 students and teachers at Virginia Tech University were murdered by a mentally ill student, Cho Seung-Hui. All the major television and radio stations covered the aftermath. Later in the week, the NBC news headquarters in New York received a package containing Cho's final manifesto.

Clearly, the media have the ability to bring crime into our living rooms. Therefore, law enforcement officers must understand how the media work and how to communicate with them effectively. Officers talk with friends and colleagues daily, and although this is a form of communicating in the public arena, distinct differences exist between this type of communication and giving a speech or being interviewed by the local television anchor. In this chapter, we examine some techniques that can facilitate a law enforcement officer's ability to effectively communicate in public situations.

PUBLIC SPEAKING

It usually takes me more than three weeks to prepare a good impromptu speech.
—MARK TWAIN

Most criminal justice professionals will be called on sometime in their careers to make presentations to the general public. Such presentations may be talks to an informal gathering of citizens at a Neighborhood Watch meeting or formal presentations to the city council. One obstacle many officers encounter when speaking to groups is stage fright. As with any other skill, however, practice makes perfect. This is not to say all officers will become dynamic and forceful speakers. Some people are better than others at appearing and communicating in public. Nevertheless, if certain basic and simple procedures are mastered, any officer can make a creditable presentation.

Law officers talk to other persons all the time. Public speaking is simply talking to more than one person. In a group setting, however, the rules of communication change. Feedback may be delayed or never received. Physical barriers, such as a nonworking microphone, may prevent persons in the back of the room from hearing. In addition, most officers typically worry about making a mistake or looking unprofessional.

Drafting the Speech

Writing a speech can be an agonizing task for many law enforcement officers. A speech, however, should be prepared differently from a term paper or a departmental position paper. Six simple rules follow for writing a speech:

1. *Prepare an outline of the topics you want to discuss.* Start with your main objective or theme. The first item to write down is what you want the audience to do as a

result of the speech. Keep this objective in mind while writing the rest of the speech.

2. *Draft an outline of the main points you want to discuss.* Only three or four major items should be on the list. If you have a laundry list of items, think about combining them or rethink what you want to accomplish with the speech.

3. *Revise the outline several times.* Then begin to add more information to your main points. Think about each piece of information that you are adding. Does it explain your main point?

4. *Remember, we write differently than we speak.* Practice your speech by speaking it aloud. After several rehearsals, you may want to revise your presentation.

5. *Prepare an outline and deliver your speech according to the outline.* You should know the subject matter well enough beforehand so that you need to refer only to the outline instead of a long, typewritten speech. Such preparation will result in a more natural delivery.

6. *When writing a speech, start at the middle or the end.* The most difficult part of a speech is the opening, which should be written last.

Once your speech is written, the next step is to deliver it. In the following section, we briefly examine some simple principles that you can follow to make your public presentations more professional.

Remembering Some Dos and Don'ts

> *Less is more only when it is recognized that the more one eliminates, the greater the importance of refining that which remains.*
> —Lewis Mumford

There are as many rules for effective public speaking as there are dynamic speakers.[1] The focus of this text is not on public speaking, nor is it our intent to include great detail on the various techniques of effective speaking. Although no single approach will work for all persons, several simple, easily mastered methods will allow most officers to make clear and meaningful presentations. The following nine rules will assist you in making oral presentations:

1. *Understand the topic of your speech.* What does the group expect to hear? If they want to be informed about the patrol functions of the department, do not deliver a speech on the records division.

2. *Know your audience and direct your speech to their interests and knowledge level.* Nothing is more boring than a speech full of technical jargon that the audience does not understand. Talk on the audience's level and the reward will be an interested audience.

3. *Humor is excellent, but it can backfire.* If you are comfortable with using humor, it can break the ice and relax the audience for the speech. However, if you cannot deliver a joke well, exclude it. A long, drawn-out joke that does not go over with the audience leaves a bad taste with everyone.

4. *Always be on time and dress appropriately.* Common courtesy requires that you do not keep the audience waiting for your arrival. Know the exact starting time and arrive a few minutes early.

5. *Do not read your speech word for word.* A speaker who drones on and on, reading from prepared notes, will be tuned out by the audience.

6. *Understand how long you are expected to speak and ensure that you do not exceed the time limit.* Even if you think you have the audience eating out of the palm of your hand, do not prolong the speech. Remember, the group may have other business, and if you are good, they will ask you to return.

7. *Whenever possible, use visual aids.* Nothing makes your point as well as visual aids. Business people have known this for years. Employees in the public sector should take the hint and use visual aids whenever possible.

8. *Rehearse as many times as your work schedule will allow.* Rehearse, rehearse, rehearse—especially at the beginning of your public-speaking career.

9. *Ask for honest feedback from the person who asked you to make the speech.* Do not simply say, "How was I?" This question will lead to the standard response, "You were great." Politely press the person to offer comments about how you could make the presentation better the next time. Once encouraged to give feedback, many people will provide helpful suggestions.

Public speaking is more of an art than a science. By following the preceding rules, however, and considering the following points, any officer can become a better public speaker.

ELEMENTS TO CONSIDER WHEN YOU ARE MAKING A PRESENTATION[2]

Appearance. A neat, professional appearance is mandatory. You will make your first impression on the audience solely on the way you look, even before you speak a word.

Stance. A speaker should walk and stand with the head up and the shoulders back, and project a quiet, confident attitude. The speaker should try to recognize and avoid any mannerism (e.g., keeping hands in pockets, crossing arms, tightly gripping the podium) that an audience may discern as nervousness.

Gestures. A speaker should ensure that his or her gestures are natural. The speaker should never allow gestures to overcome the presentation.

Facial expressions. A speaker's facial expressions should convey his or her personality along with warmth for and sincerity about the topic. If a speaker looks interested and friendly, the audience will reciprocate.

Eye contact. A speaker who develops proper eye contact will communicate more efficiently.

Voice/inflection. The speaker should modulate the tone of voice, change the pitch, and vary the pace of the speech.

Vocabulary. The speaker should always ensure correct pronunciations and provide definitions of difficult words. In addition, the speaker should use proper grammar and simple language so that the presentation remains easy to comprehend by all levels of the audience.

Enthusiasm. By choosing a topic of personal interest, a speaker can easily become excited about the topic to be shared with the audience, which will allow the speaker to concentrate on the message and convey the information as valid and important.

Speaking to a group of citizens or elected officials requires certain techniques. Different rules apply, however, when you are attempting to communicate with the media. In the next section, we examine this important aspect of law enforcement communications.

COMMUNICATION WITH THE MEDIA

Unfortunately, many police officers, administrators, and police chiefs view news reporters with distrust.[3] Just as the police have a mission to accomplish, so do the media. The Constitution prohibits the federal and state governments from passing any law that abridges the freedom of the press. The media call this the *people's right to know.* Occasionally, the media's striving to inform the public conflicts with a law enforcement agency's desire to keep certain information confidential. Only by understanding the media and their role in society can an administrator work effectively with them to present the department's position.

Relations with the Media

Understanding the media must begin with a clarification of the different types of media. The law enforcement administrator must understand that certain basic fundamental principles apply to the media in general. In addition, distinct rules, goals, and standards pertain to different types of media.

Media Types

Members of law enforcement agencies typically interact with three basic types of media: newspapers, radio, and television.

Newspapers   Newspapers usually provide more in-depth coverage than that provided by the electronic media. In addition, many newspapers cover the human aspects of a story. As discussed subsequently, electronic media professionals must use short and to-the-point stories. Newspaper editors may run a major story coupled with a sidebar that touches on another aspect of the main story. A *sidebar* is usually a short article that is placed in a column next to the main article. Many newspaper companies will employ a full-time police or court reporter. This reporter will know the officers, street language, and the law nearly as well as any police officer does.

Radio   A radio broadcast carries only the officer's voice. Radio reporters do not have to capture the scene with pictures; therefore, many interviews with the police are conducted over the telephone. Many radio stations have hourly newscasts and can therefore update the public more effectively than can newspapers, which are published daily, or television, which has evening or nightly newscasts. In this day of visual media, an effective administrator should not overlook radio as a means by which the public may be informed of the department's activities.

Television   Television is the medium people are most familiar with. It brings the action into family living rooms as it occurs. Many people have watched from the comfort of their easy chairs as hostage scenes and riots have occurred. Television is visual by its nature. A simple news release does not satisfy the television director, who wants and needs pictures: a uniformed officer speaking, a suspect being placed in a patrol vehicle, the front of a shot-up building. These types of graphic scenes are what television personnel are searching for daily. In addition, television news is short and to the point. Normally, a story on the evening news is 20 to 30 seconds long. No matter how long the reporter interviews an officer, the final broadcast will usually run no longer than one minute.

How to Deal with the Media

Understanding the distinctions between the different types of media allows the law enforcement administrator to deal with the media effectively. Chiefs, administrators, and officers will have contact with the media—sometimes daily. In many departments, the rules for these contacts have been codified by a standard operating procedure (SOP) on media relations. This procedure has three advantages. First, it assures the media and the city manager of uniformity in dealing with the press. Second, it establishes procedures that both parties know and can follow. If media representatives are consulted when the document is being drafted, they will be more understanding of its purpose and will follow the procedures more readily. Third, the SOP informs the officers on the street about how they should respond to an unexpected contact with a news reporter.

Using a *public affairs officer (PAO)* is becoming more common in law enforcement agencies.[4] A PAO is the police department's official point of contact with the media. Several approaches to using a PAO can be taken. One approach is to make the PAO the official spokesperson for the department, in which case all interviews are conducted by the PAO. Although this approach may provide continuity, it is not the most effective method for dealing with either the public or the media. Any top-level administrator who has above-average communication skills should be able to conduct a live interview with the media.

A second approach is to establish the position as an official assignment and rotate officers who fill it on the basis of their experience, intelligence, and ability. This alternative allows the public and the media to talk to a sworn officer. The disadvantage is that, depending on the length of the assignment, the media must readjust to a new officer every time officers are rotated.

Many top-level administrators have experienced sleepless nights over leaks to the press by members of their department. News reporters are ethically bound not to reveal the identity of their sources. Just as police officers will not reveal the names of their confidential, reliable informants, so news reporters carefully guard the identity of their sources. Some states have *shield laws* that prevent a news reporter from being held in contempt of court for refusing to comply with a court order to reveal a source's name. In addition, there have been numerous incidents of reporters' going to jail rather than giving up their sources' identities. By accepting that occasionally leaks to the media will occur, the effective administrator should attempt to work out a relationship with the press that minimizes the impact of a leak. On occasion, an officer may promise to keep the media informed if they will withhold the story until the appropriate time. Another technique is to appeal to the reporter's integrity and explain the consequences of releasing the story. Getting angry at the reporter or the unnamed source is fruitless. Human nature being what it is, leaks will continue as long as there is a reporter willing to listen.

Effective media relations should also include conferences among the chief or a designated representative, the news director of the television or radio station, and the editor or publisher of the newspaper. These periodic conferences can sometimes be stormy, but they allow each party to understand the other's point of view. This relationship is especially helpful if the department is on the receiving end of a story that is critical of the agency. Media representatives should always attempt to get in contact with the department for its side before the story is run. If a reporter neglects to reach the department, a call to the editor will usually provide the opportunity for a follow-up story on the department's position.

Establishing an ongoing relationship with the media is a necessary function of any law enforcement administrator. It must always be based on trust and mutual respect. Once such a relationship has been created, it will benefit both the department and the public.

The Interview

Understanding the goal of the media assists the officer in preparing for and conducting an interview. The first few times an officer or an administrator participates in a media interview can be frightening. When the newspaper reporter begins to take notes, or the radio or television reporter thrusts a microphone at the officer, the experience can be overpowering.

Preparation before the interview can help calm the officer's nerves. Being knowledgeable about the facts of the incident, as well as about the agency's position, can enhance communication. If photo opportunities are available, the officer should ensure that the media are made aware of them. Never should the officer lie or distort the truth. The officer's credibility and that of the department are on the line. An officer who does not have an answer should say so and offer to find out. If such a promise is made, the officer must keep it.

Once the officer has reviewed the facts and had preliminary discussions with the media, the actual interview will take place. By this time it may seem anticlimactic. The officer should remember to speak clearly in everyday language and avoid the use of jargon. "I observed the defendant committing a 211 and responded over the net with a 10-14" does not tell the public or the media representative what really occurred. "I saw the suspect fleeing from the convenience store with a gun in his hand and believed he had committed a robbery. I radioed for assistance and was able to arrest the suspect two blocks away" is a more complete statement.

If the officer is anxious about talking to a reporter because of being seen on the nightly news by thousands of citizens, one helpful tip is for the officer to remember that this is a one-on-one conversation. The camera is recording only what is said between the officer and the reporter. On occasion an officer will be called on to give an interview "live" instead of taped, edited, and replayed at a later time. The officer should approach this situation in the same manner as with a taped interview. He or she should be professional and communicate clearly with the reporter, not the unseen masses.

Relations with the media have traditionally been tense. By understanding the purposes and working conditions of media representatives and trying to assist them whenever possible, an officer or administrator may become an effective spokesperson for the department. This, in turn, will make the job of policing the community easier when the public understands the agency's position.

Media Access to Crime Scenes

As indicated previously, a state of distrust has historically existed between the media and law enforcement. One area that causes the most friction is media access to crime scenes.[5] The media argue that the public's right to know should allow them special privileges, including unrestricted access to crime scenes. Law enforcement's position is that unrestricted access by the media may contaminate the scene of a crime.

This conflict may have been resolved in a series of three United States Supreme Court decisions that establish the parameters of the media's First Amendment news-gathering privilege.[6] The Supreme Court stated that the right of the media to information held by law enforcement is no greater than the right of the general public and that law enforcement can prevent the media from obtaining access to information or areas not generally available to the public.

Different rules apply once the media acquire information. The courts have held that almost all attempts to prevent the media from publishing information will fail. This concept is known as *prior restraint*.[7] The Supreme Court has stated that only governmental allegation and proof that publication must inevitably, directly, and immediately cause the occurrence of an event kindred to imperiling the safety of a transport at sea can support the issuance of an interim restraining order.[8]

The media are driven by both First Amendment concerns and simple business issues of scooping other members of the press. Law enforcement officers must protect crime scenes and conduct criminal investigations. Conflict will continue between the media and law enforcement regarding access to crime scenes. Simply understanding this conflict will allow law enforcement officers to act accordingly.

RULES FOR IMPROVEMENT

Correct Word Choice

When do you use the phrase *fact that*? It is used in many legal documents, but William Strunk stated that he "quivered with revulsion" when he read the phrase. He insisted that it be revised out of every sentence in which it appears.[9]

A similar phrase is *if and when*. Use either *if* or *when*, not both.

What about the phrase *in order to*? In almost all cases, remove *in order* to tighten the sentence and make it read better.

When do you use *lawful* and when do you use *legal*? *Lawful* means "permissible under the law." *Legal* has this meaning plus the additional sense of relating to the law, as in *legal system*.

When do you use *hanged* and when do you use *hung*? *People* are *hanged* and *pictures* are *hung*.

The Paragraph

The paragraph is a convenient unit. As a general rule, if a subject requires division into topics, each topic should be a separate sentence. The beginning of a paragraph should be a signal to the reader that a new step in the development of the subject has been reached. An exception may be made for *transition sentences*, which indicate the relationship between the parts of an exposition or argument. As a general rule, single sentences should not be written as a paragraph. If the single-sentence paragraph makes the subject more readable, however, use it. Each paragraph should begin with a sentence that suggests the topic or helps the transition of the subject.

Better-Writing Drill

Officers sometimes observe, use, or seize foreign currency. Although memorizing all foreign currency denominations is not practical, some of the more commonly encountered types of foreign money are listed in the following table. Similar to the drill in Chapter 2, in this drill the country is listed in one column and the basic monetary unit is listed next to it. Try to determine the name of the foreign money and then check your results.

Country or Area	Basic Monetary Unit
Argentina	peso
Bolivia	boliviano
Canada	dollar
Ecuador	dollar
Honduras	lempira
Italy	euro
Laos	kip
Mexico	peso
Pakistan	rupee

SUMMARY

Public speaking, like any other skill, requires practice. During the early phase of any law enforcement officer's career, speeches will be more informal. As an officer rises up the promotion ladder, however, the nature of the speaking engagements will change, and more-formal rules of presentation will be required. Just as law officers learn to adapt to changing work environments, so must they learn to tailor their speeches to different types of audiences.

The media are not an enemy to be attacked or avoided. The efficient administrator will become familiar with the different types of media and their specific needs. Although tension will always exist between the media's search for the truth and the police department's requirement to keep certain information confidential, each party can learn to respect the other and work toward a common goal of providing service to the general public.

KEY TERMS

People's right to know A phrase used by the press to express that the citizens of a community have a right to know what is going on in the community and in its public agencies, including law enforcement

Prior restraint A phrase first used by the United States Supreme Court in reference to the restraint of free speech or writing prior to its being used (e.g., when a law enforcement agency attempts to prevent someone from making a speech); courts hesitate to permit prior restraint of speech or the press

Public affairs officer (PAO)   The police department's official point of contact with the media

Shield laws   Laws that protect victims from having to reveal information about their past in court (e.g., most states have rape shield laws that prevent a rape victim from being cross-examined in court about his or her sexual history unless the history is important to the case)

Sidebar   A short article that is placed in a column next to the main article in a newspaper

REVIEW QUESTIONS

1. What is the most difficult aspect of public speaking?
2. What makes one speaker more dynamic than others? List specific characteristics that you believe are essential for effective public speaking.
3. Is there any occasion that you can think of when a senior administrator should become a source for a news reporter?

PRACTICAL APPLICATIONS

1. Select five classmates and ask each to present a three-minute speech. Discuss how the speech could have been improved. What is the most common mistake made by them all?
2. Watch five television news shows in which police officers are interviewed. If you were the officer, what changes or modifications to your statements would you make? Why?
3. Using the same television shows, draft questions you would have asked the officer if you were the reporter.
4. Circle the correctly spelled word in each of the following rows.

taurama	tauram	trama	trauma
trespasing	trespassing	tresspasing	trespessing
tunge	tounge	toung	tongue
typwritter	typwriter	typewriter	typewrited
tobacco	tabacco	tobaccoo	tobaco
vormin	vernim	vernin	vermin
vandlism	vandelism	vandelesm	vandalism
vareity	variety	varetiy	varietty
vehecle	veihile	vehicle	veichle
usualy	unualluy	unsually	unusually
urene	urini	uirine	urine

5. Rewrite the following sentences as needed.
    a. Jerry and her smoked marijuana.

    _____

    b. My partner and me made four arrests last week.

    _____

c. Dave and myself found the gun.

_____

d. I run to the hurt victim.

_____

e. He did not know that the police was aware of him's conduct.

_____

6. Define and explain the following words or terms.
   a. sidebar

_____

b. media access

_____

c. position paper

_____

d. PAO

_____

e. people's right to know

_____

7. The following paragraph was taken from a police report. Make it a better paragraph.

This officer responded to the location of the parking lot of the liquor store and upon arrival saw two male subjects staring each other as if they wanted to fight each other or someone else. This officer exited the police vehicle and upon doing so subject Davis turned, dropped his weapon, and ran eastbound through the alley. At this time this officer's partner responded to subject Smith who was standing at the location and this officer yelled at subject Davis to freeze and to return to this officer.

_____
_____
_____
_____
_____
_____
_____
_____

ENDNOTES

1. For an excellent discussion of public speaking, see Steven N. Bowman, "The Practical Local Government Manager," *Public Administration* (December 1991): 22–23.
2. James E. Tilton, "Adventures in Public Speaking," *FBI Law Enforcement Bulletin* 71, no. 2 (Februrary 2002): 15–19.
3. Some of this mistrust is based on law enforcers' perception of how the media report crime; see Steven M. Chermak, "Body Count News: How Crime Is Presented in the News Media," *Justice Quarterly* 11, no. 4 (December 1994): 561.
4. See Craig A. Sullivan, "Police Public Relations," *Law and Order* (October 1993): 94, for a discussion of how one agency interacts with the media.

5. Kimberly A. Crawford, "News Media Participation in Law Enforcement Activities," *FBI Law Enforcement Bulletin* no. 64 (August 1994): 29.

6. See *Branzburg* v. *Hayes,* 408 U.S. 665 (1972); *Houchins* v. *KQED,* 438 U.S. 1 (1977); and *Press-Enterprise Co.* v. *Superior Court of California,* 106 Sup. Ct. 2735 (1986).

7. *New York Times Co.* v. *United States,* 403 U.S. 713 (1971).

8. Ibid.

9. William Strunk, Jr., *The Elements of Style,* 2d ed. (New York: Macmillan, 1972). This small book has been used for more than 30 years as a guide to better writing. It is still a required text in many English courses.

CHAPTER 7

Basic Reports

LEARNING OBJECTIVES

After reading this chapter, you should understand the following concepts:

■ The different types of reports and their purposes

■ The information that is required when you are filling out a report

■ Why reports need to be accurate, complete, and fair

INTRODUCTION

Almost everything that a police officer does must be reduced to writing.
— O. W. Wilson and Roy C. McLaren, 1972

As indicated in other chapters, administrators use law enforcement reports when making decisions about departmental policies and missions. Individual police reports form the basis for decisions by policy makers. At the other end of the spectrum is the use of reports by officers when they are testifying in court. This aspect of report writing is examined in detail in Chapter 8. (As noted earlier, the accompanying CD has actual police reports that may be reviewed.) Although court testimony is critical in convicting the offender, however, it is only one aspect of report writing. Law enforcement reports are used by individual officers in a number of ways: They are the principal source of information in conducting investigations, they provide the basis for transferring cases from one officer to another without loss of valuable information, and they are an accurate reflection of the individual officer's training, skill, and capabilities.[1]

Reports are important at all levels in law enforcement. Many types of reports must be made. Each has a designated purpose. These various reports mandate different responses and efforts by the police officer who is writing them.[2] In addition, each law enforcement agency has its own particular rules and regulations for report writing. This profusion of rules, jurisdictions, and reports makes it difficult to set forth requirements that apply to each department and report. Certain basic principles, however, do apply to all law enforcement reports. In police report writing, two important types of reports are made. In the next section, we discuss these two classifications of police records.

OCALA, FLORIDA POLICE DEPARTMENT'S JOB DESCRIPTION FOR POLICE OFFICERS

Includes the following statement regarding the report-writing duties expected of a new officer:

Writes and dictates reports in a narrative form, describing activities, events, investigations, and enforcement action taken. Completes short incident reports to record events and action taken. Prepares arrest warrants for suspects, presenting sufficient information to record the warrant. Writes application for search warrants, presenting sufficient information to gain legal approval to proceed. Makes field notes in notebook to document activities, conditions and other necessary information. Completes departmental forms to record time worked, overtime, and leave requests. Takes personal notes on assignments and information given by supervisors, and other information such as stolen vehicles and securities.

COMMON ERRORS IN REPORT WRITING

Listed next are the five most common errors in report writing. Note that most of them are the result of oversights caused by simple carelessness.

1. Failure to provide sources of information
2. Failure to report significant details
3. Failure to write neatly and clearly
4. The use of poor English
5. Failure to maintain objectivity

TYPES OF REPORTS

> *There is no distinct "right way" to complete a police report.*
> —ANONYMOUS

There are as many methods of classifying police records as there are law enforcement agencies. This is true because no single rigid system of reports will work for every police department. General guidelines exist, however, that can assist a police supervisor who is assigned the responsibility of administrating or establishing a records division.

Although all police records are aimed at accomplishing the department's mission of protecting the public and preserving the peace, some records fall into the realm of general support: records that assist in the administration of the department. Other records are operational—that is, they are directly connected to the apprehension and conviction of persons who commit crimes. Therefore, these distinctions provide a logical separation for examining police records.

Field Notes

Field notes are notes that an officer takes at the scene or immediately after leaving the scene. Field notes provide the basis for most police incident reports and should be taken as soon as practicable after an incident. These notes should be written in some type of notebook. Some organizations have prescribed notebook types that officers must use for field notes. Most officers prefer to use a loose-leaf notebook, which is easy to organize and has pages that can be removed for use in writing other reports and when testifying in court. Field notes should list the facts in the order in which they occurred or presented themselves. Because they are taken at the time the officer learned or observed the facts, field notes tend to be regarded as the most accurate report of the incident. It is important that the field notes contain an unbiased report of the facts.

Initial Police Reports

Often law enforcement agencies require the use of special forms for initial police reports. Although the reports vary among agencies, several common practices can be noted. Normally, when the police receive a call for assistance or discover a crime, they are aware of the general nature of the misconduct. Accordingly, depending on the

---

EXCERPT FROM COMMONWEALTH OF VIRGINIA DEPARTMENT OF CRIMINAL JUSTICE, POLICE/SHERIFF'S DEPARTMENT GENERAL ORDER 2-14, REVISED OCT. 30, 2004

Field notes

All formal reports begin with field notes. Field notes are important for the following reasons:

1. To create a permanent record of events.
2. To aid the investigation.
3. To ensure accurate testimony in court.
4. To protect the officer from false accusations.

---

nature of the incident or crime, one of the following standard forms is used in reporting the incident:

- Case report
- Traffic citation
- Animal control violation
- Stolen vehicle report
- Arrest report
- Juvenile arrest report
- Stolen bicycle report
- Hit-and-run report
- Vehicle accident report
- Minor property damage accident report
- Petition for emergency commitment

The *case,* or *crime, report* provides a written record of crimes reported to the police, including the details of the crime and the police action. The case report is generally used unless one of the previously listed special reports can be used. In some cases, both a case report and a special report are required.

In completing the case report, the preliminary investigator must determine whether an offense has actually been committed by determining and documenting the elements of a crime. Often, reference to particular criminal codes is used to accurately describe the offense committed. Case reports are generally coded in a manner that will alert the supervisor who reviews the reports to the seriousness of the case.

Because the investigator on the scene generally has no information about the suspect's background, standard case reports include a section to be completed by employees in the department's records section after a records check has been made.

Operational Reports

Operational reports are reports directly connected with the apprehension and conviction of persons who commit crimes. The term *conviction* is included because part of the criminal justice system involves the officer's testifying in court before a judge or a jury. In almost all instances, the officer will rely on the written report prepared at the time of the incident. The officer may not have had anything to do with the defendant's arrest, but testimony about the scene of the crime as recorded in the officer's report may be an essential part of the prosecutor's case and a necessary ingredient in the conviction of the defendant.

Two distinct types of operational reports are used: the offense report and the follow-up, or supplemental, report. The *offense report* is the original record detailing facts surrounding the commission of a crime. The *follow-up,* or *supplemental, report* sets forth information about any subsequent investigation and the results of that investigation.

Besides the two primary types of operational reports used by most law enforcement agencies, some specialized operational reports do not fit within this classification but should be considered as follow-up, or supplementary, reports. These reports concern the recording of such criminal activities as crimes involving narcotics, crimes involving intelligence, and, in some instances, sex cases. For the most part, offense reports are not used to initiate the investigation of these cases. Many of these types of crimes are handled by trained specialists who are involved in the case from the beginning to the trial of the offender.

In most of this text, we focus on the operational aspects of policing and report writing. The cop on the street, however, is unable to operate without a formalized organizational structure. This structure, the police department, utilizes administrative reports to function.

Administrative Reports

Administrative reports are just as important as operational reports. Without administrative reports, the department would grind to a halt and no law enforcement activities could be carried out.

Administrative reports may be divided into two types: those that set forth internal rules for the agency's operation and those that provide information about the agency's mission of protecting the public. The former documents involve procedures, orders, memorandums, and manuals that set forth departmental policy. The latter are usually reports to top-level management.

Administrative Reports That Establish Internal Departmental Rules

Following is a brief examination of the first type of administrative reports, which include standard operating procedures, temporary operating procedures, general orders, special orders, memos, and the duty manual.

Standing operating procedures (SOPs)   SOPs are administrative directives that establish a uniform procedure for the operation of the department in a certain area or situation. The word *standing* is a naval term used for SOPs on ships. Many individuals now use the phrase *standard operating procedures.* For purposes of this text, the two phrases are used interchangeably. SOPs are normally established for an indefinite period and may be revised or updated depending on changed circumstances. Some departments have no SOPs, whereas other departments may have 100 or more. For example, the Los Angeles Police Department has more than 100 SOPs. SOPs concern such operational matters as the use of force, authorization to go to a Code 3 response (lights and siren), and similar issues.

Temporary operating procedures (TOPs)   TOPs are short-term directives for the operation of the department. They differ from SOPs in that they have specific starting and ending dates. TOPs might be used to instruct departmental personnel on how to respond to an unusual event, such as the visit of an international dignitary or the arrival in the department's jurisdiction of a large outlaw motorcycle club. Unlike SOPs, TOPs have a definite termination date.

General orders (GOs)   GOs are administrative records used to pass information to lower-level personnel within the department rather than to set forth operational instructions. In addition, GOs have traditionally been used to define or redefine officers' duties and responsibilities. For instance, a GO might be issued that revises existing departmental policy and requires patrol officers to conduct a limited amount of the initial investigation of a crime before the case is referred to detectives.

The basic distinction between GOs and SOPs is that SOPs are concerned with specific operational situations; GOs may affect the operations of a department, but they do so indirectly. GOs may be used to pass on information about legal rulings or information received from another agency that requires coordination between that entity and the police department. This information then causes the officers to react differently in the field.

Special orders (SOs)   SOs are specific orders that are temporary. SOs are similar to GOs in that they are used to pass on information rather than to dictate direct operational policy. They might be used to inform all personnel of transfers, promotions, or upcoming promotion examination dates.

Memos (Memorandums)   Memos are documents used to pass on instructions or information from one party in the department to another. They may be of limited duration and are routinely used as a method of ensuring that all personnel understand the item being discussed. They are more effective than oral communications, especially when multiple districts and overlapping shifts exist. If the memo becomes a procedure, it should be reformatted into an SOP or a GO, depending on its content.

Duty manual   The *duty manual* is known by many names: procedures manual, department rules manual, operations manual, and so forth. This administrative record has been defined as follows:

> Duty manual: Describes procedures and defines the duties of officers assigned to specific posts or positions . . . Duty manuals and changes in them should be made effective by general order; the changes should be incorporated into the first revision of the duty manual.[3]

All SOPs and GOs should be included in the duty manual. In addition to containing a table of organization, duty manuals normally contain a job description for each departmental position. These descriptions establish the duties and responsibilities of all departmental members. For example, the duty manual lists the responsibilities of a lieutenant assigned to patrol. The manual also lists the responsibilities of a lieutenant assigned to narcotics. As can be imagined, the duties of these two lieutenants differ substantially.

Administrative Reports That Provide Information to High-Level Management about Departmental Operation

The following three types of reports fall within the second classification of administrative reports: the daily report, the monthly report, and the annual report.

Daily report   The *daily report* is an up-to-date report of the major crimes reported during the last 24 hours. This report usually includes statistics showing the number of major crimes committed during the month to date, the number of major crimes committed during the year to date, and the number of major crimes committed in the last year up to the date of the report.

Daily reports also include information about the number of arrests for the same time periods. This type of report is an extremely effective tool for informing the chief of police and the department's upper management of the extent of criminal activity within their jurisdictions. The daily report serves as the basis for compiling the monthly and annual reports.

Monthly report   The monthly report is a key management tool. Whereas the daily report keeps the police administrator informed of the extent of criminal activity, the *monthly report* is a document that allows administrators to determine trends in both departmental functions and criminal behavior. For example, the monthly report may indicate a sudden increase in the number of burglaries. This fact could alert the department to the need to adjust patrol boundaries within a district or might cause the burglary division to start inquiring on the street as to whether a new gang is operating in the area. The information contained in the monthly report forms the basis for the annual report.

Annual report   The *annual report* is a document that presents information about the operation of the department for the preceding year. It is considered an indispensable management tool in the profession.[4]

In this section, we described various types of police records that are found in most law enforcement agencies. In the following sections, we examine the types of information that may be contained in these reports.

REQUIRED INFORMATION

As indicated previously, different reports are used for different purposes. All initial reports, however, should contain certain building blocks of information. This information forms the basis for any arrest, follow-up investigation, and presentation of the case to the district attorney. The officer should use certain building blocks of information to ensure that everything is included and that *who, what, when, where, why,* and *how* are covered in each report.

Who

Who is much broader than *who committed the crime.* This type of information is an all-inclusive category that requires special attention by the responding officer. The question *who* is not answered by simply listing the name of the person suspected of committing the crime.

Who requires the officer to identify certain persons involved in the offense. *Who is the victim?* Many times, officers respond to a call and talk to a witness to a potential crime but discover that finding the victim may be time consuming and, in some situations, futile.

Who is the offender? Is the person known to the victim, the witness, or other persons? Can the officer obtain a name, a description, or other information that may identify the offender?

Who are potential witnesses? Will they volunteer information, or are they afraid of retaliation by the offender? They should be identified by name, address, employment, and other information that will assist other officers if a follow-up investigation or a second interview of the witnesses is required.

The officer must also ensure that law enforcement personnel who responded to the scene of the crime are identified. *Who was the first officer on the scene? Who conducted the investigation? Was any evidence collected and who was it turned over to?* All officers involved in the investigation must be identified and their roles explained.

Answering the question of *who* involves identifying the complaining party, the victim, the suspect, the witnesses, and any involved law enforcement personnel. This identification should include home and work addresses and telephone numbers, physical descriptions, and occupations when appropriate.

What

What is a broad question that covers a number of areas. The officer must ensure that all these aspects are answered in any report. Many times citizens will call and report what they believe to be a certain type of crime. For example, a citizen may call and report being robbed. The officer who responds and interviews the victim may discover that the citizen has been the victim of a burglary instead of a robbery. Therefore, the type of offense reported and the offense actually committed may differ. Injuries, damage, or other physical aspects of the crime or the crime scene that are observed by the officer must be included in any report.

The officer must determine what evidence is available and what evidence was not obtained. The evidence may be oral, visual, or physical. *What was done with any evidence?* Is there a chain of custody? Has it been properly marked, tagged, stored, and disposed of according to departmental policy and regulations?

The officer must also review what, if any, further police actions are required. *What agencies responded to the call? What agency assumed jurisdiction for the crime? What section or officers will conduct any necessary follow-up investigation?*

What type of offense was committed? Was it a crime against a person or property? an accident, a natural disaster, or an intentional act?

When

The question of *when* is more than the date, day, and time of the offense. The officer must examine this question from the perspectives of the offense, the citizens involved in the offense, and the law enforcement agency responding to the call for assistance. Each of these areas should be reviewed and basic information documented about when it became involved.

When was the offense committed or discovered? When was it reported? Was there a significant delay between discovery and reporting? If so, the officer needs to inquire into the reasons for this delay.

What persons were observed at the scene of the crime is a critical piece of information. *What time did they arrive, how long did they stay,* and *when did they leave* are questions to which the officer should seek answers. Was the victim at the scene or did he or she arrive at that location at a certain time? Did any witnesses have an opportunity to view the scene of the crime before the officers arrived? If so, what was the time and how long did they view the scene? Did they observe the incident? If so, for how long and from what location?

When did law enforcement officers arrive at the scene of the crime? How much time had passed since the commission of the crime, the report of the crime, and the arrival of the police? *When did the officer get in contact with the victim, the witnesses, or other parties and take their statements?* Recording this information may be critical if the victim or witness later changes the story. The fact that the officer obtained a statement within minutes, hours, or days immediately after the incident, when the crime was fresh in these individuals' minds, may become important in court if the witnesses or the victim testifies differently during the trial.

Where

Where must cover the offense, the persons involved in the incident, and police agencies. In the police report, the officer must answer questions about the location of all these variables.

The most obvious question to be asked is *where was the offense committed?* The officer should not automatically assume that the location of the property or the body is where the offense occurred. *Where the crime occurred, where it was discovered,* and *where it was reported* may be three distinct locations. For each of these factors, the officer should ensure that any report clearly indicates the location and type of activity involved.

The location should be described by street address, intersection, or exact location in any building. The officer should ensure that the location is clear and understandable by any person who reads the report. For example, what is the difference between a living room and a family room?

The officer should ensure that all available information is obtained about persons involved in the incident. The locations of the victim, the witnesses, and the suspect are critical to any investigation. Where they reside, their work addresses, all telephone numbers, and other information necessary to get in contact with them should be gathered and recorded by the officer. In addition, the locations of all the parties at the time of the crime is important. Exactly where they were located may have a significant impact on their testimony. For example, a witness who was located across the street may not have been able to observe the suspect's eye color.

The locations and activities of the police should also be carefully recorded. Where they interviewed victims, witnesses, and suspects is important. Where they arrested the suspect may become critical. If it was inside a residence, did they have a warrant? Where evidence was observed, marked, and stored is important to follow-up investigators. Thus, simply listing where the crime occurred is only the beginning of answering the query *where*.

How

How the offense was committed is important for modus operandi files. What tools were used and how they were used are often critical pieces of evidence that may tie the offense into similar crimes. *How was the offense discovered? How was it reported?*

How various persons were involved in the crime is often overlooked by inexperienced officers. *How was the victim transported to the hospital? How did the suspect arrive and depart the crime scene? How did witnesses happen to be at the location of the incident?*

How police agencies responded at the scene of the crime is also important. *How did the officer identify the victim, the suspect, and the witnesses? How did the officer locate these individuals?*

Why

Motive, or *why a person commits a crime,* is not traditionally one of the elements of any offense. However, prosecutors and jurors want to know why the crime was committed; therefore, officers should attempt to answer this question if possible. *Why was the offense reported?* Was it for insurance purposes, to seek revenge, or for other reasons? *Why did the suspect commit the crime in that manner?* Was an easier method available to accomplish the crime, and why did the suspect not use it? *Why did witnesses come forward?* Is there any bias, prejudice, or motive to their cooperation?

As the preceding discussion indicates, several ways of asking the same question exist. If the officer approaches report writing by using this method, doing so will ensure no gap or missing piece of information in the report. Simply put, gathering information is only the first step in writing a complete report. Once the information is obtained, the officer must organize it.

RECORDING ORAL STATEMENTS OF WITNESSES

Principle: The record of the witness' statements accurately and completely reflects all information obtained and preserves the integrity of this evidence.
Policy: The investigator shall provide complete and accurate documentation of all information obtained from the witness.
NIJ TECHNICAL WORKING GROUP FOR EYEWITNESS EVIDENCE (OCTOBER 1999)

An essential element of any police investigation is the recording of witness recollections. During the interview or as soon as reasonably possible afterwards, the investigator should:

- Document the witness's statements (e.g., audio or video recording, stenographer's documentation, witness's written statement, written summary using witness's own words).

- Review written documentation; ask the witness if there is anything he or she wishes to change, add, or emphasize.

Complete and accurate documentation of the witness's statement is essential to the integrity and success of the investigation and any subsequent court proceedings. Point-by-point consideration of the components of a statement may enable the officer to judge which are most accurate. This is necessary because the witness may remember each piece of information independently of other elements.

The investigator should review the individual elements of the witness's statement to determine the accuracy of each point. After conducting the interview, the investigator should:

- Consider each individual component of the witness's statement separately.
- Review each element of the witness' statement in the context of the entire statement. Look for inconsistencies within the statement.
- Review each element of the statement in the context of evidence known to the investigator from other sources (e.g., other witnesses' statements, physical evidence).

A point-by-point consideration of the accuracy of each element of a witness's statement can assist in focusing the investigation. This technique avoids the common mistake of predicting the accuracy of an individual element of a witness' description by the accuracy of another element.[5]

ORGANIZATION OF REPORTS

All departments or agencies have standard forms that assist the officer in organizing and writing reports. Many of these reports have boxes or spaces for specific information about the crime and further information gathered by the officer. This format is used to ensure consistency and completeness in law enforcement reports. After the first page of these reports is filled in, however, the officer is expected to write a summary or detailed account of the crime. Doing so requires that the answers gathered during the initial investigation be organized and set forth in a clear and readable fashion.

Drafting the Report

The officer must learn to quickly and accurately place the information obtained at the crime scene into a readable document. This report should flow logically and be a complete record of the officer's involvement. To accomplish this, the officer should follow four principles in drafting any report: (1) start at the beginning, (2) write in chronological order, (3) place details in supplemental reports, and (4) write in the past tense. By using these principles, the officer will avoid omitting valuable information and ensure that any person reading the report will understand what occurred.

The officer should begin any summary or narrative with his or her initial involvement: "Responded to a call for assistance" and so forth. Such information sets the stage for the reader to follow the officer's actions from the beginning to the end of the report. It also establishes when the officer became involved in the incident.

The officer should then proceed to write the report in chronological order. Starting at the beginning, the officer can proceed to the present time or the end of the report. Following this principle gives an easy order to the material and ensures that the officer does not forget an item of information that might be left out if the report jumped from the beginning to the end and back to the middle of the officer's involvement.

Following are 21 rules for good report writing.

General Rules for Report Writing

1. Law enforcement reports are generally written about past events. Accordingly, under most circumstances they should be written in the past tense. Rather than write that the car is black, state that the car was black. (It may have been repainted since then.)

2. Be specific in quantifying an individual's behavior in your reports. Although the subject may be *aggressive* or *combative,* those words have different meanings to different people. For example, reporting that the subject "took a boxer's stance, tightened his lips across his teeth, was breathing rapidly, and brought up clenched fists" is a better description of the subject's conduct than the comment that the subject was "combative."

3. The officer writing the report should write in the first person. Report writing should be similar to speaking. When speaking to a colleague, you would not say "this officer." The third-person "fly on the wall" report is more cumbersome to write and not as easy to grasp by officers being trained how to write reports.

4. When you are writing reports that contain the statements of others (witnesses, suspects, or other officers), use the third person to refer to the others: "Officer Smith stated that the weapon belonged to him."

5. Use complete sentences in your report. All sentences should have subjects and verbs and convey complete thoughts. Do not write sentence fragments. Sentence fragments are groups of words that begin with capital letters and end with periods but are not complete sentences.

6. If the subject is singular, the verb in that sentence should also be singular. If the subject is plural, the verb must also be plural.

7. Collective nouns are always singular; therefore, their verbs should also be singular.

8. Indefinite pronouns are always singular.

9. Use adjectives to alter, give additional meaning to, or modify nouns and pronouns. Use adverbs to alter, give additional meaning to, or modify verbs, adjectives, and other adverbs.

10. Most words ending in *-ly* are adverbs. *Not, never,* and *very* are also adverbs.

11. When deciding whether to use an adjective or an adverb, find the word being modified. If the word is a noun or a pronoun, use an adjective. If the word is an adjective or an adverb, use an adverb.

12. Do not use run-on sentences. Run-on sentences are two or more sentences joined into one long sentence.

13. Eliminate comma splices. Comma splices occur when two complete sentences are joined with commas without connecting words such as *and* or *but.*

14. Use correct punctuation in your reports. Poorly punctuated reports can be confusing and misleading.

15. Use apostrophes to show possession. Possessive pronouns (e.g., *his, hers, ours, yours, theirs,* and *its*) do not need apostrophes.

16. Many people do not understand the rules for using brackets. Accordingly, as a general rule do not use them in law enforcement reports.

17. Use quotation marks in reports only to enclose exactly what a person said.

18. Do not use abbreviations that can be confusing to people who are unfamiliar with the subject matter. When in doubt, spell it out.

19. Poor spelling creates doubt about the report. One method of eliminating misspelling is through your word choice.

20. If force was used, the report should contain all the specifics of how and why the officer used force.

21. If handcuffs were used, the officer should report this fact. For example, one career law enforcement officer recommends the use of language similar to the following:

> Mr. Jones submitted to my handcuffing him. He was handcuffed with his hands behind his back with his palms facing outward. I then checked the handcuffs to see that the handcuffs were on properly and double-locked the handcuffs and checked that they were double-locked. I asked Mr. Jones how the handcuffs felt and he did not reply to my question. I placed the tip of my right little finger between each of Mr. Jones's wrists and the handcuffs were on properly.[6]

The officer should cover only the main points in the initial report. Other details should be included in supplemental, or follow-up, reports. This procedure allows the reader to gain a quick understanding of the incident without getting bogged down in details. In addition, the officer can concentrate on explaining exactly what happened without weaving numerous details into the report. Details are important and may be critical for solving the case or convicting the offender. They belong in supplemental reports rather than in the initial crime report, however.

The officer should write the report in the past tense because the event has already occurred. Doing so also assists the officer in maintaining the chronological order of events.

Understanding the Report Format

As indicated previously, most law enforcement agencies have standard forms that the officer will use to draft reports. Filling in these forms is relatively simple. Unfortunately, there is not an accepted form for all reports in the United States. Normally, however, the different forms used by various agencies include the following sections.

Front Sheet

The front sheet is a preprinted form with short, empty spaces; boxes to be checked; and space for short names, addresses, and other information. This portion of the report is relatively easy to fill out because it requires the officer to fill in the blanks and limits the choice to a few common selections.

The records department uses the front sheet to maintain statistical information about the type and number of crimes within the jurisdiction. The front sheet also provides any reader with a quick summary of the parties, the nature of the crime, and other pertinent information.

Narrative Section

The narrative section is a blank portion of the report that the officer uses to flesh out the front sheet information. It provides a chronological history of the officer's involvement.

The officer should follow the principles set forth previously when drafting the report in this section. It must be clear, concise, and understandable. This section does not include every conceivable detail about the crime. Within the narrative section, the officer will refer to other portions of the report or separate supplemental reports for more details or additional information.

Conclusions and Recommendations

The conclusions and recommendations section allows the officer to express opinions and/or recommend a course of action. At this point, the officer may state, "Recommend case be referred to the D.A. for filing of P.C. 459 [burglary]." This is the officer's opinion or conclusion that a crime has been committed and that further action is necessary.

In addition to these three basic portions of any police report, many departments include three other sections in initial reports. These are separate sections that detail witnesses' statements, the property involved, and the evidence collected by the officer or other officers.

Witness Statements

The witness statements section sets forth any witness statements. Whenever possible, the officer should use direct quotations and not substitute words for those of the witness. In this section, facts must be separated from opinions. The witness may state, "I heard two loud sounds." The officer should record this statement and not substitute "I heard two gunshots." If the witness states, "I heard two shots," the officer should follow up with questions as to why the witness knew or recognized the sounds as gunfire. Doing so adds to the witness's credibility and saves everyone embarrassment later.

Property

In the property section, any property that was stolen or damaged is described. The property should be listed separately and described in detail. For example, if the property stolen was a man's watch, "One man's watch" does not fully identify the property. A more complete description would be: "One man's yellow-gold watch, Baldwin, Model No. 334, Serial No. 55555."

The nature and extent of any injury to the property should be explained in detail. If photographs were taken, refer to them and where they are located; for example, "Photographs attached" or "Photographs taken and maintained by crime lab personnel; contact Technician Smith."

Evidence

The evidence section refers to any evidence obtained during the investigation. It should be itemized, it should be identified, and its locations should be listed. If possible, photographs or photocopies of any physical evidence should be attached to the report.

All this information is critical to allowing other officers to continue any follow-up investigation. Forms provide a standard format and flow of information that is easy to understand and ensures that vital information is not omitted. In the next section, we examine the content of any law enforcement report.

REPORT CONTENT

In this section, we do not discuss how to write the numerous reports required of law enforcement officers; rather, we explain how this information should be set forth. As indicated in previous chapters, police reports serve a variety of purposes. To meet these various objectives, they are read, reviewed, and acted on by different individuals and agencies. Therefore, any police report must contain all the necessary information. Police reports must also be *accurate, complete,* and *fair.*[7] In the following subsections, we discuss each of these concepts.

Accuracy

Accuracy in a police report requires that it be written objectively. The officer must verify information contained in the report. An item as simple as the date versus the day can be critical in a police report.

Accurate reports must be understandable. Correct spelling, proper grammar, and good sentence structure add to the accuracy of any report. The use of correct grammar ensures that the reader understands what the officer is attempting to communicate. The difference between *there* and *their* may not seem like a major mistake to a civilian, but it can make a difference in a police report.

Accuracy also implies that the report is turned in to the department in a timely manner. Adding information to the initial report after it has been filed is unacceptable. If additional information is discovered after the initial report has been completed, the officer should submit a supplemental report and explain why the information was not included in the initial report.

Completeness

All police reports should be complete. The reader should be able to pick up any initial report and answer all the questions listed previously. Although the report must be complete, however, the officer must not be so detail oriented as to confuse the reader. Therefore, completeness includes the principle of *conciseness*.

The officer must learn when to leave information in the main body of the report and when to place it in a supplemental report. The report cannot be so brief and full of references that the reader must constantly flip back and forth between different attachments. Likewise, the report should not be so lengthy and full of details that the reader must wade through the unimportant to find the useful information.

Fairness

Doing so is difficult, but the officer must constantly keep in mind the obligation to be fair to everyone involved in the criminal justice system—including the suspect. The officer is not an advocate for one side or another. Joe Friday of *Dragnet* fame used to say, "Just the facts." This instruction applies to report writing.

Fairness in a police report requires combining accuracy and completeness to ensure that all relevant information is reported. The officer's credibility and reputation will outlive any single report; therefore, integrity should never be compromised on any case. The report should clearly distinguish among facts, inferences, opinions, and judgments. *Facts* are items that can be independently verified. Facts are information the officer has obtained or observed. *Inferences* are suppositions of what "probably" occurred. They are statements the officer makes that are drawn from facts. Personal *opinions* are the officer's personal beliefs and should never be placed in a report. The officer may, however, record witnesses' or victims' personal opinions in the report as long as they are clearly indicated as opinions and not facts. The officer's personal approval or disapproval of certain acts are considered *judgments* and do not belong in police reports.

RULES FOR IMPROVEMENT

Becoming a Speedy Writer

The purpose of this section is to help you develop a comfortable writing style and help make you a speedy and correct writer. Too often, people waste time by reacting to each situation as if it were new. If you develop certain habits in your writing style, you will gain both speed and accuracy. Checklists become automatic, and you will be less likely to omit essential items from your report. A clear-cut plan for conducting and writing an investigative report will make your report easier to write, faster to read, and less likely to contain errors or omissions. The habits that you develop should normally include the following eight:

1. Always use checklists. For example, develop checklists for specific crimes.
2. Form habits for referring to yourself, referring to others, and describing others.
3. Form a system for listing and describing evidence and other items.
4. Form habits for checking and describing places, locations, trademarks, and modi operandi (MOs).
5. Be objective. Descriptions should be of observations rather than interpretations. For example, if a person is limping, indicate that the person was limping. Do not describe the individual as having a broken foot or a sprained ankle.
6. Get into the habit of placing in quotation marks all word-for-word statements made by individuals. Make sure that the report clearly identifies the individuals making the statements.
7. Always list your sources of information in your report. For example, ". . . according to witness Black, 'Jones threw the first punch.' "
8. Do not use long, complicated sentences. Reports are written to provide information, not to entertain the reader.

People

How should you refer to yourself? How should you refer to others? Unless your agency dictates rules regarding these questions, make your choice and stick to it. The current trend is to always refer to yourself in the first person. Always describe others in the same way, in a preset order, and use a checklist. For example, always describe a person from head to foot. Use a checklist that includes name, sex, age, height, weight, build, telephone number, occupation, business address, home address, clothing, and so forth.

Property

Use checklists to describe the various types of property. For example, when describing an automobile, start with the license plate number, the make of the car, the model or type of car, the year, the color, and any peculiarities.

Places

Often, people are not specific enough when describing places. Do not assume that a street address is sufficient. If possible, include room numbers, apartment numbers, and so forth. Make it a habit to be precise in describing locations of incidents. Get into the habit of describing a location in a standard, sequential method. For example, if you always survey a room from left to right, always describe it in the same way.

Using the Comma

Seven general rules for using the comma are listed next.

1. Use a comma to separate words and phrases in a series.
   The officers studied hard, worked long hours, and were effective.
2. Do not use a comma when the conjunction connects all the words in a series.
   Blue and white are common colors of police vehicles.
3. Use a comma to separate pairs of words in a series.
   Official and unofficial, national and state agencies attended the convention.
4. Use a comma to set off words in apposition.
   The minimum required equipment of officers, such as weapons, differs among departments.
5. Do not separate compound personal pronouns from the words they emphasize.
   The officer himself called the station.
6. Use a comma to separate a name from the title or degree that follows it.
   Larry Brown, Chief of Police of Los Angeles, made the first speech at the convention.
   [*Note:* Omit the comma when the appositive has become part of a proper name: William the Conqueror.]
7. Use a comma to set off a contrasted word, phrase, or clause.
   Studying, not playing, will prepare you for the promotion examination.

SUMMARY

Every agency has its own special rules for writing reports. Many agencies, however, incorporate certain basic principles or require the same or similar information in their reports. Every law enforcement officer must understand how to approach the report-writing task. Like many other personal skills, effective report writing is achieved only with practice and a conscious effort to improve.

All reports should contain the basic information necessary for supervisors to make informed decisions. This information includes who, what, when, where, how, and why. This information is necessary for various reasons, including modus operandi, follow-up investigations, and departmental use.

Officers must ensure that all reports are accurate, complete, and fair. As is discussed in other chapters, the officer's credibility may depend on his or her ability to write an intelligent report. Report writing is probably one of the least favorite and most avoided activities in a police agency. The benefit of a well-written police report, however, may be the conviction of a violent criminal.

KEY TERMS

Administrative reports   Reports that may be divided into two types: those that provide information about the agency's mission of protecting the public and those that set forth internal rules for the agency's operation. The former documents are usually reports to the top-level management; the latter documents involve procedures, orders, memorandums, or manuals that set forth departmental policy.

Annual report   Document that presents information about the operation of the department for the preceding year

Building blocks   Memory tools designed to ensure that the officer covers *who, what, when, where, why,* and *how* in each investigative report

Case, or crime, report   A form that provides a written record of crimes reported to the police, including the details of the crime and the police action

Daily report   An up-to-date report of the major crimes reported during the last 24 hours

Duty manual   A codification of the written rules of the police agency; also referred to as the *procedures manual*

Field notes   Notes made at the scene of a crime that compile facts in the order in which they presented themselves

Follow-up, or supplemental, report   A report that sets forth information about any subsequent investigation and the results of that investigation

General orders (GOs)   Administrative records used to pass information to lower-level personnel within the department rather than to set forth operational instructions

Memos (Memorandums)   Documents used to pass on instructions or information from one party in the department to another

Monthly report   Document that allows administrators to determine trends in both departmental functions and criminal behavior

Offense report   The original record detailing facts surrounding the commission of a crime

Operational reports   Reports directly connected with the apprehension and conviction of persons who commit crimes

Special orders (SOs)   Specific orders that are temporary

Standard operating procedures (SOPs)   Administrative directives that establish a uniform procedure for the operation of the department in a certain area or situation

Temporary operating procedures (TOPs)   Short-term directives for the operation of the department

REVIEW QUESTIONS

1. What is the most important fact in any report—*who, what, when, where, how,* or *why?* Justify your answer.
2. If *why* a person commits a crime is not part of the elements of the crime, why should police officers be required to spend their time attempting to answer this question?
3. Which of the four principles of report drafting is the most important? Why? If you had to eliminate one of these principles, which would you choose? Why?
4. Explain why departments have separate reports for different aspects of a crime, such as a separate sheet for witness statements.

5. The section dealing with content lists three basic areas that all police report writers should ensure are present—*accuracy, completeness,* and *fairness.* Which is the most important and why?

PRACTICAL APPLICATIONS

1. Select a class that you are attending. On a specific date, record your activities and observations from the time you enter the class until you leave it. Describe what occurred and, using the principles set forth in this chapter, draft a complete initial crime report.
2. Pick two other students in your class and describe any jewelry they are wearing. After you write the description, ask them to comment on its accuracy. If you were given this description, could you locate the property?
3. Change each of the following statements from an interpretation to an observable fact:

   Jerry Jones was angry.

   Harry Smith was ill.

   Jerry wanted to leave.

   Sue Walton had a broken leg.

4. Each of the following sentences was taken from a police report. Write a question that arises in your mind when you read each sentence.

   The middle suspect was caught by automobile.

   The accused was uncooperative and angry.

   The suspect indicated that he wished to leave.

   The subject engaged in a verbal dispute with the other subject.

5. Circle the correctly spelled word in each of the following rows.

questionaire	questioneaire	questionnere	questionnaire
quantity	quantety	quantitiy	quanitity
stanard	standerd	standard	stendard
punisheble	pusnishable	punishble	punishable
singuler	singeler	singular	singlar
separete	saparate	seprete	separate
suffocation	suffacation	sufocation	suffocatione
sucessful	succesfull	successful	successfull
strungulation	strunglation	stranglation	strangulation
stifening	stifenent	stiffening	stifen

6. Rewrite the following sentences as needed.
   a. Because it was written without any support it is an opinion and should not be used in the report, next try to include the key facts.

   _____

   _____

   b. In view of the fact that he was only five years out of school I did not believe him.

   _____

c. The two suspects got into a physical altercation and then into a fight.

d. This officer responded to the accident scene quick.

e. I advised the suspect who spoke only Spanish of his rights in English.

7. Define and explain the following words or terms:
   a. daily report

   b. special orders

   c. TOPs

   d. SOPs

   e. initial police report

ENDNOTES

1. Michael T. D'Aulizio, "Instituting Quality Control Measures for Police Reports," *The Police Chief* 57, no. 10 (October 1992): 129–32.
2. Myron Miller and Paula Pomerenke, "Police Reports Must Be Reader Based," *Law and Order* (September 1989): 66–69.
3. O. W. Wilson, *Police Administration* (New York: McGraw-Hill, 1963), 33.
4. Jerome R. Wolff, "The Police Department Annual Report," *The Police Chief* 47, no. 3 (April 1980): 22.
5. See National Institute of Justice (NIJ) Technical Working Group for Eyewitness Evidence, *Eyewitness Evidence: A Guide for Law Enforcement* (U.S. DOJ, Office of Justice Programs, October 1999).
6. Edward Nowicki, "Report Writing: Keep Excessive Force Litigation at Bay," *Police* (November 1999): 48.
7. For an excellent discussion of the purposes of basic police reports, see "Records—Part III," International Association of Chiefs of Police Training Key Series, no. 198 (Alexandria, Va., 1973).

CHAPTER 8

Drafting Affidavits and the Use of Reports in Court

LEARNING OBJECTIVES

After reading this chapter, you should understand the following concepts:

■ What should be in an affidavit

■ What you should do to prepare to testify in court

■ What is expected of witnesses during direct examination

DRAFTING AFFIDAVITS

There are two types of affidavits: those that serve as evidence to assist the court in the decision of an issue or the determination of certain facts, and those used to invoke the judicial process. A certificate (or affidavit) of service is considered to be the second type of affidavit. A certificate of service is used in civil courts to provide evidence that a party has been officially notified of the pending court proceeding, generally a necessary step before a civil court has jurisdiction of a party. In this section of the chapter, we will examine a special type of affidavit: the one that is required before a search or arrest warrant may issue.

THE U.S. CONSTITUTION, FOURTH AMENDMENT

The right of the people to be secure in their persons, houses, papers and effects against unreasonable searches and seizures, shall not be violated, and no warrant shall issue, but upon probable cause, supported by oath or affirmation particularly describing the place to be searched and the persons or things to be seized.

The Fourth Amendment states that no warrant shall issue but upon probable cause supported by an oath or affirmation that particularly describes the place to be searched and the persons or things to be seized. *A search warrant must be issued by a neutral and detached magistrate.* It is the magistrate, not the police, who determines that probable cause exists. In determining whether probable cause exists to issue a warrant, the magistrate bases the decision on *the facts, not opinions*, contained in a sworn affidavit submitted by the police officer requesting the warrant. To see an affidavit used to support a search warrant, examine the examples contained in the CD that accompanies this text.

As noted in *State* v. *Spencer*, 510 P.2d 833, 1973 Wash. App. LEXIS 1165 (1973), an affidavit supporting a search warrant must be sufficiently comprehensive to provide facts from which the issuing magistrate can independently conclude there is probable cause to believe the items sought are at the location to be searched. Further, these facts must be current, not remote in time, and sufficient to justify the magistrate's concluding that the property sought is probably on the person or premises to be searched at the time the warrant is issued. In the Spencer case, the only evidence offered in the affidavit to support the warrant was the officer's opinion that controlled substances were stored on the premises to be searched. This opinion was not supported by any statement of fact. The court stated that a mere expression of an officer's opinion, without more evidence, cannot form the basis for issuance of a search warrant.

The issuing magistrate must be informed of the source of the information contained in the affidavit. If the source is something other than the affiant's personal knowledge, the affiant must also set forth some of the underlying facts and circumstances that led to the informant's conclusions so that the magistrate may ascertain the informant's credibility. While the issuing magistrate may draw common-sense inferences from the facts and circumstances contained in the affidavit, a substantial factual basis must exist to conclude that the items sought are probably located at the place to be searched.

In *Ray* v. *State*, 43 Okla. Crim. 1, (1929) the court stated that three forms of affidavits for search warrants are more or less prevalent:

- Affidavits on mere information or belief
- Affidavits that assert positive knowledge of the possession of the instruments or things used or obtained in violating the law
- Affidavits that set out facts showing probable cause for a belief that the accused has violated the law and that the accused is in possession of the instruments used in its violation or of the products of its violation

The first form of affidavit is always bad. The second form may be employed if the affiant can truthfully state from personal knowledge that the law has been violated and that the accused is in possession of physical evidence demonstrating that fact. The third form is sufficient in every case, and is therefore the safest type.

An affiant should swear to facts showing probable cause for his or her belief. That does not mean, however, the affiant must know absolutely that the person is a thief, has liquor in his possession, or is guilty of some other offense. Making an affidavit based on positive knowledge of guilt is in many instances impossible, but the affidavit should state the facts upon which the affiant's belief is founded. The court opined that most sheriffs and peace officers (also some county attorneys) do not comprehend the true purpose and requisite features of an affidavit for a search warrant. The court also stated: "to obviate this misconception we make these further explanations: In every instance the affidavit should state some fact or facts showing probable cause, as a basis or foundation for an affiant's belief."

An affidavit upon which a search warrant was issued in *State* v. *Campbell,* 282 N.C. 125, (1972) read in pertinent part as follows:

> Peter Michael Boulus, Special Agent; N.C. State Bureau of Investigation; being duly sworn and examined under oath, says under oath that he has probable cause to believe that Kenneth Campbell; M. K. Queensberry and David Bryan has on his premises certain property, to wit: illegally possessed drugs (narcotics, stimulants, depressants), which constitutes evidence of a crime, to wit: possession of illegal drugs. . . .
>
> The property described above is located on the premises described as follows: a one story white frame dwelling .9 miles from the Coats city limits on Hwy. 55 west toward Angier; on the right side of the hwy. directly across from Ma's Drive In also known as Bill's Drive-in.

What facts are stated in the above affidavit to allow the magistrate to determine that probable cause exists for the issuance of a search warrant? Compare that affidavit with the affidavit involved in *Cole* v. *United States* (on the CD accompanying this text).

USE OF REPORTS IN COURT

Numerous television shows attempt to portray what courtrooms are like. Police officers are sometimes shown as cool professionals who do not recant their positions under fierce cross-examination. Unfortunately, real life bears little resemblance to television. Many times, officers do become frustrated and flustered on the witness stand, especially if they have not prepared properly for the hearing. In court, officers have identified the wrong person as the perpetrator, forgotten to mention important details, and made other embarrassing and avoidable mistakes. Many of the mistakes made during court hearings are the direct result of an officer's either failing to prepare for court or failing to discuss the case with the prosecutor before taking the stand.

The following dialogue is an example of what can happen in court if several key words are incorrectly spelled in the police report:

> *"Now officer, will you explain to the court why you attacked the victim after she had already been injured?"*

"I did not attack the victim."

"But isn't this your signature on the report as the reporting officer?"

"Yes."

"Now, officer, your report reads, 'I raped her in a blanket and called for an ambulance.'"

"But sir, I meant *wrapped*."

"Then your report is in error?"

"Yes, sir."

"How many other errors are in your report?"[1]

The criminal legal process begins with the apprehension of the suspect. Once an arrest is made, the officer must fill out a report, have the sergeant approve it, and file it with the records division. The report and any follow-up are then forwarded to the city attorney or district attorney's office for review so that a determination can be made about whether a criminal case should be filed.

The prosecuting attorney may reject the case for a violation of some technical rule or simply for insufficient evidence. Alternatively, the case may be returned to the arresting officer or to the detectives assigned to the case for additional follow-up prior to filing. Finally, the prosecutor may file the case.

Once the case is filed, a series of hearings are held regarding the defendant's plea, bail, and willingness to settle the case. During this process, the arresting officer and assigned detectives continue to work on other cases or assignments. The legal system is notorious for moving slowly. Days, weeks, and months may pass before the officer is called on to appear in court. For a police officer, the court appearance is the final step in the criminal justice process. It will tax the officer's communication skills to the limit.[2]

THE COURT APPEARANCE

Police officers—good police officers—do not simply arrive in court the day of the trial, do battle with the defense attorney, and convince the jury they are telling the truth and the defendant is lying. They prepare for court. During their careers, officers can expect to testify in court about everything from simple traffic tickets to homicides. Although the magnitude of the cases may differ, the principles for effective trial preparation are the same.

Preparing for Court

Prior to going to court, the officer should review the report in detail. The officer cannot expect to sit in front of a judge in a court trial, or a jury in a jury trial, and read the report. Citizens do not understand that the officer may have made numerous other arrests since this one. After all, the defendant's liberty is at stake and the defendant will testify to remembering the incident clearly; therefore, the reasoning goes, so should the officer. Depending on the seriousness of the case and how well the officer remembers the scene, the officer may want to drive by it prior to going to court. The officer should be able to pronounce the defendant's name and be familiar with any other unique pronunciations of words in the case. Doing so adds to the officer's credibility.

Dress regulations for court appearances vary according to the jurisdiction. Some departments require the officer to appear in court in uniform. Others give this discretion to the officer. Prosecutors have their own personal beliefs about how an officer should dress for court. Some prosecutors believe that the police uniform adds an aura of credibility; others believe it makes the officer look like the gestapo. If the officer is to appear in uniform, it should be clean and pressed. When wearing civilian attire, the officer should strive for a professional, conservative look. Remember, the jurors should pay attention to the testimony and not what the officer is wearing. Flashy clothes, rings, gold chains, or other out-of-the-ordinary dress may cause a juror to concentrate on the officer's clothing at a critical part of the testimony instead of listening. The officer does not have to wear a three-piece suit with a white shirt, but he or she should dress in a manner acceptable for court. Cowboy boots, jeans, or a leather miniskirt is unsuitable—unless the officer was working undercover and the prosecutor believes the jury needs to see how the officer was dressed when the arrest was made.

Coordinating with the Prosecuting Attorney

On receiving the summons to appear in court, the officer should attempt to contact the prosecutor. In most large cities and counties, prosecutors—like the police—are overworked and understaffed and may not return any telephone calls before meeting the officer in the court hallway. The officer should not depend on the prosecutor to make the job of testifying easy. The prosecutor may not have examined the file prior to appearing in court and may be depending on the officer to carry the day. If a critical aspect of the case is not evident from reading the report, the officer should ensure that the prosecutor is informed of it *prior* to the start of the trial—not just before the officer takes the stand. The reason is this: the prosecutor may be engaged in last-minute plea bargaining or may make an opening statement to the judge or jury that will later prove to be false if he or she is not made aware of all the important facts surrounding the case.

Depending on the jurisdiction, the officer may be given the opportunity to sit next to the prosecutor during the trial and act as an *investigating officer* or a *trial assistant.* Instead of thinking of this experience as wasted time away from normal assignments, the officer should rejoice. This situation is an opportunity to observe the trial from start to finish. The experience gained from acting as an investigating officer on a case will improve the officer's courtroom demeanor immeasurably.

After discussing the case with the prosecutor, the officer will await his or her turn to testify. Depending on the nature of the case, and the prosecutor's preference, the officer may testify first or last. If at the counsel table as the investigating officer, the officer should remain attentive and assist the prosecutor whenever possible. If in the seats reserved for the general public, the officer should also remain attentive and professional. Although jurors are told not to consider anything that is not admitted into evidence, they will sometimes form unofficial opinions of persons on the basis of their observations. If the officer is required to remain outside the courtroom, he or she should also remain attentive and professional. In addition, the officer should avoid joking with other officers—and especially avoid laughing with the defense attorney. Jurors who observe these antics may believe that the officer is not serious about what is occurring in the courtroom and therefore may discount the officer's testimony.

Having reviewed the report, refreshed the memory, and talked with the prosecutor, the officer is ready to take the stand and testify.

TESTIMONY IN COURT

Some law enforcement officers are uncomfortable standing or sitting in front of a group and talking. This skill, however, is exactly what every police officer must master. Occasionally, an officer may be required to testify in a deserted courtroom with only the court personnel present, such as in a closed hearing in which the officer is testifying about a confidential informant. The majority of an officer's testimony, however, will occur in public. Moreover, the officer will be subjected to cross-examination by the defense attorney, who will attempt to destroy the officer's credibility.

Even if not members of the debating team in high school or college, all law officers, with proper training, can learn to communicate in a professional manner while testifying. This oral skill can be mastered with practice, but only if the officer is familiar with the purposes of both direct examination and cross-examination. In the following subsections, we briefly discuss this aspect of the criminal justice process.

Direct Examination

Understanding the Goals of Direct Examination
To testify in court effectively, all officers should understand the aims or goals of direct examination. Most prosecutors attempt to satisfy two generally accepted objectives during all direct examinations:

1. To present all legally sufficient evidence to support the charges filed against the defendant
2. To convince the fact finder of the integrity of the evidence and, ultimately, the truth of the charge

Direct examination is the prosecutor's opportunity to present favorable evidence to the jury. The officer is responsible for telling the truth and leaving the jury with a good impression of professionalism and honesty. Many prosecutors hand out to lay witnesses lists outlining what is expected of them during direct and cross-examination. Unfortunately, prosecutors assume that because police officers have been through academy or other formal training, they understand what occurs in a courtroom. This assumption is not always true.

Knowing the "Ten Commandments" for Witnesses
Following is a list of what have been called the "Ten Commandments" for witnesses:[3]

1. *Tell the truth.* In a trial, as in all other matters, honesty comes first.
2. *Do not guess.* If you do not know, say so.
3. *Be sure you understand the question.* You cannot possibly give a truthful and accurate answer unless you understand the question.
4. *Take your time and answer the question asked.* Give the question as much thought as is required to understand it, formulate your answer, then give the answer.

5. *Give a loud, audible answer.* Everything you say is being recorded. Do not nod your head yes or no.

6. *Do not look for assistance when you are on the stand.* If you think you need help, request it from the judge.

7. *Beware of questions involving distance and time.* If you make an estimate, make sure everyone understands that you are making an estimate.

8. *Be courteous.* Answer yes or no, and address the judge as *Your Honor.*

9. *If asked if you have talked to the prosecutor, admit it freely if you have done so.*

10. *Avoid joking and making wisecracks.* A lawsuit is a serious matter.

These commandments are as valid for a seasoned police officer as they are for a rookie. Each rule is based on both common sense and years of court experience by prosecutors.

The first and most basic rule of testimony requires that the officer tell the truth. Although the idea that peace officers should always tell the truth seems obvious, reality and emotions can sometimes cause officers to slant their testimony to assist the prosecutor or to ensure that the defendant is portrayed in a bad light. Failure to testify truthfully has several consequences. The most obvious issue is that the officer is sworn to tell the truth. Violation of this oath can lead to criminal charges or the destruction of the officer's reputation. In addition, the officer's credibility may be destroyed in front of the court or jury, with the result that they disbelieve all of the officer's testimony and acquit the defendant. This result is the exact opposite of what was intended by slanting or stretching the truth to help out the prosecutor or place the defendant in an unfavorable light. Who can forget the problems caused in the O. J. Simpson case when everyone learned that Detective Mark Fuhrman of the Los Angeles Police Department had "forgotten" using racial slurs in the past?

Close to the first rule is the second, which requires that the officer not try to help the case by guessing. If the officer is unsure, a simple statement to this effect is sufficient. Such a statement shows the jury that the officer is human and may not have the answer to every question.

The third rule simply requires that the officer understand the exact question that is asked. At first glance, this rule appears simple to follow; however, many times attorneys will ask several questions in one sentence. If the officer is unsure of the exact question, a request should be made to repeat or clarify the question.

The fourth rule requires the officer to think through both the question and the answer instead of blurting out a response. Taking a few seconds to form your answer in your mind before responding to the question is a good practice.

The fifth requirement mandates that the officer answer in a loud and clear voice. Remember, appellate courts have only the written transcript of what occurred when they review a case on appeal. The court reporter will not transcribe a nod of the head or estimate the distance between the officer's hands when he or she is demonstrating a gesture or an action of either the officer or the defendant. If the officer uses motions during the testimony, they should be accompanied by an accurate oral description.

The sixth commandment may seem harsh, but it exists for the officer's benefit. The officer must understand that no one but the judge can intervene during direct examination or cross-examination. The attorneys may raise objections, but the court must decide whether the objections are valid.

The seventh rule is one that every rookie will violate at least once. Typically, the officer states a distance during direct examination. For example, in response to the prosecutor's question about the distance between the officer and the defendant, the officer may state, "The defendant was 20 feet from me when I observed the weapon." On cross-examination, the defense attorney may ask the officer to point out an object in court that is 20 feet from the witness stand. If the officer is mistaken about this distance, the defense attorney will clearly point out this mistake and will then ask how the officer could be certain about the distance between the officer and the defendant on the night in question when he or she cannot even make an accurate estimate in the calm and secure setting of a courtroom.

The eighth commandment is also basically common sense, but it can also build an officer's credibility. The officer should be seen as a professional and not as someone who does not respect authority.

The ninth rule ties in with the first rule because it requires the officer to answer a question truthfully. Discussing the case with the prosecutor before you testify is not improper.

The last commandment also pertains to the officer's credibility. The defendant's liberty is at stake during the trial. The officer should be professional and calm when answering every question.

Being on the Witness Stand

Once called to testify, the officer should approach the witness chair or, as it is sometimes called, *witness box,* and turn to the clerk or judge to be sworn in. The officer will be asked to swear or affirm to tell the truth, the whole truth, and nothing but the truth. Once the officer is sworn in, the prosecutor, clerk, or judge will tell him or her to be seated. The officer should wait for this invitation because doing so shows respect for the court and allows the prosecutor to appear to be in control of the courtroom.

Once the officer is seated, the prosecutor will ask a series of questions about the officer's knowledge of the crime or the defendant. This questioning is known as *direct examination.* Following is a series of preliminary questions most prosecutors use to start the questioning:

- Would you state your full name for the record?
- What is your occupation?
- How long have you been employed by the X Police Department?
- On the (date and time in question) what was your assignment?
- On that date and time did you observe anything unusual?
- At what location did you observe this occurrence?
- Is that location in the (city, county, state) of X?

The purpose of these questions is to allow the officer to become comfortable on the stand and to give the jury some background information about the officer. Such questions also set the stage for the more critical testimony about the officer's observations and reactions. In some jurisdictions these questions are known as *foundational questions* because they establish the officer's jurisdiction and authority to act.

When a party—in this instance, the people of the state through the prosecutor—calls a witness, the party is allowed to ask only direct questions (with some minor exceptions that are not relevant to this text). Such questioning is accomplished through direct examination. A direct question is open ended and does not suggest the answer to the person being questioned. Once the prosecutor finishes with direct examination, the defense attorney has a right to cross-examine. *Cross-examination* allows asking either direct or leading questions. A *leading question* is phrased in a way that suggests an answer to the person being questioned.

After establishing the jurisdiction for the officer to act, the prosecutor will question the witness about his or her knowledge of the crime. The officer should listen to each question and ensure that he or she understands what is being asked. If not clear about what the question is, the officer should state this fact and ask the prosecutor to restate the question. "I'm not certain I understand your question; would you please restate it?" is one way to ask for clarification. A review of the previous chapters will indicate that such a question is a form of feedback.

If the question is understood, the officer should pause for a second and then answer. This pause should follow every question; as is discussed subsequently, it becomes extremely important during cross-examination.

When answering the question, the officer should answer only what was asked. Following is an example of an officer's answering more than was asked:

Did you observe anyone at that location?

Yes, as I pulled up to the service station, he saw me and fled from the scene. I then lost sight of him for several minutes, but observed him one block from the scene of the crime.

Not only is the officer's response defective on several grounds, but it creates more questions than it answers. Furthermore, without clarifying some of the issues in the officer's answer, the prosecutor may have opened the door for the defense attorney to question whether the defendant was the same person who fled from the service station. Following is a specific series of questions dealing with the issues the officer raised:

Did you observe anyone at that location?

Yes, I did.

Whom did you observe?

I saw the defendant.

Would you point to that person if he or she is in court and, for the record, describe what the person is wearing?

Yes, it is the person sitting next to the defense attorney, wearing a blue suit.

How far away were you when you saw the defendant?

I was about fifteen feet from him.

What was he doing when you first saw him?

He was backing out of the service station office.

What, if anything, did he do next?

He looked toward my marked patrol vehicle and fled.

Where did he go?

He ran south on Broadway Street.

What did you do at that time?

I entered the service station to check on the welfare of the people inside and was informed by Mr. Smith that the defendant had just robbed them at gunpoint.[4]

Once you heard this, what did you do?

I called for backup on my police radio.

Is that the only thing you did—call for backup?

No, I broadcast a description of the defendant, including his height, weight, race, and clothing.

Where did you receive this information?

I observed the defendant when I drove into the location, and I broadcast that information.

What did you do next?

I proceeded south on Broadway and observed the defendant standing behind some boxes in the alley.

After you saw him, what did you do?

I pulled my service weapon and ordered him to put his hands in the air and turn around.

The difference between the two sets of questions is apparent. The second set provides the jury with more complete facts surrounding the incident and establishes why the officer could recognize the defendant even though he or she lost sight of the defendant for several minutes.

Cross-Examination

Once the officer has answered the questions posed by the prosecutor, the defense attorney has the right to ask questions on cross-examination. Unlike trials in the movies, cross-examination seldom results in witnesses breaking down and recanting their previous testimony. Rather, it is a series of questions designed to attack the credibility of witnesses by showing weaknesses in their original testimony or by establishing a motive or bias on their part.

Cross-examination has several purposes. All officers should be aware of these objectives so that they can better understand the questions being asked of them by defense attorneys. Depending on the jurisdiction, some questions or issues may not be raised on cross-examination.[5] The general objectives of cross-examination, however, include, but are not limited to, the following nine points:

1. To develop favorable matters that were left unsaid on direct examination
2. To introduce all of a conversation or document, if the witness has testified to only a part of the content
3. To demonstrate that the witness is lying
4. To establish that the witness could not have seen or heard what he or she has claimed
5. To test the witness's ability to hear, see, remember, and relate facts with accuracy
6. To establish the witness's bias or prejudice
7. To establish any interest the witness may have in the outcome of the case
8. To impair the witness's credibility
9. To impeach the witness by any means permitted by law

Just as with direct examination, the officer should pause before answering any question. This pause is critical because it allows the prosecutor to object to the question and prevent its answer from coming before the jury. Defense attorneys can and will use numerous tactics or techniques to discredit the officer's testimony. This chapter, however, is not on courtroom survival. Rather, it concerns communication; therefore, only general principles are discussed.

The officer should know the facts surrounding the case. An unprofessional and embarrassing response by the officer is to say, "I don't recall, but I put it in my report." Rest assured, the defense attorney will know the facts—and will have the opportunity to read the report again while the officer is testifying. In addition, the defense attorney has the defendant's version to draw on. Even though defendants do not always tell their attorneys the complete truth, the defense attorney is provided with another perspective on the facts that can be used to attack the officer.

Furthermore, the officer should always maintain a professional, courteous attitude. Some attorneys will argue with witnesses, others will be condescending, and some may even sneer. No matter what tactic is used, the officer should never lose his or her temper. The officer must be prepared for these types of defense ploys and respond in a positive manner. Positive responses in such situations reinforce in the jury's mind that the officer is a professional simply doing a job.

If the officer makes a mistake during testimony and is caught by the defense attorney, the officer should readily admit to the mistake. Nothing damages your credibility more than letting a defense attorney lead you down a path of rationalizations in an attempt to justify an obvious mistake.

The officer's voice and body language should convey the attitude of a calm professional. The voice should be loud enough for all the jurors to hear, but not so loud as to distract from what is being said. The officer should also avoid squirming on the witness stand. If the testimony has proceeded for more than two hours and the officer must use the rest room, the officer should politely ask for a brief recess.

The officer should not despair if the defense attorney appears to be "winning." After cross-examination, the prosecutor is allowed to conduct a *redirect examination,* which is the prosecutor's opportunity to clarify any issues raised during cross-examination.

Preparing for and testifying in court are everyday experiences for some officers. Even when it becomes a common occurrence, the officer must understand that unless the information can be conveyed to the jury in the proper manner, all the work done during the arresting, questioning, and charging of the defendant may be wasted. This experience can be one of the most challenging and exciting aspects of police work.

RULES FOR IMPROVEMENT

Editing is a critical part of any written communication. Editing requires more than just using the spell checker on your word-processing program. Editing is rewriting to improve the document. Ernest Hemingway once stated that he rewrote the last paragraph of *For Whom the Bell Tolls* 39 times. When asked what problems he had with the last paragraph, he merely stated that the problem was with the "words."

Terri LeClercq developed certain tips that writers can use to shorten a document and to "power edit" their work.[6] Her suggestions are as follows:

- If possible, eliminate qualifying adverbs such as *very* and *many* that mask weak verbs and adjectives.
- Because *there* is generally followed by a *to be* verb, the weak and wordy combination can be replaced by the use of a stronger verb.
- Often, *to be* verbs (*is, are, was, were, am, will be, has, had, have, be,* and *been*) can be replaced with vibrant verbs that carry a stronger message.
- Common words that can often be eliminated include *that, the, by, of,* and *to. Draft:* Writers can gain power by editing unnecessary verbiage. *Better:* Writers can gain power editing unnecessary verbiage.
- Some words and phrases are inherently redundant (e.g., *co-conspirator, in order to, the fact that, the question as to whether, unless and until,* and *lease agreement*).

SUMMARY

The law enforcement officer's testimony in court is the final step in the criminal justice procedure. The officer should carefully prepare for this event and always remember to present a professional image to the court and the jury. The officer's professional reputation—and the department's—goes on the line every time the officer testifies.

Preparing to testify is as important as the actual testimony. The officer must never assume that the case will be easy or that the defendant's attorney will not attack the officer's credibility. Whenever possible, the officer should discuss the case with the prosecuting attorney before entering the courtroom.

Direct examination and cross-examination have distinct purposes. The officer should be prepared for both types of questioning and follow the "Ten Commandments" as closely as possible. All officers should remember certain techniques when testifying. These will become second nature to most officers after they have testified in court several times.

KEY TERMS

Affidavit   A written or printed declaration or statement of fact, made voluntarily and confirmed by the oath or affirmation of the party making it. It is taken in the presence of an officer having authority to administer the oath

Cross-examination   The defense attorney's opportunity to attack a witness's credibility or establish a motive or bias on the witness's part; questions are either direct or leading questions

Direct examination   The prosecutor's opportunity to present favorable evidence to the jury; questions are open ended and do not suggest the answer to the person being questioned

Exclusionary rule   A rule of evidence that excludes from being admitted in a criminal trial evidence on the question of defendant's guilt or innocence that was obtained in violation of the defendant's constitutional rights

Foundational questions Preliminary questions most prosecutors use to start the direct examination

Leading question A question phrased in a way that suggests an answer to the person being questioned

Magistrate A judicial officer or judge with the authority to issue warrants

Probable cause A situation in which the facts and circumstances within an officers' knowledge and about which there is reasonably trustworthy information are sufficient to warrant a person of reasonable caution believing that an offense has been or is being committed

Redirect examination The prosecutor's opportunity to clarify any issues raised during cross-examination

Search A government intrusion into an area of interest where a person has a reasonable expectation of privacy

REVIEW QUESTIONS

1. What is the most appropriate attire for an officer testifying in court? Why?
2. Which of the "Ten Commandments" is the most important? Why?
3. If you had to delete one of the "Ten Commandments," which would you delete? Why?
4. Which is more important—direct examination or cross-examination? Why?
5. What effect can a simple reporting error have on an officer's testimony?

PRACTICAL APPLICATIONS

1. Form five-person teams and require everyone to write down their observations for a 30-minute period when they are alone. Have each member of the team testify in front of the others about their observations. How accurate is the testimony?
2. Watch a television show in which an officer testifies. How many of the "Ten Commandments" did the officer violate? Be prepared to explain what occurred and why you believe the testimony was flawed.
3. Circle the correctly spelled word in each of the following rows.

anxeity	anxiety	anixety	anexity
bagage	baggage	bagaged	baggageed
benefitted	benefited	benfited	benfeted
carpose	coprse	coper	corpse
coroborate	corroberate	corroborate	corroborete
begueath	bequaeth	bequeth	bequeath
behavior	baveor	bahevior	bahavor
corresponde	correspond	correponde	corespond
councelman	cuncilman	councileman	councilman
corperal	coparel	corporal	corparele

4. Rewrite the following sentences as needed.

a. The very young child victim wore a bright red colorful shoes and a bright red colorful dress.

_____

_____

b. Today is worse than yesterday which was worse than tomorrow and both were better than friday.

_____

_____

c. The crooked illegal card dealer deal the card from the bottom of the deck.

_____

d. Please bringed the coffee to me when you are going by home.

_____

e. The report written by this officer contain several mistakes and it won't happen again.

_____

_____

5. Define and explain the following words or terms.

a. direct examination

_____

b. cross-examination

_____

c. leading question

_____

d. foundational questions

_____

e. redirect examination

_____

ENDNOTES

1. Tom E. Kakonis and Donald K. Hanzek, *A Practical Guide to Police Report Writing* (New York: McGraw-Hill, 1977): 72–73.
2. Much of the material in this chapter is based on the authors' experiences as a prosecutor, defense attorney, and police officer.
3. "Direct Examination: A Prosecutor's Workshop," County of San Diego, Calif., District Attorney's Office (November 15, 1995).
4. In some jurisdictions, Mr. Smith's statement to the officer might be considered hearsay. In others, however, it will be admitted, not for the truth of the matter stated, but for the limited purpose of showing the officer's state of mind.
5. "Cross Examination: Trial Techniques Training Program," County of San Diego, Calif., District Attorney's Office (January 29, 1977).
6. Terri LeClercq, "Power Editing," *Texas Bar Journal* 52, no. 3 (March 1994): 22–24.

CHAPTER 9

Questioning

LEARNING OBJECTIVES

After reading this chapter, you should understand the following concepts:

■ The difference between an interview and an interrogation

■ The rationale for requiring *Miranda* warnings to be given to crime suspects

■ The different techniques police use when they question a witness to a crime

■ How to interview a crime victim

■ The various techniques police use when they question a suspect

INTRODUCTION

Interviews and interrogations are unique forms of communication that usually occur only in a law enforcement agency. These information-gathering techniques are critical for apprehending and obtaining criminal convictions. They are distinguished from each other by purpose and by the circumstances surrounding the collection of the desired information.

An *interview* is a systematic questioning of an individual to gather information about an actual or a suspected crime. An *interrogation* is a systematic questioning of an individual *who is in custody or is deprived of freedom in any significant way* for the purpose of gathering information about an actual or a suspected crime. As these definitions indicate, the difference between the two types of inquiry is that during an interrogation the person is not free to leave. In the following sections, we examine, compare, and contrast the interview and the interrogation and analyze special issues that arise concerning a law enforcement officer's communication skills.

MIRANDA AND ITS EFFECT

Before the U.S. Supreme Court decided *Miranda* v. *Arizona,* confessions and the accompanying interrogations were decided case by case. In this approach, the circumstances surrounding the interrogation were reviewed to determine whether the police broke the suspect's will. The interrogation was considered improper if it violated the suspect's due process rights.

Pre-*Miranda* Techniques

In *Brown* v. *Mississippi,* the defendant was taken to the crime scene, where he was questioned about his involvement in a murder.[1] After denying guilt, he was hung (by the neck) by a rope from a tree. He continued to claim innocence and was tied to the tree and whipped. He was released but subsequently seized again and whipped until he finally confessed. The court held that the interrogation and confession were products of coercion and brutality and violated the defendant's Fourteenth Amendment due process rights.

In *Ashcraft* v. *Tennessee,* the defendant was taken to the police station and questioned continuously for two days about his wife's murder.[2] The officers questioned Ashcraft in relays because they became exhausted during the interrogation; however, the defendant was denied rest and sleep the entire time. The court held that the prolonged interrogation of Ashcraft was coercive and, therefore, the confession was involuntary and inadmissible.

In *Spano* v. *New York,* the defendant was suspected of a murder.[3] Spano informed a friend (a rookie police officer) that he had killed the victim. Spano was arrested, and the rookie officer was instructed to tell Spano that he (the officer) was in trouble and might lose his job unless Spano confessed. Spano finally confessed to the killing. The U.S. Supreme Court held that the use of deception as a means of psychological pressure to obtain a confession was a violation of the defendant's constitutional rights; therefore, the confession was ruled involuntary and was suppressed.

In *Escobedo* v. *Illinois,* the defendant was arrested for murder and interrogated for several hours at the police station.[4] During the interrogation, Escobedo repeatedly requested to see his attorney—who was also at the police station, demanding to see his client. The police refused both requests and finally obtained the confession. The court held that Escobedo was denied his right to counsel and, therefore, no statement obtained from him could be used at a criminal trial.

The *Escobedo* case was confusing because one factor was unclear: when the right to counsel attached during the interrogation. Trial courts began interpreting the meaning of *Escobedo* differently. Thus, the stage was set for the U.S. Supreme Court to clear up the confusion that resulted from its previous rulings.

Miranda

In *Miranda* v. *Arizona,* the U.S. Supreme Court established certain safeguards for individuals who are being interrogated by police.[5] Most people know that the *Miranda* decision requires police officers to advise defendants of their constitutional rights. In reality, *Miranda* established a four-pronged test that must be satisfied before a suspect's statements can be admitted into evidence. The test requires affirmative answers to all four of the following questions:

1. Was the statement voluntary?
2. Was the *Miranda* warning given?
3. Was there a waiver by the suspect?
4. Was the waiver intelligent and voluntary?

In *Miranda,* the defendant was arrested at home in Phoenix, Arizona, in connection with the rape and kidnapping of a female and was taken to a police station for questioning. At the time, he was 23 years old, poor, and basically illiterate. After being questioned for two hours, he confessed to the crime. The U.S. Supreme Court issued its now-famous *Miranda* warning requirement:

> We hold that when an individual is taken into custody or otherwise deprived of his freedom . . ., the privilege against self-incrimination is jeopardized. . . . He must be warned prior to any questioning that he has a right to remain silent, that anything he says can be used against him in a court of law, that he has a right to an attorney, and that if he cannot afford an attorney one will be appointed for him prior to any questioning if he so desires.

The *Miranda* decision drew a distinct line for admissibility of confessions and admissions obtained during investigations. It changed the way police interrogate suspects. The decision was wide in scope, but it nonetheless left some questions unanswered.

In *Berkemer* v. *McCarty,* the U.S. Supreme Court held that the *Miranda* warning must be given during any custodial interrogation.[6] The Court held that a person subjected to a custodial interrogation must be given the warning regardless of the severity of the offense, but questioning a motorist at a routine traffic stop does not constitute custodial interrogation.

Since its inception, the *Miranda* decision has generated both support and criticism. Supporters argue that it protects the rights of individuals accused of crimes, whereas detractors claim that it allows the guilty to go free because an officer may not have followed all the rules. In recent years, the courts have begun to allow statements to be admitted into evidence despite the absence of the *Miranda* warning.

The Eroding of *Miranda*

Miranda did not prevent statements obtained in violation of its rules from being used to impeach the credibility of a defendant who takes the witness stand. In *Harris* v. *New York,* the court held that using such statements was proper so long as the jury was instructed that the confession was not to be considered evidence of guilt but could be used to determine whether the defendant was telling the truth.[7]

Furthermore, voluntary statements made by a defendant who did not receive the *Miranda* warning are admissible if the defendant is later advised of his or her rights and waives these rights. In *Oregon* v. *Elstad,* the defendant was picked up at his home as a suspect in a burglary and made incriminating statements without receiving his *Miranda* warning.[8] After being advised of his rights, he waived them and signed a confession. The U.S. Supreme Court held that the self-incrimination clause of the Fifth Amendment did not require suppression of the written confession because of the earlier unwarned admission.

In *Illinois* v. *Perkins,* the U.S. Supreme Court held that an undercover officer posing as an inmate need not give a jailed defendant the *Miranda* warning before asking questions that produce incriminating statements.[9] The Court held that no coercive atmosphere is present when an incarcerated person speaks freely to someone whom he believes is a fellow inmate. The Court added that the *Miranda* warning does not forbid strategic deception by taking advantage of a suspect's misplaced trust.

In *Arizona* v. *Fulminante,* the U.S. Supreme Court held that the harmless error rule is applicable to cases involving involuntary confessions.[10] The *harmless error rule* holds that an error made by the trial court in admitting illegally obtained evidence does not require a reversal of the conviction if the error was determined to be harmless. The burden of proving harmless error rests with the prosecution and must be proved beyond a reasonable doubt.

In *Davis* v. *United States,* the U.S. Supreme Court considered the degree of clarity that is necessary for a suspect to invoke his *Miranda* rights.[11] Agents of the Naval Investigative Service were questioning the defendant in connection with a sailor's death. The defendant initially waived his rights, but approximately 90 minutes later stated, "Maybe I should talk to a lawyer." The agents asked clarifying questions; when the defendant stated that he did not want an attorney, the interrogation resumed, eliciting incriminating statements. The Court held that an equivocal request for a lawyer is insufficient to invoke the right to counsel and that clarifying questions need not be asked before an officer proceeds with the interrogation.

After years of allowing suspects to avoid police interrogation by invoking their *Miranda* rights, the U.S. Supreme Court is beginning to take a more reasonable and practical approach to this controversial issue.[12] Nevertheless, police officers must carefully tailor their interrogations so that they obtain information while also protecting the suspect's constitutional rights.

INTERVIEWS

Interviews are a key part of any investigation. Various techniques are used during interviews to elicit information from the different types of witnesses. No single method will work for all officers or be effective with all witnesses. Although the general rules regarding interviews also apply to crime victims, special consideration must be given to the victims' needs and feelings. A successful interview is composed of tact, sensitivity, and determination.[13]

Interviewing Witnesses

A witness interview does not occur without preparation and hard work on the part of an officer. Before a witness can be interviewed, however, one must be found.

Identification of Witnesses

One of the cardinal rules of law enforcement interviewing is to locate witnesses to a crime as soon as possible. Two reasons exist for this principle. First, locating and interviewing witnesses immediately after the commission of the crime allows officers to broadcast the suspect's description to other officers. The longer the time lapse between the incident and the witness interview, the greater the chance that the witness will not recall all that was observed. A second reason for interviewing witnesses as soon as possible after the crime is to prevent them from comparing stories with other witnesses and changing their accounts of what they saw.

Witnesses may be located in a number of places; however, the crime scene is the most obvious place to begin. Normally, people who remain at crime scenes are willing to provide information to the police. The officer should approach the most obvious witness first; this person will usually be someone who is excited or talkative. The officer should avoid asking, "Did you see what happened?" A more open-ended question will elicit a wider response. A question such as "What happened here?" may lead to other witnesses. The first question may be answered by a simple no, whereas the second question may provide other information: "I didn't see who fired the shot, but the janitor saw everything." Thus, how the initial question is posed may determine the citizen's answer or level of cooperation.

Officers should consider revisiting the crime scene daily for a week after the crime was committed. If possible, this visit should occur at the time when the crime originally occurred. Pedestrians, schoolchildren, and other people who may have been in the area at the time of the crime should be questioned. The officer should approach these citizens with an understanding attitude and stress the need to cooperate with the police during this time period.

Another technique for locating witnesses is canvassing the neighborhood. Such canvassing normally occurs only after a serious crime, such as homicide, has been committed. Because this is a staff-draining exercise, the police administrator will be called on to justify this use of officers. When contacting neighbors, the officer should present identification, explain the reason for the visit, relate the time of the crime, and ask if the witness saw or heard anything unusual. If the answer is yes, the officer can then proceed to more-specific questions about the crime.

Finally, the victim's or suspect's friends or relatives should be interviewed in an attempt to locate witnesses. The officer should approach these citizens in a professional manner and begin the interview with open-ended, nonspecific questions. If one of these persons has any knowledge about either the victim or the suspect, the officer should then proceed to specific areas of inquiry. This approach allows the officer to develop a well-rounded picture of either the victim or the suspect.

Identifying potential witnesses is only the first step in the process of interviewing witnesses.

Interview Preparation

The officer cannot always select the interview location. Therefore, the officer must rely on communication skills and control the communication process to elicit the needed information. The officer must obtain as much information as possible before conducting any interview. Depending on the situation, the officer may conduct the interview at the crime scene, at a witness's home, or at the police department. The officer should control the interview and ensure that critical items of information are obtained. At the same time, the officer must not be so rigid in questioning as to miss a witness's offhand remark that might lead to information that will assist in the suspect's arrest.

In situations involving numerous distractions, the officer should attempt to obtain only the basic facts and should schedule a follow-up interview to gather other information. A basic description of the suspect, what the witness observed, and the witness's name, address, and both work and residence telephone numbers may be all the information the officer can obtain in these situations.

The follow-up interview is a vital phase of the interviewing process. To prepare for it, the officer should first review all available information. The normal procedure for such an interview is to follow a structured or logical questioning sequence. Random questioning is rarely used because it lacks direction and fails to obtain all pertinent information. Witnesses should be allowed to relay all the information in their possession before the officer begins to ask questions. When a witness is interrupted during a statement, he or she may forget a fact or pick up the narrative at a different point.

Preparation is critical to the efficient, productive interview of witnesses. The officer must be prepared for the interview by knowing the facts surrounding the incident. The officer must also know when and where a brief interview is appropriate and when a more thorough interview is necessary.

Conducting the Interview

The actual interview should flow smoothly if the officer has prepared properly. The officer must remember to remain courteous, attentive, and professional. If the witness is uncomfortable relating the facts of the incident, the officer should offer supportive comments. If the witness seems reluctant to talk, the officer can remind the witness of a citizen's obligations. An officer may use many techniques during the interview process, but his or her primary duty is to make sure the lines of communication with the witness remain open.

Evaluating Witnesses

One of the interviewing officer's tasks is to evaluate the witness's credibility. *Credibility* can be defined as the "believability" of the witness. In other words, what personal characteristics render this witness's testimony worthy of belief by an impartial party? These characteristics include truthfulness, the opportunity to observe, accuracy in reporting what was observed, and motive for testifying.

Four factors may determine credibility: opportunity, attention, personal knowledge, and physical characteristics. The officer should evaluate each factor when judging a witness's credibility.

1. *Opportunity* refers to the witness's awareness of his or her surroundings. Was he or she in a location that allowed an unobstructed view of the crime? Did he or she see only part of the act? Can he or she contribute facts that, although not specific to the crime, assist the investigators in putting together a complete picture of the incident?

2. *Attention* requires that the witness be aware of the incident. What brought the event to the witness's attention? The witness may have paid attention to only part of the incident, and the officer must resist the temptation to put words in the witness's mouth about something that the witness did not observe. For example, if a witness states, "The first time I saw him was when he shoved the shotgun in the teller's face," the officer should not attempt to have the witness testify about when the suspect entered the bank.

3. *Personal knowledge* relates to the facts that the witness observed or experienced. The officer should ensure that the witness actually observed what he or she states he or she saw, heard, or felt. To do this, the officer may want to determine where the witness was located in relation to the incident, the location of other persons, and any other facts that may show that the witness was where he or she states he or she was and that the witness had an unobstructed view of the crime scene.

4. *Physical characteristics* concern the witness's ability to observe and relate what he or she saw. Does the witness wear glasses, contact lenses, a hearing aid? Is the witness color-blind? If so, is this fact critical to the witness's testimony?

Once the interviewing is completed, the officer should compare the witnesses' statements against one another to assist in evaluating their credibility.

Successfully interviewing witnesses is more an art than a science. General principles regarding the interview process, however, will assist the officer in communicating with witnesses. Locating witnesses, preparing for the interview, conducting the interview, and evaluating the witnesses' credibility are necessary steps in this process.

Interviewing Victims

Many of the same techniques discussed in the preceding section apply when an officer interviews crime victims. In many situations, victims are also witnesses to the crime. Victims, however, must be treated differently than witnesses for a variety of reasons.

Some victims will experience emotional or mental problems as a result of the crime. In many crime victimization studies, researchers have examined the effects of sexual assault on victims, but consensus is developing among experts that victims of serious nonsexual crimes may also experience demonstrated psychological effects as a result of the offense.

Post-traumatic stress syndrome came into our consciousness as a result of the Vietnam War. Returning veterans reported flashbacks, severe depression, and other symptoms. Post-traumatic stress syndrome is now recognized as a mental disorder. Some confusion might exist about the words *syndrome* and *disorder*. *Syndrome* connotes a collection of symptoms, whereas *disorder* is the clinical diagnostic term. According to the *Diagnostic and Statistical Manual of Mental Disorders—IV,* the essential feature of *Post-Traumatic Stress Disorder (PTSD)* is the development of characteristic symptoms following a psychologically distressing event that is outside the range of usual human experience. The victim usually experiences intense fear, terror, and helplessness. The characteristic symptoms involve flashbacks in which the patient relives the experience, avoidance of stimuli associated with the event, or numbing of general responsiveness.[14]

In several studies, researchers have found that many victims of violent crimes suffer from PTSD.[15] Dean Kilpatrick and his associates found that more than 57 percent of all victims of rape and 27 percent of victims of nonsexual assault suffered from PTSD within one month after the assault.[16] Crime victims have reported experiencing anger, fear, anxiety, intrusive imagery and nightmares, sleep disturbance, guilt, and impairment in social functioning following the crime.[17]

We must stress that victims suffering from PTSD are not necessarily psychotic or deranged; rather, they are attempting to cope with a highly stressful event or series of events in their lives. An understanding and awareness of a crime's psychological impact will help peace officers obtain information and investigate the case. Investigators should understand that, as with other forms of trauma, a victim suffering from PTSD may not exhibit a total disappearance of the symptoms with time; rather, the victim will feel a reduction in their frequency and intensity.[18] As these symptoms lessen, crime victims may be able to resume their places in society, but they will often harbor terrifying memories. Law enforcement officers can assist victims in this transition by being sensitive to their needs, concerns, and fears.

INTERROGATIONS

The key to success in interrogating suspects is careful preparation. Just as preparation for interviewing witnesses is necessary, a complete review of all facts is required for an effective interrogation. As with many aspects of police work, interrogation is more of an art than a science; however, certain broad guidelines will assist officers in this area.

Unlike in the movies, successful interrogations do not always end with a confession. Statements given by a suspect may be exculpatory. That is, the suspect may deny any wrongdoing or guilt. The suspect may also admit guilt but plead justification for those actions. Finally, an interrogation may produce a complete confession. The various kinds of statements that come from an interrogation require investigating officers to effectively use their communication skills to the fullest extent possible.

Interrogations should occur in a location free from distractions or interruptions. Most modern police departments have rooms that are designated as interview or interrogation rooms. Many are equipped with tape recorders and some have one-way mirrors that enable superiors or other officers working on the case to view the questioning. These rooms should be sparsely furnished, well lit, and secure.

Interrogation Techniques

Numerous interrogation techniques are available to police officers. Normally, an interrogation is conducted by two officers. One officer is the primary interrogator and the second officer acts as a recorder and witness. Depending on the suspect's reaction, the officers may switch roles during the interrogation. Before the interrogation, the officers should agree on which role each will take. Following is a brief summary of some of the more common interrogation techniques.

Factual Technique

The factual interrogation technique is a straightforward approach in which the officer points out all the facts that show the suspect committed the crime. The officer explains the nature of the evidence and how it conclusively proves the suspect committed the act. The officer then explains that the suspect's only alternative is to cooperate with the police and that doing so is in the suspect's self-interest. The interrogation should be conducted in a businesslike manner, with the officer displaying little or no emotion. The officer should not make any deals or indicate that the suspect's cooperation will be brought to the attention of the district attorney.

Sympathetic Technique

With the sympathetic technique, the officer acts understanding toward the suspect's position or justification for carrying out the acts. The officer should speak in a mild voice, should sit close to the suspect, and may want to occasionally touch the suspect in an understanding way. This approach offers the defendant a friendly face during the interrogation.

Face-Saving, or Justification, Technique

An officer using the face-saving, or justification, approach encourages the suspect to state the reason for committing the act. Again, the officer should never indicate that the defendant will receive a lesser sentence or go free after explaining the reasons for the act. However, the officer can ask questions in a manner that implies that what the suspect did was a natural, everyday occurrence—that anyone in the same circumstances would do the same thing.

These interrogation techniques are usually not used in a strict, mechanical method. The officer may need to switch from one approach to another depending on the suspect's reaction or mental state. Veteran police officers understand the need to remain flexible in this critical area of law enforcement investigation and use their interpersonal and communication skills to the maximum.

Recording Techniques

How the suspect's statement is recorded affects the communication process between the officer and the defendant. Several of the more common techniques used to record a suspect's statement follow.

Interrogating Officer Records Statement

When the interrogating officer records a suspect's statement, the officer must take notes while conducting the interrogation. This note taking can be distracting to both the suspect and the officer. It may interrupt the free flow of the discussion and cause the suspect to become concerned about what the officer is writing down. One advantage to this approach is that the officer can testify to having personally recorded the suspect's statement. The disadvantages of this method, however, outweigh this simple fact, and this technique is not used when two officers are available to interrogate the suspect.

Assisting Officer Records Statement

One of the most common methods used to record the suspect's statement is for the officer who is not doing the talking to write down what the defendant says during the interrogation. The problem with this approach is that unless the suspect is ready to give a complete confession, the situation might require both officers to ask questions at different times during the interrogation. One advantage of this technique is that it allows for uninterrupted questioning by one officer while the other takes notes. The questioning officer can concentrate on the suspect and not be diverted by having to write down what is said.

Statement Is Transcribed by Court Reporter

One of the most accurate ways to record the suspect's statement is to have a court reporter transcribe the statement. But this method is normally used only when the officers believe that the suspect is ready to confess. Usually, the suspect must agree to this method. The disadvantage of this approach is that it requires a certified court reporter to take the statement from the suspect. In addition, because the suspect usually must agree to this procedure, it is not used until a confession has been obtained.

Statement Is Tape Recorded

Two alternatives are available for tape recording a suspect's statement. In the traditional method, a common cassette tape recorder is used. With the advent and increased use of videotape recorders, however, modern police departments are increasingly turning to this approach to record interrogations. This method may be either clandestine or obvious. With the clandestine method, the video camera is usually placed behind a one-way mirror. With the obvious method, the suspect's permission must be obtained prior to taping the interview. With either approach, the officer should state the time, date, and location of the recording.

The advantages of this approach are clear: A video is a pictorial record of the suspect's demeanor as well as the statement. Also, videotapes are now used by average citizens, and jurors are more understanding and appreciative of the medium.

Accurately recording the suspect's statement is vital to the successful prosecution of the criminal case. The interrogating officers should ensure that the suspect is treated courteously and that the suspect's rights are preserved. Interrogating a suspect is one of the most critical stages of any criminal investigation and requires the officer to react appropriately at all times. Interrogation skills, like interviewing skills, take time and practice to develop. Once sharpened, however, they will serve the officer and the department well.

RULES FOR IMPROVEMENT

Characteristics of a Well-Written Report

A well-written report is factual, accurate, objective, complete, concise, clear, and timely. Four basic steps to writing a good report are as follows.

1. Investigate, interview, and observe—gather the facts.
2. Record the facts by using field notes and so forth.
3. Organize the information and report it using a systematic procedure.
4. Edit and proofread the report. [*Note:* Using the spell checker on your computer does not negate the need to edit.]

Report Evaluation

When evaluating a report, use the following criteria:

> Is the report factual?
> Is the report accurate?
> Is the report objective?
> Is the report both complete and concise?

Sentence Structure Checklist

For letter sentences, use the checklist below:

- Write in complete sentences; include both a subject and a verb.
- Avoid sentence fragments.
- Avoid complex sentences.
- Do not run sentences together.
- Combine only related ideas into single sentences.

Spelling Checklist

The checklist below should help improve your spelling:

- Memorize words frequently used in law enforcement reports.
- Memorize frequently misspelled words.
- Know the following basic spelling rules:
  - Use *i* before *e* except after *c* or when sounded as *a*.
  - To make the plural of words ending in -*y*: If the *y* is preceded by a vowel, add *s*; if the *y* is preceded by a consonant, change the *y* to *i* and add *es*.
  - To add a suffix to words ending in silent *e*: If the suffix begins with a vowel, drop the *e*; if the suffix begins with a consonant, keep the *e*.
  - If a word is monosyllabic or accented on the last syllable and ends in a single vowel and a single consonant, double the final consonant before a suffix beginning with a vowel.

Capitalization Checklist

Use capital letters for:

- The first word in a sentence
- The names of specific people and members of national, political, racial, regional, or religious groups
- Geographic names
- Names of organizations and institutions
- Specific street, building, ship, plane, and train names
- Trademark names
- Names of historical periods, events, or special events
- Days of the week, months, and holidays
- Titles used before a name

Do not capitalize:

- General words
- Directions
- Names of seasons
- Titles following a name
- Words showing family relationship preceded by a possessive pronoun

SUMMARY

Conducting an interview is an essential step in any criminal investigation. This encounter provides law enforcement officers with vital facts surrounding the commission of a crime. Many times, the interview will take place in an atmosphere charged with emotion. Victims of violent crimes may be under a great deal of stress and law enforcement officers must be sensitive to their plight, yet at the same time must proceed, gathering enough information to go forward with the investigation. This dilemma requires police officers to use all the communication skills they possess to obtain the necessary information.

Interrogating a suspect is more an art than a science. Although officers can learn the mechanics of an interrogation, knowing when to switch approaches comes only with experience and knowledge. No one technique will work for all suspects. The officer must understand this fact and pattern the interrogation accordingly. Even when interrogations do not produce confessions, they provide law enforcement officers with sufficient information to request the prosecutor's office to file charges.

KEY TERMS

Harmless error rule   A rule used by appellate courts to indicate that the trial court made an error but that if the error did not harm the accused, the conviction need not be reversed

Interrogation   Systematic questioning of an individual *who is in custody or is deprived of freedom in any significant way* for the purpose of gathering information about an actual or a suspected crime

Interview   Systematic questioning of an individual to gather information about an actual or a suspected crime

Post-Traumatic Stress Disorder (PTSD) The development of characteristic symptoms following a psychologically distressing event that is outside the range of usual human experience

REVIEW QUESTIONS

1. Explain the rationale behind the *Miranda* decision.
2. Do you believe the *Miranda* warning is still a valid concept? Why?
3. What are some of the keys to success in interrogating a suspect?

4. How are interviews and interrogations distinguished from each other?
5. Explain some of the popular techniques used for interviewing potential witnesses.

PRACTICAL APPLICATIONS

1. List a series of questions that are open ended. Ask a classmate to answer them. Did you obtain the information you sought when you drafted the questions?
2. Practice the various interrogation techniques and list those you are most comfortable using. Explain why you prefer these techniques to the others.
3. Circle the correctly spelled word in each of the following rows.

cornor	coroner	corenor	corner
counselor	counseler	counsolor	conseler
continous	continuous	continnous	conitinous
disipation	disipetation	dissipaten	dissipation
environement	enveronment	environment	enviroment
exccepted	excception	excetion	exception
hurried	huryed	hurred	hurrid
horzontal	horizontal	horizontale	horizonal
hispanice	Hispanic	Hispanc	Hespanic
humeliate	humelate	humileate	humiliate

4. Rewrite the following sentences as needed.
   a. The building was burned to the ground by four juvenile kids.

   _____

   b. I detected the odor of smoldering smoke and then placed a call to the local fire department and requested that they send help.

   _____

   c. Jerry said that he had discovered his television set missing after being gone from his home only ten minutes that day.

   _____

   d. This officer attempted to contact the suspect by telephone and then in person.

   _____

   e. The suspect was taller and lived with his mother and father who were retired.

   _____

5. Define and explain the following words or terms.
   a. interview

   _____

   b. interrogation

   _____

   c. post-traumatic stress disorder

   _____

   d. *Miranda* decision

   _____

   e. *Berkemer* v. *McCarty* rule

   _____

ENDNOTES

1. 297 U.S. 278 (1936).
2. 322 U.S. 143 (1944).
3. 360 U.S. 315 (1959).
4. 378 U.S. 748 (1964).
5. 384 U.S. 436 (1966).
6. 468 U.S. 420 (1984).
7. 401 U.S. 222 (1971).
8. 470 U.S. 298 (1985).
9. 495 U.S. 292 (1990).
10. 111 Sup. Ct. 1246 (1991).
11. 114 Sup. Ct. 2350 (1994).
12. Kimberly A. Crawford, "Invoking the Miranda Right to Counsel: The Defendant's Burden," *FBI Law Enforcement Bulletin* 64, no. 3 (March 1995): 27–32.
13. Anne C. Binge, "The Cognitive Interview Technique: An Effective Investigative Tool," *Law and Order* (November 1994): 39.
14. American Psychiatric Association, *Diagnostic and Statistical Manual of Mental Disorders*, 4th ed. [*DSM-IV*] (Washington, DC: American Psychiatric Association, 1994), 424.
15. A. W. Burgess and L. L. Holmstrom, "The Rape Trauma Syndrome," *American Journal of Psychiatry* 131 (1974): 981.
16. D. G. Kilpatrick, B. Saunders, A. Amick-McMullan, C. Best, L. Vernonen, and H. Resnick, "Victim and Crime Factors Associated with the Development of Post Traumatic Stress Disorder," *Behavioral Therapy* 20 (1989): 199.
17. D. S. Riggs, C. V. Dancu, B. S. Gershuny, D. Greenberg, and E. B. Foa, "Anger and Post-Traumatic Stress Disorder in Female Crime Victims," *Journal of Traumatic Stress* 5 (1992): 613.
18. Aphrodite Matsakis, *I Can't Get Over It: A Handbook for Trauma Survivors* (Oakland, Calif.: New Harbinger Publications, 1992).

CHAPTER 10

Interviewing and Interacting with Victims of Crime

LEARNING OBJECTIVES

After reading this chapter, you should understand the following concepts:

- The problems involved in interacting with recent victims of violent crime

- The need for police officers to be sensitive and knowledgeable regarding victims so they obtain all the necessary information without revictimizing the victim

- How victims have traditionally been treated by the criminal justice system

- Various types of reactions that victims may experience

- How to recognize Acute Stress Disorder (ASD)

- Rules for interacting with victims of crime

INTRODUCTION

The victim is the forgotten member of the criminal justice system. Most criminal justice texts and many criminal justice classes focus on law enforcement, the prosecution, courts, and the offender. Only within the last ten years have some criminal justice texts begun to include chapters on, or discussions of, victims of crime. There would be no need for the criminal justice system, however, if we did not have victims. This chapter will discuss victims of crime and how they interact with law enforcement officers. Officers must be sensitive and knowledgeable regarding victims. This enables officers to obtain all the necessary information and at the same time not revictimize the victim by asking inappropriate questions or acting in a insensitive manner.

History of Victims and the Criminal Justice System

Primitive laws were the rules used by preliterate societies to govern the tribe, clan, or other gathering of individuals. These rules or regulations represent the foundation on which the modern legal system is built. Primitive laws were marked by three characteristics: (1) Acts that injured others were considered private wrongs, (2) the injured party was entitled to take action against the wrongdoer, and (3) this action usually amounted to in-kind retaliation. These types of laws encouraged blood feuds and revenge as the preferred method of making the victim whole.

As society continued to evolve, the art of reading and writing was invented. One result of this invention was the development of written codes of conduct. Many of these codes treated certain wrongs (e.g., theft or assault) as private wrongs, with the injured party being the victim.[1]

The Code of Hammurabi

The Code of Hammurabi is considered one of the first known attempts to establish a written code of conduct. King Hammurabi ruled Babylon around 2000 B.C. He was the sixth king of the First Dynasty of Babylonia and ruled for nearly 55 years. During that period of time Babylon was a commercial center for most of the known and civilized world. Because its fortune lay in trade and other business ventures, the Code of Hammurabi provided a basis for order and certainty. The Code established rules regarding theft, sexual relationships, and interpersonal violence and replaced blood feuds with a system sanctioned by the state.[2]

The Code of Hammurabi was divided into five sections:

1. A penal code or code of laws.
2. A manual of instruction for judges, police officers, and witnesses.
3. A handbook of rights and duties of husbands, wives, and children.
4. A set of regulations establishing wages and prices.
5. A code of ethics for merchants, doctors, and officials.[3]

The Code established certain obligations and objectives for the citizens of Babylon to follow. These included the following:

1. An assertion of the power of the state. This was the beginning of state-administered punishment. Under the Code, the blood feuds that had occurred previously between private citizens were barred.

2. Protection of the weaker from the stronger. Widows were to be protected from those who might exploit them; elder parents were protected from sons who would disown them, and lesser officials from higher ones.

3. Restoration of equity between the offender and the victim. The victim was to be made as whole as possible and, in turn, the victim was to forgive the offender.

Of note in the Code is its concern for the rights of victims.[4] In fact, this code may have contained the first "victim rights statute" in history. It was relatively short-lived, however. Victims were again to be neglected in society's rush to punish the offender. This meant that victims' rights would not resurface until the twentieth century.[5]

Other Early Codes and Laws

The Mosaic Code, which is based on the belief that God entered into a contract or covenant with the tribes of Israel, had a long lasting impact on Western civilization. According to tradition, Moses returned from Mount Sinai carrying the Ten Commandments, which were inscribed on two stone tablets. These commandments subsequently became the foundation of Western morality. The Mosaic Code also became the basis for many of the laws in modern society: The prohibitions against murder, perjury, and theft, for example, were all present in the Mosaic Code thousands of years before the founding of the United States.[6]

Another important milestone in the development of modern law was ancient Roman law. Roman law was derived from the Twelve Tables, which were compiled and written circa 450 B.C. These laws had existed for centuries as unwritten law, and their interpretation and enforcement were limited to the ruling patrician class of citizens. The plebeian class, who were the workers and artisans of Rome, protested, bringing commerce to a standstill. These citizens wanted the law to apply to all citizens of Rome.[7] As a result the laws were inscribed on twelve wooden tablets and prominently displayed in the forum for all to see and follow. These laws were basic rules governing the conduct of family, religious, and economic life.

In the middle of the first century A.D., England was conquered by Roman legions. The conquerors imposed Roman law, customs, and the Latin language on the English people during the next three centuries. From this period until the Norman conquest of 1066, the legal system in England was very decentralized. There was little written law except for crimes against society. Western society had forgotten or moved away from the teaching of the Code of Hammurabi, and crimes during this period were again viewed as personal wrongs.

The Norman Conquest under William the Conqueror established royal administrators who rode a circuit and rendered justice. These royal judges used local custom and rules of conduct as a guide in rendering judgments. This system, known as *stare decisis* (Latin for "to stand by the decided law"), would have far reaching effects on modern American criminal law.

The next major development in the history of law was the acknowledgment of the existence of common law, a traditional body of unwritten legal precedents created by court decisions throughout the Middle Ages in England. Early English common law forms the basis for much of our present-day legal system.[8] During the Middle Ages, when cases were heard, judges would start their deliberations from past decisions closely related to the case under consideration. In the eleventh century, King Edward the Confessor proclaimed that common law was the law of the land. Subsequently, court decisions were recorded and made available to lawyers, who could then use them to plead their case. This concept is one of the most important aspects of modern American law.

Modern Codes and Laws

The Magna Carta of England and the United States Constitution stand as seminal documents in the history of law. The Magna Carta was signed on June 15, 1215, and was later interpreted as granting basic liberties for all British citizens. The U.S. Constitution established certain individual rights, defined the power of the federal government, and limited punishment for violation of laws.

American law combines both common law and written statutes. Statutory laws are enacted by state legislatures and Congress, and are the major source of American criminal law today. These laws are usually compiled in various codes and are subject to revision by the legislatures.

Another source of American criminal law is constitutional law. The U.S. Constitution does not define new crimes (the only crime defined in the Constitution is treason). Rather, it sets limits on laws as they apply to individuals. An example of this principle is the U.S. Supreme Court's ruling on flag burning. This practice had been proscribed as criminal conduct by a state statute, but now is protected under the First Amendment right of freedom of expression.

Significantly, many of the codes we have discussed, with the exception of the Code of Hammurabi, lacked any laws providing crime victims with protection and respect. This absence of protection in our laws has caused many victims to be revictimized by the system. The following sections will discuss various aspects of law enforcement's interaction with victims.

VICTIMS' REACTIONS

To communicate effectively with victims of crime it is important to understand the various types of reactions that they may experience. This section discusses the more common mental reactions that victims may have either immediately after the crime or at a later date.

Crisis

Many scholars consider Eric Lindemann to be a pioneer in the study of the effects of crisis on mental health and emotional well-being.[9] Lindemann offered a new understanding of the dynamics of crisis as well as a systematic approach to treating crisis victims.[10] His study on the survivors' grieving process in the 1942 Coconut Grove fire in Boston is the foundation on which much knowledge concerning the grief process has been built. Lindemann believed that acute grief was a natural and necessary reaction to significant loss. Another scholar, Gerald Caplin, extended Lindemann's theories to include all human reactions to traumatic events and not just the grieving process as a result of loss.[11]

Individuals react differently to different situations, so a crisis to one person may be only a minor annoyance to another. As a result, the term *crisis* has many valid meanings. In medicine crisis has a pathological meaning, whereas psychiatry uses the term with a different connotation. A number of scholars have given different definitions of the term as well. Consequently, rather than adopt a sociological, medical, psychological, or legal definition of the term, we will view it from the perspective of victims' reactions to crime. We therefore define crisis as a specific set of temporary circumstances that results in a state of upset and disequilibrium, characterized by an inability to cope with a particular situation using customary methods of problem solving.[12]

Authorities differ regarding the number of steps in the crisis reaction. One of the most common analyses divides this process into three stages: impact, recoil and reorganization.

The Impact Stage

This phase occurs immediately after the crime. Victims feel as if they are in shock. Some cannot eat or sleep, while others may express disbelief that the crime actually occurred. Statements such as "I can't believe this happened to me!" are common during this stage. Many victims feel exposed and vulnerable or express feelings of helplessness.

The impact phase may last for several hours to several days after the crime and is often punctuated by episodes of severe mood swings. The victim may appear to be in control one moment, and the next moment exhibit disorganized and uncontrolled emotions. A crime victim is especially vulnerable at this time and susceptible to the influence of others. The victim may interpret innocent statements offered by friends as blame for being the victim.

The Recoil Stage

During this phase, victims attempt to accept or adapt to the crime and begin to reintegrate their personalities. Victims commonly experience a wide variety of emotions including guilt, fear, anger, self-pity, and sadness. Sometimes victims struggle to accept the pain caused by the crime; at other times they deny experiencing these feelings at all. Caplin explained this process as victims needing to rest from wrestling with their situation, but who must eventually awake and return to considering the problem.[13] In essence, victims become emotionally exhausted after trying to cope with their feelings about the crime, so they put these feelings aside to rest, recover, and begin the healing process. Later, they can examine their feelings about the crime with renewed emotional resources.

Many victims are in denial during the recoil phase. This emotional detachment sometimes is an extension of the shock of the impact phase. Such detachment allows victims to gradually become immune to feelings that would overwhelm them if they faced them all at once. Victims may believe that they must seal off any feelings to get on with their lives. Some victims defend against feelings during this phase by immersing themselves in work or other projects. Other victims accomplish the same end by becoming almost obsessed with the criminal justice system, learning about procedures, criminal laws, parties, and so on.

During this phase victims begin to deal with their feelings about the crime. Some victims mentally re-examine every detail of the crime. They may talk about the crime endlessly or dream about it. As victims confront the reality of the criminal act, they may re-experience the fear. Some victims allow themselves to feel the full intensity of their fear only after the immediate threat of the crime has passed. This fear can be immobilizing. Victims must verbalize their fear and other intense emotions associated with the criminal act to begin the healing process. With time, most of the trauma associated with these feelings will lessen.

Another common feeling during the recoil stage is anger toward the criminal. Victims may experience rage but be unable to vent it. Some victims, especially those who have suffered from a violent attack, may think about revenge for hours on end. Victims must understand that the desire for revenge is natural and a normal part of the healing process. Many victims also try to rationalize their victimization. These victims search for the answer to the question, "Why me?"

The Reorganization Stage

The recoil stage eventually gives way to the reorganization stage. The victim's feelings of fear and rage diminish in intensity, and the victim then has the energy to confront life's daily activities. The victim's need to deny the victimization lessens. Eventually he or she can put the experience in perspective and spend his or her energy living in the present.

Victims will never forget their experience and, as indicated earlier, they respond in various ways. The discussion to this point has focused on one reaction to the crisis resulting from victimization. Other victims may experience different feelings. Acute Stress Disorder, which we discuss next, is another reaction that victims of crime may experience.

Acute Stress Disorder

Acute Stress Disorder (ASD) is acute stress that is experienced in the immediate aftermath of a traumatic event. This newly categorized disorder was first listed in *Diagnostic and Statistical Manual of Disorders,* 4th edition (DSM-IV) in 1994.[14] The characteristic feature of ASD is anxiety, dissociative symptoms, and other manifestations that develop within one month after exposure to the traumatic event. To receive a diagnosis of ASD the victim must have experienced, witnessed, or been confronted with an event that involved actual or threatened death, serious injury, or physical danger to the victim or others. Additionally, the victim's response to such a condition must involve intense fear, helplessness, or horror. This diagnosis requires that the victim report experiencing several of the symptoms of Post-Traumatic Stress Disorder (PTSD) and experiencing three of the five PTSD dissociative symptoms (derealization, depersonalization, dissociative amnesia, subjective sense of numbing, and reduction in awareness of surroundings) during or immediately after the traumatic incident. These symptoms must persist for at least two days, but no more than 30 days. If these symptoms last longer than 30 days, the victim may be suffering from PTSD.

Post-Traumatic Stress Disorder

PTSD was first identified when some Vietnam veterans began experiencing flashbacks of events that occurred during combat. This disorder is defined as the development of characteristic symptoms following a psychologically distressing event that is outside the range of usual human experience.[15] These events include, but are not limited to, military combat, violent personal assault, kidnapping, being taken hostage, terrorist attack, torture, incarceration as a prisoner of war, natural or manmade disasters, severe automobile accidents, or being diagnosed with a life-threatening illness. This definition requires that the person has experienced, witnessed, or been confronted with an event or events that involved actual or threatened death or serious injury, or a threat to the physical integrity of self or others. The person's response should also have involved intense fear, helplessness, or horror. The victim may experience the following symptoms: re-experiencing the traumatic event, avoidance of stimuli associated with the event, numbing of general responsiveness, and increased agitation.[16]

Victims of any crime can experience PTSD. Several scholars, however, have researched the effect of rape on victims.[17] Victims of rape have reported or been diagnosed as suffering from PTSD. Rothbaum's study found that 94% of rape victims displayed classic symptoms of PTSD one week after the assault. This figure dropped to 47% 12 weeks after the incident.[18] Kilpatrick's study, *Rape in America,* reported that 11% of all women raped still suffer from PTSD. The authors estimated that 1.3 million women in the United States currently suffer from PTSD as a result of a rape or multiple rapes.[19]

Long-Term Crisis Reaction

Long-term crisis reaction is the name of a condition identified by the National Organization for Victim Assistance (NOVA). NOVA is considered one of the early leaders in the victim rights movement. This group has responded to a number of crises throughout the world. Professionals from NOVA working with crisis victims have observed this reaction on a number of occasions. A long-term crisis reaction occurs when victims do not suffer from PTSD, but may re-experience feelings of the crisis reaction when certain events in their lives trigger recollection of the trauma.[20] These trigger events may include anniversaries of the crisis; birthdays of loved ones lost during the trauma or holidays; significant life events such as marriage, divorces, births, and graduations; media events that broadcast similar types of incidents; and involvement in the criminal justice system.

The intensity and frequency of long-term crisis reactions usually diminish with time. As the victim develops coping mechanisms to deal with the trauma, these resources may lessen the victim's reactions to triggering events. The victim eventually learns to function despite these reactions.

Other Mental Disorders

Victims of crime may suffer various mental disorders as a result of their victimization. Consequently they attempt to regain the mental equilibrium lost as a result of the traumatic event. The following sections briefly discuss two common mental problems faced by victims of crime.

Depression

A major depressive episode is a period of at least two weeks during which the victim has either feelings of despondency or a loss of interest, or pleasure, in nearly all activities. Possible symptoms include changes in appetite, weight, sleep, and psychomotor activity; decreased energy; feelings of worthlessness or guilt; difficulty in thinking, concentrating, or making decisions; and recurrent thoughts of death or suicide. The victim must experience clinically significant distress or impairment in social, occupational, or other important areas of functioning.

Substance Abuse

The essential feature of this disorder is a maladaptive pattern of substance use. This pattern leads to significant adverse consequences related to repeated use of substances. Normally, these substances are drugs or alcohol. The victim may frequently fail to fulfill major role obligations, repeatedly use substances in situations in which substance use is physically dangerous, incur legal problems related to the use of substances, and have social and interpersonal problems.

Other Effects

Different victims of the same crime react differently to that crime, and conversely, victims of different crimes may suffer similar reactions. There is no "clear bright line" that law enforcement officers can use to determine which symptoms victims will suffer. Researchers, however, have established broad general categories of problems suffered by victims of certain crimes. Susman and Vittert's text, *Building a Solution: A Practical Guide for Establishing Crime Victim Service Agencies,* lists specific crimes and typical reactions.[21] While individual crime victim's reactions vary depending on a number of factors, Table 10.1 summarizes these findings.

TABLE 10-1

Burglary	Robbery	Assault	Sexual Assault
Home is no longer a safe haven	Fear of walking alone on the streets	Anger and/or bitterness	Embarrassment
Reluctant to leave home	Relief at survival	Realization of mortality	Difficulty in describing the incident
Reluctant to stay home	Realization of mortality	Physical injury	Concern about STD/pregnancy
Express lots of "I shoulds"	Frustration at loss of personal effects	Medical bills	Bills for the medical exam
Heavy financial loss	Fear of intimidation	Time loss from work	Fear of telling family members
Sorrow at loss of senimental items	For commercial robberies, fear of loss of job	Fear of reprisals	Fear the neighbors will find out
Disgust with destruction that occurred during the burglary		If assailant is a family member, feelings of betrayal	Fear of media publicity
Realization of isolation		If a result of a traffic incident, fear of driving	Recurring nightmares, changes in sleeping patterns, loss of appetite
Frustration with police who don't investigate thoroughly		If a result of jealousy, feeling of vulnerability	Decision to prosecute
Expense of securing home		For male victims, shame at losing a "fight"	Fear that they will have to testify about prior sexual history
			Bitterness against the offender
			Sexual dysfunction

Battered Women	Survivors (e.g., Relatives) of Homicide Victims	Child Victims	Elderly Victims
Decision to stay	Acceptance of death	Parent's reaction	Fear of crime
Decision to leave	Funeral arrangements	Signs of emotional distress	Acute financial loss
Financial worries	Financial problems when breadwinner is killed	Guilt	Change in lifestyle
Decision to prosecute	Delayed emotional reaction	Parent's unconcern	Loneliness
Desire counseling for batterer and/or themselves	Reaction of children	Difficulty in describing incident	Family reactions
For separated couples, visitation offers opportunities for further attacks	Need for information on the criminal case	Fears about testifying	Reluctance to get involved in the criminal justice system
Isolation	Media publicity	Incest—decision about family future	
Helplessness	Feelings of powerlessness in the criminal justice system	Incest—mixed reaction by mother	
Psychological dependence	Ordeal during trial	Reaction of other children	
Fear of reoccurrence	Loneliness	Fear of intimidation	
Feeling of personal failure	Can't stop ruminating		
Fear for safety of any children	Desire for revenge		

The passage of time and intervention techniques may lesson or alleviate the mental and emotional consequences associated with the trauma of a criminal act. The victim, however, may never be the person he or she was before the crime.

INTERACTION WITH VICTIMS

By understanding the various reactions that crime victims go though, officers can be more sensitive and supportive of victims. This in turn helps officers obtain more accurate and complete information from the victim.

The officer should always ensure the victim is safe and not in danger or injured in any manner. If the victim is injured it may be necessary to transport him or her to a hospital and continue the questioning there. The officer should make certain the victim understands that he or she is now safe and the perpetrator can no longer harm him or her.

RULES FOR INTERACTING WITH VICTIMS OF CRIME

1. Never tell a victim that you know how they feel. Simply put, you do not know how they feel. Even if you have been a victim of the same crime, each person is different.

2. Never tell a victim that time will heal their suffering. Some victims never get over the effects of the crime.

3. Never tell a survivor that the victim of a homicide is in a better place and no longer suffering.

4. Be compassionate and supportive without becoming emotional yourself.

5. Always carry out any promise you make to the victim.

6. Never forget that the victim is the most important person in the criminal justice system.

The officer should never hurry or rush the interview unless it is necessary to get a description of the suspect and immediately broadcast it to other officers or agencies. In that case the officer should reassure the victim that more information will be gathered after the suspect's description has been furnished. On occasion, the victim may ask the officer questions. The officer should answer all questions fully and in a professional manner. The officer should never speculate. If the officer does not know the answer to a question, he or she should say so and reassure the victim that the answer is being sought.

If the victim cannot answer questions because of his or her mental or physical state, the officer should not "force" the victim to talk. Rather, the officer should inform victim that the officer will return at another time for the interview or that other officers, such as detectives or investigators, will be contacting the victim for information.

Depending on the crime, victims of crimes may be very disoriented, angry, or suffering from grief. The officer should always approach victims with an attitude of "C&P"—Compassion and Professionalism. This will ensure the victim is treated with respect and caring. This, in turn, will result in more complete information, which may assist in the investigation and apprehension of the suspect.

DEATH NOTIFICATION PROCEDURES

On occasion law enforcement officers may have to inform a parent, spouse, sibling, or child of the death of a loved one as a result of a criminal act. One of the most traumatic moments in a survivor's life is receiving notification of the loved one's death.[22] The notification by itself is a devastating event, but it can become even more traumatic if it is carried out in an insensitive manner.[23] Some authorities believe that a uniformed officer should deliver the death notification because most people gerenally perceive that person as an authority figure. Some communities, however, employ crisis intervention workers. These workers are usually members of the local victim assistance staff. These persons accompany the officer on the notification call. This procedure creates a notification team that can work together to ease the survivor's pain.

Whoever makes the notification call should have as much information about the death as possible. The team should be able to tell the survivor what happened, when it occurred, how the victim died, and who identified the victim. The notification team should never, if at all possible, make a death notification by telephone. The team should never take the victim's personal items with them on the call. These items will only add to the survivor's suffering. At a later time, however, the officer or victim service provider should offer to retrieve and return all the property of the deceased.

When making a call, the notification team should ask to enter the home. The team should do this by indicating that they have important medical information that they would rather discuss inside the house. Once inside the home, the team should ensure that they are talking to the appropriate relative. If a child has been murdered, the team should speak to both parents at the same time if at all possible. A team member should ask the survivors to be seated and then sit down next to them. The message should be clear, direct, and simple. For example, the team spokesperson may tell the parents, "I have some very bad news for you. Your son, John, was shot during an armed robbery. He died immediately." Terms such as "expired," or "passed on" should not be used as they can confuse the survivors and leave room for doubt or false hope.

Members of the notification team should not be shocked by the responses their news might elicit from the survivors. The survivors may cry, faint, laugh, or simply withdraw. The notification team should focus on the survivors' immediate needs and help them contact close relatives or friends to get assistance. An important aspect of the notification process is furnishing all available information to the survivors. This simple act may alleviate some of the suffering and allow the survivors to understand exactly how and why the death occurred. This process is one of the hardest duties a law enforcement officer has to perform. It's not a task that gets easier with experience, but it can provide survivors with the information they need to begin the healing process.

SUMMARY

Dealing with victims of crime is a critical part of any law enforcement officer's duties. If an officer treats a victim with disrespect or insensitivity, the result probably will be a lack of information or cooperation from that victim. Many officers are very adept at conducting high-speed chases, firing their weapons, and interrogating suspects, but unfortunately are clumsy when discussing intimate details with a crime victim.

Victims may suffer various responses as a result of the crime. Officers must understand these responses so they can properly interact with the victim during questioning. Officers must approach victims with compassion and always maintain their professionalism. This both assists the officer in interviewing the victim and helps the victim better cope with the impact of the crime.

REVIEW QUESTIONS

1. Which early law codes gave victims rights against the perpetrator?
2. Describe the various stages of crisis that victims go through.

3. What is the difference between Acute Stress Disorder and Post-Traumatic Stress Disorder?
4. What is the minimum number of people that should make a death notification call?

PRACTICAL APPLICATIONS

1. Draft a series of laws that protect victims of crime. Make sure you include a process that helps victims deal with law enforcement officers.
2. Have someone act as a victim and question him or her regarding a crime. The victim should go through the various stages of crisis reaction.
3. Prepare a script and conduct a death notification call on one of your classmates in front of the class. Have the class critique your technique.

ENDNOTES

1. Sir Henry Summer Maine, *Ancient Law,* 10th ed. (London: John Murray, 1905).
2. S. Schafer, *The Victim and His Criminal* (New York: Random House, 1968).
3. Masters and Roberson, *Inside Criminology* (Englewood Cliffs, NJ: Prentice-Hall, 1985).
4. Gordon, *Hammurabi's Code: Quaint or Forward Looking,* (New York: Rinehart, 1957).
5. G. O. Mueller & H. H. A. Cooper, "Society and the Victim: Alternative Responses," in I. Drapkin & E. Viano, Eds., *Victimology: A New Focus,* Vol. 2 (Lexington, Mass.: D. C. Heath, 1974), 85–102.
6. S. A. Cook, *The Laws of Moses and the Code of Hammurabi* (London: Adam and Charles Black, 1903).
7. O. W. Mueller, "Tort, Crime and the Primitive," *Journal of Criminal Law, Criminology, and Police Science*, 43 (1955): 303.
8. S. T. Reed, *Criminal Justice,* 3rd ed. (New York: Macmillan Publishing Company, 1993).
9. Albert R. Roberts and Sophia F. Dziegielewski, "Foundation Skills and Applications of Crisis Intervention and Cognitive Therapy," in *Crisis Intervention and Time-Limited Cognitive Treatment,* Albert R. Roberts, ed. (Thousand Oaks, California: Sage, 1995).
10. E. Lindemann, "Symptomatology and Management of Acute Grief," *American Journal of Psychiatry* 101 (1944): 141–148.
11. C. P. Wing, *Crisis Intervention as Psychotherapy* (New York: Oxford, 1978) and Gerald Caplin, *Principles of Preventive Psychiatry* (New York: Basic Books, 1964).
12. See Albert R. Roberts, *Crisis Intervention Handbook: Assessment, Treatment and Research* (Belmont, Calif.: Wadsworth, 1990) and Morton Bard and Dawn Sangrey, *The Crime Victim's Book,*" 2nd ed. (New York: Brunner/Mazel, 1986).
13. Caplin, *Principles of Psychiatry,* 46.
14. *Diagnostic and Statistical Manual of Mental Disorders,* 4th ed. (Washington D.C.: American Psychiatric Association, 1994).
15. *Diagnostic and Statistical Manual of Mental Disorders* 4th ed. (Washington D.C.: American Psychiatric Association, 1994), 427–429.
16. DSM-IV, pp. 427–429.
17. For an excellent discussion of the effects of rape on victims, see Bruce Taylor, "The Role of Significant Others in a Rape Victim's Recovery: People Who Are More Likely to Be Harmful Than Helpful," paper presented at the 1996 ACJS Annual Meeting, Las Vegas, Nevada, March 1996.
18. B. O. Rothbaum, E. B. Foa, T. Murdock, D. S. Riggs, & W. Walsh,"A Prospective Examination of Post-Traumatic Stress Disorder in Rape Victims," *Journal of Traumatic Stress* 5 (1992): 455–475.

19. D. G. Kilpatrick, C. N. Edmunds, & A. K. Seymour, *Rape in America: A Report to the Nation* (Arlington, VA: National Victim Center, 1992).

20. Marlene A. Young, "Crisis Response Teams in the Aftermath of Disasters," in *Crisis Intervention and Time-Limited Cognitive Treatment,* Albert R. Roberts, Ed. (Thousand Oaks, Calif.: Sage, 1995).

21. Jarjorie Susman & Carol Holt Vittert, *Building a Solution: A Practical Guide for Establishing Crime Victim Service Agencies* (National Council of Jewish Women, St. Louis Section, 1980).

22. For an excellent in-depth discussion of this process, see "Survivors of Homicide Victims," *NOVA Network Information Bulletin* 2, no. 3 (October 1985).

23. Lula M. Redmond, *Surviving When Someone You Love Was Murdered* (Clearwater, Florida: Consultation and Education Services, Inc., 1989).

CHAPTER 11

Interviewing as an Art

LEARNING OBJECTIVES

After reading this chapter, you should understand the following concepts:

■ The importance of properly preparing for an interview

■ Differences between an interrogation and an interview

■ The need for a proper interview setting and location

■ When to use the various types of questions

■ Physical conditions that influence the questioning session

■ Three commonly used general questioning techniques

■ When to use free narrative questions

■ Limitations on using direct questioning

INTRODUCTION

I keep six honest serving men
They taught me all I knew
Their names are What and Why and When
And How and Where and Who
—RUDYARD KIPLING

What you know is important. What is even more important is what you do when
you do not know.
—PROFESSOR MARY LEE BRETZ, RUTGERS UNIVERSITY

In Chapter 9, we discussed questioning. In this chapter, we continue to look at the practical aspects of interviewing and interrogation. This chapter is a modification of a handout that author Cliff Roberson uses in his seminar on interviewing. The two chapters have some overlap, but the repetition should aid you in learning the art of questioning.

Felix Lopez, a personnel specialist, once stated, "Interviewing is very much like piano playing; a fair degree of skill can be acquired with the necessity of formal instruction. But there is a world of difference in craftsmanship, in technique, and in finesse between the amateur who plays 'by ear' and the accomplished concert pianist."[1] Once you understand the basics of human behavior, you can move beyond gut instinct and guesswork. The techniques and tactics presented in this chapter will give you the skill to gain an unprecedented edge in any interview or interrogation.

Questioning can be classified as either interviewing or interrogation. *Interviewing* is the nonconfrontational type of questioning, and interrogation is the confrontational type. *Interrogation* is essentially an accusatory conversation between the interrogator and the person being interrogated. The basic purpose of interviewing is to obtain information about a factual situation and about the person being interviewed. An interrogation is usually conducted to secure an admission or a confession from a person who has committed or is suspected of committing a crime. Devallis Rutledge defines *interrogation* as "a controlled questioning calculated to discover and confirm the truth from the responses of an individual, in spite of his intentions and efforts to conceal it."[2]

Questioning has long been considered to be more of an art than a science. For many years, this has been true. With several advances in psychology, however, we can see the tide turning quickly and dramatically. Although experience is required to obtain a degree of expertise in the art of questioning, the psychological techniques described in this chapter will decrease on-the-job training time and significantly increase the questioner's ultimate degree of proficiency.

Developing the art of questioning requires that the individual learn from each situation. Many individuals repeat their experiences over and over without learning. Accordingly, these individuals, rather than having ten years' experience, have one year's experience relived ten times. This book will guide the serious student into building on his or her experiences and greatly accelerate developing the skill of an expert practitioner.

Developing the art of questioning is based more on positive human qualities and a deep understanding of human nature than on any academic achievements. To be a successful questioner, you need to be emotionally mature, mild mannered, likeable, impassive, and soft spoken, with the ability to display feeling and compassion. Emotional maturity is necessary to prevent your feeling anxiety, frustration, irritation, and rejection. Symptoms of emotional immaturity such as apathy, sullenness, resentment, and arrogance hinder the flow of information from the individual being questioned.

The questioner's behavior is essential to the process and will always have a crucial effect on the type and quantity of information received. The techniques provided will allow you to learn two essential skills. First, you will learn precisely what to say and how to say it to get the information that you want. Second, through knowing advanced techniques for interpreting human behavior, you will be able to quickly and effectively gauge any response for truthfulness and accuracy.

Comedian Groucho Marx once said, "There's one way to find out if a man is honest— ask him." If this solid advice fails you, you will need a backup plan. To be successful, comedians must be perceptive individuals who can see humor and truth in people. The ability to be perceptive and recognize the truth is also crucial to the interviewing process. You will learn, however, how to take perception to an entirely new level, expanding your ability to include new levels of awareness. Otherwise, no matter how glaring something may be, if you do not know to look for it, you will not see it.

INTERVIEW PLANNING

When you watch the casual performance of a skilled questioner, you may wrongly assume that the relaxed atmosphere indicates that no appreciable planning occurred prior to the questioning session. Prior planning is essential. Planning for a questioning session includes conducting background checks on the person being interviewed and obtaining as much information as possible on the subject matter of the session, including any reasons that the individual may have to present the information in one manner or another. Knowledge of the individual's personal background, cultural attitudes, habits, character, and reputation will provide useful information for determining the tactics to be used in the questioning session. Background information is also useful during a questioning process when the individuals being questioned have hidden agendas that may taint the information they provide. If another person has previously questioned the individual, you should know in advance any previous problems or attitudinal responses of the individual.

Consider what attitude the individual being questioned is likely to take. Attempt to anticipate any behaviors such as anger, suspicion, sullenness, or contempt and plan the questioning to fit the situation.

If an interpreter is necessary, do not use a female interpreter when the individual being questioned is from a country where women are considered inferior. The interpreter should act merely as a vehicle for accurately passing the information between the questioner and the person being questioned. Brief the interpreter that no conversation should occur with the individual being questioned other than what you tell the interpreter and the responses from the individual being questioned. No matter what the individual's responses, they should be relayed to you. You, not the interpreter, evaluate their worth. This rule applies to even the most trivial comments or remarks by the person being questioned.

The first four minutes of the contact session may determine the success of the entire session. The clothes that the questioner wears communicate a message to the individual being interviewed. Consider what would be best for the questioning session. For example, for a male interviewer, appearing in shirtsleeves with a tie that is loosened or in a sport shirt—or for the female interviewer, similar casual wear—rather than in a business suit may enhance an informal questioning session.

Likewise, never allow the seating arrangement to be a matter of chance. Numerous studies indicate that sitting next to someone, rather than across from him or her, establishes good rapport more effectively. Therefore, predetermine the seating arrangement to your advantage. If you are interested in a nonconfrontational, easy interview, sit together on the same side of the desk (or without a desk). With only a few exceptions, every interview and interrogation should be conducted this way.

INTERVIEW LOCATION

The location of the interview should be selected with care. The location provides the individual with an indelible first image of the questioning session. Select a location that will provide privacy and that will be available for the duration of the questioning, even if the questioning takes longer than planned. The location should be nonthreatening, be neutral, and have a certain degree of warmth. In most situations, the location should reduce the level of seriousness and give the appearance of a business meeting rather than a police interrogation.

Any items or distractions that could influence the interviewee's responses should be removed. Closing the blinds, unplugging the telephone, and putting up "Do Not Disturb" signs should also be considered. Prior to the arrival of the individual to be questioned, the questioner should choose seats for both him- or herself and the interviewee, and then view the room from both positions. Doing so will allow the questioner to determine any distractions that may influence the questioning.

Although friendly witnesses may be interviewed in their homes or offices, most individuals should be interviewed at an unfamiliar location. Persons feel more secure and are more content in their homes or at friendly locations. A strange location prevents the individual from becoming too comfortable.

In certain cases, leaving items such as pencils or paperclips on the table within the individual's reach may create additional variables that may be helpful to the questioner. For example, does the individual's playing with these items rather than maintaining eye contact mean that he or she is lying? Is it a sign of nervousness? In some cases, an individual may play with the items in an attempt to buy time before answering the question. Throughout this book, you will see exactly what these actions mean and how to use them to your advantage.

NOTE TAKING

When to take notes during a questioning session is critical. Note taking is generally not recommended in the early stages of the session, before you have established the desired rapport. Often the best method is to gain the information first, then take notes as you review the information with the individual.

QUESTION FORMULATION

Think as wise men do, but speak as common people do.
—ARISTOTLE

Asking the appropriate questions is essential to having a productive interview or interrogation. Questions are your tools. The quality and quantity of information that you obtain will depend to a degree on the quality of your questions. In general, your questions will be based on assumptions; therefore, the assumptions should not be based on faulty information. Certain general rules should be followed in the construction of questions. Thirteen rules, which are not absolutes because exceptions should be made when you are using certain techniques, are set forth next.

General Rules for Question Construction

1. Make your questions short.

2. Limit each question to only one topic. Avoid complex questions. They tend to confuse and may lead to unintended false answers.

3. Use clear and easily understood questions.

4. Do not use harsh and threatening terms such as *murder, dope addict, embezzler,* and so forth.

5. Use precise questions unless you are on an exploring expedition. Precise questions tend to result in precise responses.

6. If possible, use discerning questions that are designed to produce information directly on the matter under discussion.

7. When seeking new information, do not use questions that may be answered with either yes or no.

8. Do not use questions that suggest the desired answer (leading questions). Leading questions tend to influence the responses and should be avoided when you are seeking new information.

9. As a general rule, design your questions to progress from general to specific. First, seek general information about an event or a situation—that is, explore. Next, start inquiring about specific information on the basis of the answers to the general questions.

10. Ask questions in a logical sequence. Usually, doing so requires a sequence of specific questions to resolve an issue or a fact. In addition to providing logical links, the sequencing of questions should generally be from known to unknown—for example, "You stated earlier that you knew Mrs. Smith. How long have you known her?"

11. Consider the manner in which you will ask your questions. If possible, conduct a practice session prior to the actual questioning. Use a tape recorder during the rehearsal. Afterward, listen to your tone of voice, speed of delivery, and word selections. Many times reviewing the recording will demonstrate that you are using a tone or a delivery style that conveys a message different from what you intended.

12. Design your questions so that the individual being questioned will understand them. To do this, you will need to know the individual's understanding of the language, trade terms, and local expressions. Try to use language that the individual will be comfortable with and will easily understand.

13. Do not talk down to the individual. Keep the language at his or her comfort level.

Many times, an individual will pretend an inability to comprehend your questions. If possible, prior to the session, make inquiries of persons who know the individual's ability to understand the language in which the questioning will occur. If the alleged inability to communicate does not surface until the start of the questioning session, the pretense may be discovered by staging a conversation with another person in front of the individual and observing his or her facial expressions and other unspoken signs of reaction.

PHYSIOLOGY AND ITS INFLUENCE

Physical conditions will have an influence on the questioning session. For example, the brain depends on the circulatory system for food and waste elimination. All information received by any party to the questioning session is transmitted to the brain by sensory organs. Brain activity is influenced by existing and anticipated conditions of the body. Unfavorable physical conditions for a productive questioning session should be neutralized as much as possible, and favorable conditions enhanced.

Whether to permit or encourage smoking during the session is a difficult decision to make. If possible, ascertain early whether the individual is a smoker and, if so, at what level. Smoking decreases a person's physical and mental efficiency. If it is desirable to dull the individual's mental efficiency, smoking may be encouraged. If you want maximum mental efficiency from the individual, you may want to limit the smoking. If the individual is a heavy smoker, however, preventing the smoking may cause physical discomfort, which is also not conducive to maximum mental efficiency.

Alcohol is a cytological poison. Accordingly, it produces ascending paralysis of the brain and the nervous system. Alcohol tends to remove some of an individual's inhibitory powers. In the earlier stages of intoxication, the individual often exhibits a marked decrease of self-control and a weakening of willpower. In addition, persons in a mild state of intoxication generally have a reduced ability to fabricate deception, and their reasoning power is decreased. The questioner should be extremely cautious of any responses obtained from persons who are intoxicated.

Coffee and tea with caffeine are physical and mental stimulants. The rule of thumb is to offer coffee or tea to friendly witnesses but not to individuals being cross-examined or interrogated. Fatigue reduces the efficiency of the body and often makes the individual more receptive to persuasion and less alert under cross-examination or interrogation.

Hunger and thirst are generally distractions, which interfere with questioning. As a general rule, both the questioner and the individual should have adequate food and nonalcoholic beverages before the questioning session.

QUESTIONING TECHNIQUES

Three general questioning techniques are usually used: free narrative, direct questioning, and testing-type questioning. *Free narrative* occurs when the individual is allowed to provide a continuous account of an event or incident—for example, "Tell me what happened." This technique is often used to get a quick overview of what the individual knows about the event or incident or to determine what the individual is willing to tell about the matter. It also provides useful information that can be used to frame specific questions. When you use the free narrative technique, be sure to minimize interruptions. Often the individual will give valuable clues about the matter while discussing information that may not seem directly on point. In addition, what may seem like "wandering" (deviating from anticipated information) may result in useful background information.

Direct questioning is the asking of systematic, direct questions designed to yield specific information about a matter. Direct questioning is often used to fill in details omitted during free narrative. Direct examination is generally conducted by using this technique. As a general rule, you should begin the direct questioning phase by asking nonhostile questions that are not likely to alienate the individual. [*Remember:* You can easily become confrontational, but going from hostile to considerate is extremely difficult. Therefore, always present yourself as warm and ingratiating.]

When you use direct questioning, frame each question so that only one answer is required, and ask only one question at a time. In most cases, direct questions should be asked in an order that will develop the facts in their order of occurrence. Ask straightforward questions and give the individual sufficient time to answer. Do not rush the individual being questioned.

Try to help the individual remember, without suggesting the answer. You may need to repeat or rephrase the question to get the facts. If you do not understand the answer or the answer lacks clarity, ask the individual to explain or interpret the response. Provide an opportunity for the individual to qualify his or her answers. If possible, have him or her give comparisons by percentages, estimates of time and distance, and so forth, so that you can ascertain the accuracy of the responses.

Get all the facts. If the free narrative approach was used before the direct questioning, ask questions about every item discussed during the free narrative. Ask questions about minor details. These questions will often provide clues that were previously unreported. After the individual has answered all your questions, ask the individual to summarize the responses.

Testing-type questioning is similar to cross-examining a witness in court. It is not loud, abusive, or "third-degree" questioning, however. The purpose of this technique is to test previous responses for correctness and completeness and to resolve any conflicting information. Use of this technique should be limited to special cases in which you have an indication that the individual is not telling the complete truth or is a hostile witness. Clues that should be explored during this phase include attempts to evade answers, vague answers, conflicts in the information, and apparently inaccurate information. Unlike direct questioning, testing-type questioning involves asking questions designed to expand the knowledge of details in a random order. In addition, questions asked during direct questioning may be asked again in a different manner or context.

During this latter phase, it may be appropriate to use suggestive questions or ask about known information as if it were unknown. Explore areas that are vague or what appear to be evasions. Point out any conflicts or inconsistencies in the responses.

If appropriate, point out any unspoken behavior that the individual uses. For example, if the individual appears nervous or has sweaty hands, you may want to point out that this conduct is generally a sign of being less than truthful. Rationalize with the individual. Ask the individual to imagine that he or she is asking the questions and ask how he or she would judge the answers.

During the questioning session, be careful not to use your facial expressions and other unspoken behavior to imply that any particular response is desired.

ACTIVE LISTENING

Probably one of the most powerful actions for implying acceptance of someone is to listen. . . . Good listening takes practice; it's actually a discipline.[3]

Be an active listener. Listen to all that the witness says before you respond. Do not interrupt or finish sentences for the person. Listen for feelings as well as for facts. Create an open and receptive atmosphere with your body language. Listening involves concentrating on what is and what is not being said, both orally and nonorally. Listening also involves being and looking alive and alert. As stated by Jesse Nirenberg, "Listen as though you think interviewees have something worthwhile to offer."[4]

Charles Stewart and William Cash attribute six functions to active listening:[5]

1. To aid the individual being questioned in opening up
2. To aid the individual in accurately expressing feelings
3. To assist the individual in defining the situation
4. To allow a response to the individual's total communication
5. To help pinpoint specific problems
6. To help locate areas or information that needs clarification

INTERVIEW TACTICS

An important force in social interaction is the tendency for one person to communicate, orally and nonorally, his or her expectations to another person. The second person then tends to respond consciously or unconsciously to these expectations.[6]

Some people are naturally gregarious and will try to answer your questions any way they can. Other persons are more reticent and must be gently prodded. Some will be highly uncooperative and maybe even hostile when they do not want to get involved. Tactics may include feeding the witness's ego by making the witness think his or her help would be invaluable.

How close should you be to the individual being questioned? Anthropologist Edward T. Hall contends that definite distances should be maintained between people for different purposes and that these distances vary according to culture.[7] Hall states that when you get too close to an individual, you violate his or her "personal space bubble." Americans usually reserve the space to 18 inches from their body for intimate conversations and from 18 inches to 48 inches for normal, casual interactions.

Charles L. Yeschke suggests three distances for questioning. The *intimate location* is for in-depth-type interviews requiring intense interpersonal communications and for interrogations. The intimate location can be the most stressful or reassuring depending on how the session is conducted. This location creates the greatest interpersonal dynamics and should be reserved for sessions that require the expression of deepest human empathy and encouragement. The *moderate location* brings participants close enough to allow a gentle touch of an arm or shoulder if appropriate. Yeschke states that most questioning should take place within the moderate location. The moderate location leaves space from 18 to 48 inches between the questioner and the individual being questioned. The *conversation location* is where the participants are situated in a safe location just outside physical reach. This location leaves about four to six feet between the participants. In the conversation location, no obstructions should exist between the questioner and the individual being questioned.

Yeschke also recommends that the questioner's chair, in relationship to the individual's chair, be to the left front or right front at an angle of about 45 degrees.[8] Rarely should you start a session within the intimate location. An invisible boundary will always exist around the person being questioned. Accordingly, start at a distance and move into the moderate location as the individual relaxes. Rushing into the moderate location may cause undue stress and block the flow of communications.

As a general rule, you should open the questioning session with a friendly, noncombative statement about the purpose or objective of the questioning session—for example, "John, thank you for taking time from your busy schedule to help me determine what happened on Tuesday night. I am looking for any information that will me in making clear recommendations to___ regarding the ____."

Establishing rapport is crucial but takes effort. The following rules will help you do so.

Rules for Establishing Rapport

- Introduce yourself.
- Establish friendliness by talking briefly about a subject of apparent interest to the individual.
- If possible, wait until the individual appears to be friendly and cooperative before beginning the questioning process.
- Keep the conversation informal and light.
- Avoid directly challenging the individual (at least during the early stages of the interview).
- Appear interested and sympathetic to his or her circumstances.
- Do not try to hurry the individual.
- Display pleasant emotional responses without exhibiting unspoken clues about the expected content of the responses.
- Allow and encourage expressions of feelings and facts without the individual's feeling threatened.

The questioner should present a positive image to the individual being questioned. In appropriate situations, the questioner must be able to pretend anger, fear, joy, and numerous other emotions. He or she must demonstrate sympathy and sincerity. Sympathy gives the appearance of being in accord with the individual or understanding his or her situation. Individuals can sense insincerity and sham on the part of the questioner. If the individual concludes that the questioner is insincere, the rapport will be destroyed and will be difficult to repair.

Additional images that the questioner should strive to establish are those of impartiality, empathy, and firmness. The questioner should never voice views or opinions on matters involved in the questioning. Neutrality is necessary to create impartiality. Empathy is often created by conveying a genuine understanding of the individual's situation or problems. The presence of empathy will create an aura of understanding in the individual's mind. Thus, the questioner needs the "bedside manner of a doctor" and the "charm of a politician." The questioner must also project firmness. Any sign of weakness on the questioner's part will compromise the session and may result in the individual's taking control of the session.

In most situations, the questioning should be broadly based to allow information that is not actively solicited to also come out. The individual being questioned must decide whether to talk about what he or she knows. The critical part of this decision is often determined by the individual's evaluation of the questioner. If the individual sees phoniness or that the questioner does not match the image that he or she is trying to portray, the individual will become suspicious and reluctant to provide all the information he or she has.

General Tactical Guidelines

General tactical guidelines that a questioner should use include the following:

- Do not exhibit any personal prejudices during the session.
- Keep an open mind and be receptive to all information.
- Never underestimate the mentality or physical endurance of the individual being questioned.
- Do not take on a contemptuous attitude.
- Be a good listener.
- Never raise your voice.
- Be patient and gentle, but persistent.
- Display only one motivation: the search for truth.

Interpretation of Unspoken Behavior

All behavior is meaningful: it is only the true meaning that may not be evident to the observer.[9]

In all questioning sessions, two basic channels of communications are used: oral and unspoken. Oral communications encompass the words that are spoken, including the choice of words used, the tone of voice, and the speed of delivery. Unspoken communications consist of facial expressions, body movements, body positioning, and posture that are used in place of words. More often than not, unspoken communications are the result of unconscious activities of the individual, who may be unaware of the behavioral clues he or she is exhibiting.

In addition to normal unspoken behavioral clues, consider the following:

* What the individual indicates, both orally and nonorally
* How the individual says what he or she says
* What he or she fails to say

Frequently after talking to someone, you feel that the individual is not telling the truth. This feeling is your interpretation of the individual's spoken and physical behavior. The ability to articulate behavioral clues and their meaning is a critical asset for a competent questioner.

Unspoken behavior does not occur by chance. Each time an individual engages in an unspoken behavior, it has a meaning and is caused by something. Thus, the individual is providing clues that are as important as the replies to your questions.

When you observe unspoken behavior, consider the individual's entire body. How the individual sits in the chair is one of the first clues that you are likely to observe. As a general rule, truthful individuals have good posture. They sit in an upright position with their shoulders squared and parallel to the questioner's shoulders. Their arms are usually loose and hang away from their bodies. In contrast, the untruthful individual is usually uncomfortable, and fear of detection generally makes the individual assume a defensive posture that is more comfortable and conceals the vulnerable parts of the body. Most people feel uncomfortable in the abdominal region. Thus, the untruthful individual often will turn so that the trunk is not exposed to the questioner or use the hands and arms as a barrier to protect the abdominal cavity and relieve the stress of sitting across from the questioner.

Untruthful individuals will also posture themselves in a slumping position, extending the feet and legs toward the questioner. This posture extends the distance between the individual and the questioner. If there is a desk or table, the untruthful individual may slump over and put his or her weight on the table, using the hands to support the head. The position of the legs when crossed may also reveal clues to the presence of deception. As a general rule, the more defensive an individual becomes, the higher the knee rises to protect the trunk.

If the individual uses grooming gestures, the timing of these gestures can reveal whether they are related to deception. The untruthful individual often tenses his or her

---

TERMS USED IN THE INTERPRETATIVE PROCESS

Congruence means the quality of being "equal" or "equivalent." Congruence occurs when the words correspond with the unspoken clues. Usually when this occurs, the individual is being truthful.

Incongruence refers to when the words do not match the unspoken clues. When this situation occurs, the unspoken behavior is incongruent, or not equal, with the words (i.e., the individual is not being truthful).

Leakage occurs when an individual's true feelings or attitudes leak out through uncontrolled, unspoken behavioral clues.

Emblems are unspoken clues that can be directly translated into or substituted for words. An example would be shaking your head to indicate yes or no.

Illustrators are hand and arm movements the individual uses to illustrate or additionally describe what the individual is saying.

muscles, which causes jerky and abrupt movements. Hands are also used to screen the eyes during deception.

In most cases, the head and the face are the most expressive parts of the body. The face can display hundreds of expressions and movements to illustrate and add depth to oral communications. When the head is upright and held straight, with its weight supported on the neck, it is in a neutral position. Tilting the head to one side is an indication of interest. Tilting the head down may indicate a negative attitude. The untruthful person tends to put the head back or forward out of the plane of the shoulders, and the head movements are jerky or abrupt. The truthful individual tends to nod the head in a gentle, fluid motion. Often an untruthful person will roll the head around the neck to loosen tension in the neck and shoulder muscles.

Truthful individuals usually make good eye contact. Good eye contact is when the individual has direct eye contact with the questioner 40 to 60 percent of the time. In most cases, the eyes of a truthful individual have warmth and depth, which allows the questioner to look below the surface of the eyes. Conversely, the eyes of a deceptive individual often have a flat look that does not allow the questioner to look beneath the surface of the eyes. In addition, many deceptive persons exhibit rapid eye movements.

The trained questioner must be able to assess behavioral clues and ascertain their true meanings. Individuals may provide different behavioral clues that indicate different methods of lying. Some individuals can even fake truthful behavioral clues.

Although behavioral clues provide essential information, be aware that no single behavioral clue is always a reliable indicator of truth or deception in all people.

THE SEARCH FOR TRUTH

Sigmund Freud once remarked, "Man cannot keep a secret," and criminologist Hans Gross stated, "The way must be paved for a man to tell the truth." Aubry and Caputo contend that we were born to tell the truth. It is only our environment that teaches us that the truth may frequently lead to grief. For example, the schoolboy who admits to throwing a spitball quickly finds himself rewarded with punishment.[10] Nevertheless, the compulsion to tell the truth is strong. The competent questioner should be aware that an individual cannot bury the truth too deeply in the labyrinth of his or her mind. One of your duties in questioning is to lessen the individual's resistance to providing truthful answers.

TOOLS REQUIRED FOR SUCCESSFUL QUESTIONING

1. Common sense
2. An understanding of psychology
3. Empathy
4. Attentive listening
5. Nonjudgmental acceptance
6. Patience
7. Positive eye contact
8. Anger suppression
9. Flexibility
10. Positive attitude
11. Sensitivity

PRACTICE

Like any other art or skilled act, learning questioning techniques requires extensive practice. Ronald Fisher and Edward Geiselman's experience in training Israeli investigators indicates the importance of practice. Fisher and Geiselman discovered that after a short lecture on interviewing techniques, investigators often thought they understood the logic of the procedure and that practice was unnecessary. When required to conduct a questioning session, however, they could not implement it as easily as expected. Only after repeated practice did they become skilled questioners.[11] Thus, Fisher and Geiselman recommend practice exercises in questioning. They also recommend that the learner use a building-block approach, progressing to the next set of skills only after mastering the skills already learned.

SUMMARY

As discussed previously in this chapter, the skills needed to be a successful questioner include the following:

- Establishing rapport
- Being an active listener
- Asking appropriate questions
- Providing sufficient response time
- Not interrupting
- Exploring by use of detailed questions
- Interpreting unspoken behavior
- Evaluating the responses received

As mentioned, these skills may be developed in building-block practice sessions. For example, in the first block of practices, concentrate on developing the skills of building rapport, being an active listener, and not interrupting. Second, work on the development and delivery of questions. Delay the evaluation and interpretation of both oral and nonoral communications practices until after the other two blocks have been mastered. Practice sessions will be more productive if each is divided into several short sessions. Each session should focus on only one or two skills. If possible, videotape the sessions for your review.

REVIEW QUESTIONS

1. Is interviewing an art or science?
2. Why are physiological factors important in questioning a witness?
3. What steps may an interviewer take to establish rapport?
4. Why is it important to be an active listener when interviewing a suspect?
5. What steps may officers take to improve their skill as interviewers?

PRACTICAL APPLICATIONS

1. Divide the class into groups and practice interviewing a suspect.
2. Attend a court trial and evaluate the attorneys' ability to question both friendly and hostile witnesses.
3. Read the available literature and establish a list of ten or more steps that you could take to become a better interviewer.

ENDNOTES

1. Felix Lopez, *Personnel Interviewing* (New York: McGraw-Hill, 1975), 1.
2. Devallis Rutledge, *Criminal Interrogation: Law and Tactics,* 3d ed. (Incline Village, Nev.: Copperhouse, 1996).
3. James Mallory, Jr., *The Kink and I* (Wheaton, Ill.: Victor Books, 1977), 146.
4. Jesse S. Nirenberg, *Getting through to People* (Upper Saddle River, NJ: Prentice Hall, 1963).
5. Charles J. Stewart and William B. Cash, Jr., *Interviewing Principles and Practices* (Dubuque, Iowa: William C. Brown, 1974).
6. *Productivity and the Self-Fulfilling Prophecy: The Pygmalion Effect* (New York: McGraw-Hill Films, 1975).
7. Edward T. Hall, *The Hidden Dimension* (Garden City, NY: Doubleday, 1966).
8. Charles L. Yeschke, *Interviewing: An Introduction to Interrogation* (Springfield, Ill.: Charles C. Thomas, 1987).
9. David E. Zulawske and Douglas E. Wicklander, *Practical Aspects of Interview and Interrogation* (New York: Elsevier, 1992), 51.
10. Arthur S. Aubry, Jr., and Rudolph R. Caputo, *Criminal Interrogation,* 3d ed. (Springfield, Ill.: Charles C. Thomas, 1980), xiii–xiv.
11. Ronald P. Fisher and R. Edward Geiselman, *Memory-Enhancing Techniques for Investigative Interviewing* (Springfield, Ill.: Charles C. Thomas, 1992).

CHAPTER 12

Hostage Negotiations

A. Introduction
B. Communication in Hostage Situations
    1. Goals in Hostage Situations
    2. Profile of Hostage Negotiation Teams
    3. The Critical Incident Negotiation Team
C. Summary
D. Review Questions
E. Practical Applications
F. Endnotes

LEARNING OBJECTIVES

After reading this chapter, you should understand the following concepts:

■ The three primary informational goals a negotiator strives for in a hostage situation

■ The relationship that develops between a negotiator and the perpetrator in a hostage situation

■ Why time is not of the essence in a hostage situation

INTRODUCTION

U nfortunately, greed, misplaced ideals, or simple incompetence can lead to situations in which a criminal takes an innocent party hostage. Negotiation with individuals or groups holding citizens as hostages requires special communication skills. These skills are discussed in this chapter.

Hostage negotiation is one of the most publicized actions of law enforcement agencies, not only in the United States, but throughout the world. It is also one of the most misunderstood actions that peace officers undertake. Hostage negotiation is truly a test of a law enforcement officer's communication skills.

The terrorist acts of September 11, 2001, highlighted the need for training on dealing with hostage takers. Before that time, on February 28, 1993, in Waco, Texas, agents of the Bureau of Alcohol, Tobacco, and Firearms (ATF) attempted to serve a search warrant on David Koresh, leader of the Branch Davidian group, at the group's compound. The raid on the compound involved more than 100 federal agents and was deemed a failure by some: four ATF agents and six Branch Davidians died. For the next 50 days, federal agents attempted to negotiate with Koresh for his surrender. Finally, on April 19, 1993, agents fired tear gas into the compound. Within moments, the building was in flames and more than 70 sect members died inside.

In another situation, the FBI was involved in a standoff at Ruby Ridge, Idaho, with Randy Weaver, an alleged white separatist. In August 1992, marshals went to Weaver's cabin to arrest him for failing to appear on a gun-related charge. A gunfight broke out, and Weaver's son and a federal deputy marshal were killed. The next day, Weaver's wife was accidentally shot by a federal agent as she stood unarmed in the cabin's doorway. Weaver subsequently surrendered after an 11-day standoff.

Although the Branch Davidian and Weaver incidents may not have involved hostages in the traditional sense, both situations highlight the importance of effective communication skills during critical situations. The Good Guys in Sacramento, the *Achille Lauro* hijacking, the bombing of TWA Flight 840, the Rome and Vienna airport attacks, and the Atlanta and Georgia prison sieges by Cuban inmates are examples of well-known hostage situations. Just listing these hostage situations recalls memories of terror, death, and, in some cases, failure to save the hostages.

COMMUNICATION IN HOSTAGE SITUATIONS

The FBI divides hostage situations into four broad categories: the terrorist situation, the prison situation, the criminal situation, and the mentally disturbed situation. The techniques used in each case, however, are the same.[1] All officers should have a fundamental understanding of hostage negotiations because they may find themselves involved in such situations at some time in their career and because hostage negotiations are a specialized form of communication. Police administrators must also understand these principles to effectively supervise their departments.

Police officers are trained to take charge of and control the situation. They are taught that their lives and others' lives may depend on their ability to manage any situation. When officers are involved in a hostage negotiation situation, however, they must understand that their ability to completely control events may be limited. The officer on the scene must attempt to contain the situation until trained negotiators arrive. Thus, an officer's communication skills play a critical part in hostage negotiations. The officer must attempt to get the suspect to talk. The ability to communicate with the suspect is an absolute requirement in a hostage situation.

If hostage negotiators are part of a team, they should train together as often as possible.[2] Doing so builds trust and effectiveness within the hostage negotiation team. All training should be evaluated and constant efforts made to improve each team member's performance.

Training for hostage negotiators should be wide ranging, including briefings from the local telephone company on new designs and features of any communications system, as well as training by mental health professionals and clergy members on personality disorders and techniques for communicating with distraught individuals. The department's legal adviser or the county prosecutor should discuss the legal aspects of hostage negotiations and update team members on any changes in the law. Hostage negotiators should also attend critiques of actual incidents.

Goals in Hostage Situations

The officer must strive for three primary informational goals in setting the stage for a successful negotiation. First, the officer must attempt to obtain specific information about the incident so that the department can negotiate with the suspect realistically. The officer should attempt to determine the motivation and intent of the hostage taker through discussions with the suspect. Is the hostage taker mentally ill and suffering from delusions? Is he or she wanted by the police and attempting to use the hostages as leverage? Was he or she caught in the act of committing a crime and is he or she holding the hostages as a reaction to the situation? The answer to why the suspect is holding the hostages allows the officer to react according to the suspect's demands. The negotiator should also obtain as much information as possible about the suspect from outside sources. All this information helps the officer find triggers to the suspect's personality and understand what personal tack to take.

The second goal is to gain as much information as possible from the suspect during the negotiations. The officer should not ask closed-ended questions that the hostage taker can answer with a simple yes or no. A question such as, "We can't get you a million dollars; will you accept five hundred thousand?" can be answered quickly in the positive or negative by the suspect. A question such as, "We will try to get the million. But if we can't get all of it, what else do you want?" requires explanation, however, and engages the suspect in a discussion with the officer. In addition, this type of question adds to the suspect's belief of being in control of the situation and able to dictate the negotiation terms.

The final goal of any communication effort is for the officer to express interest in what the suspect is saying. Although police officers should avoid face-to-face negotiations whenever possible, the situation might arise in which the officer is in close contact with the suspect.[3] The officer will want to obtain as much information as possible about the situation if a chance to meet the suspect arises. The officer must also remain attentive, however. Spoken and unspoken skills come into play in this situation. Maintaining eye contact with the hostage taker instead of looking around and casing the location will give the impression of being sincerely interested in what the suspect is saying. By appearing to be interested in the suspect, the officer will take the first step toward establishing a relationship.

The relationship between the suspect and the officer who negotiates for the release of the hostages is delicate. The officer must appear to be professional and neutral. The suspect will realize that a hostage taker's goals and those of the officer are distinctly different, but may begin to trust the officer if the officer appears willing to enter into a neutral relationship to gain the release of the hostages. The hostage taker understands the officer's objectives and the mission of the police and will, therefore, constantly evaluate the officer's statements and actions during the negotiations. The suspect will not readily believe the officer, but will hesitantly accept the officer's role, because the suspect needs the officer as a means to accomplish goals and to reach an acceptable settlement.

A suspect who believes the officer is lying will not proceed with negotiations. The officer should attempt to maintain credibility by agreeing only to the demands that the suspect could reasonably make. For example, the officer should not agree to give the suspect the Hope diamond. The officer might be able to convince the suspect, however, that several one-carat diamonds could be obtained. Open and credible communication between the officer and the suspect leads to the beginning of a relationship. The officer has taken the first step toward establishing that relationship by being able to rationally discuss alternatives with the suspect.

Time is not of the essence in hostage negotiations. Just the reverse is true—the officer should do everything possible to consume time. From a tactical perspective, the longer the negotiations take, the more likely the suspect will make an error leading to apprehension.

The lapse of time allows the officer to establish a relationship with the hostage taker. One technique is to explain to the suspect that all requests must be cleared by headquarters. This allows for a delay between receiving a request and acting on it. Delaying the negotiation will wear down the suspect. The passage of time requires the suspect to continue watching the hostages, anticipate police responses to demands, and worry about the consequences of these actions. This stress on the hostage taker may allow the officer to negotiate a deal. Delaying tactics can be a two-edged sword, however, because stress may also cause the suspect to act irrationally and harm the hostages. The officer must be able to anticipate the suspect's moods and intentions and react accordingly.

In the best of all possible worlds, the officer should be able to offer the suspect a deal in which the hostage taker perceives that both parties win. A win-win solution is extremely difficult to achieve. Hostage negotiation is simply a bargaining process in which each side has a bottom line. Most negotiations center on moving from stated unrealistic demands to appropriate points of agreement. The negotiator must attempt to steer the suspect's demands away from absolutes to acceptance of certain realistic demands in exchange for other alternatives. For example, in a situation in which a hostage needs medical attention, the negotiator may obtain the release of the hostage in return for a minor concession in another area, such as giving the suspect special food. This bargaining process is part of establishing a relationship between the suspect and the officer. Many negotiators, however, do not believe offering the suspect access to a radio or television is a wise tactical decision. They like to cut suspects off from the outside world and, therefore, make them more dependent on the negotiator. In addition, they believe news media coverage of the situation might impair negotiations.

Normally, the officer is replaced by trained negotiators during the incident. But the officer must be prepared to carry out all the negotiations if no other trained personnel are available, and the officer must be ready to accept the suspect's surrender at any time. If the suspect indicates a desire to surrender, the officer must communicate the procedure in a clear, professional manner that is reassuring to the suspect. If certain concessions or agreements with the suspect were made as part of the surrender, the officer should endeavor to abide by them whenever practical. For example, if the officer agreed to allow the suspect to meet with a representative of the media, this agreement should be honored, if possible. The purpose of honoring such agreements is simple—other potential hostage takers will understand that the police keep their promises in such situations.

Profile of Hostage Negotiation Teams[5]

In February 1992, hostage negotiators and members of special operations teams gathered to exchange information and experiences. Few comprehensive data exist about hostage negotiation activities in the United States. Therefore, members attending the February conference agreed to complete a survey to learn more about the needs of hostage negotiation teams.

The survey was a 44-page questionnaire including specific questions about issues that affect negotiation teams. The survey was based on input from FBI hostage negotiators and was reviewed by these negotiators, as well as other experts, to ensure its accuracy. The survey revealed that few females served on hostage negotiation teams and that the ethnic composition of the teams was primarily white. Most team members were assigned to investigation or patrol, with some in administration. Only 41 percent of those surveyed stated that their department had any written negotiator selection policy. Once selected to serve on a hostage negotiation team, few members received more than ten days of training. Once a team member, the amount of training did not increase. Most team members received fewer than five days of in-service training each year.

The results of this survey point out the importance of effective communication in hostage situations. Many hostage negotiation teams may have little training in crisis

---

GUIDELINES FOR NEGOTIATION[4]

- Stablilize and contain the situation.
- Select the appropriate time to make contact.
- Take your time when negotiating.
- Allow the subject to speak; being a good listener is more important than being a good talker.
- Do not offer the subject anything.
- Be as honest as possible; avoid tricks.
- Never dismiss any request as trivial.
- Never say no.

- Soften the demands.
- Never set a deadline; try not to accept a deadline. If a deadline is set, let it pass without comment if possible.
- Do not make alternative suggestions.
- Do not introduce outsiders (non–law enforcement) into the negotiation process.
- Do not allow any exchange of hostages; especially do not exchange a negotiator for a hostage.
- Avoid negotiating face to face.

Hostage Negotiations   **169**

management; therefore, the ability to communicate with the perpetrator becomes critical. Failure to communicate effectively may have deadly results.

The Critical Incident Negotiation Team

In 1985, the Crisis Management Unit at the FBI Academy established the Critical Incident Negotiation Team (CINT).[6] This team is a small, highly trained, and mobile group of experienced FBI negotiators. The FBI negotiates approximately 45 bank robbery and hijacking hostage incidents each year. The original CINT members were selected from more than 350 FBI agents nationwide on the basis of law enforcement background, personal interviews, psychological testing, and negotiation experience. Twenty-five negotiators were selected. The Crisis Management Unit arranged and coordinated semiannual training seminars for team members.

The FBI deploys CINT negotiators both within and outside U.S. boundaries. Negotiators have been used at Ruby Ridge, Idaho; at Waco, Texas; and in other high-profile, emotionally charged situations. In addition, negotiators have assisted in the release of American hostages held in Ecuador, Chile, El Salvador, and other countries.

CINT negotiators also train international police forces. They meet with police forces from around the world to provide training in crisis management as it pertains to kidnapping and hostage incidents.

Protracted hostage situations require special skill and training. The CINT is one federal agency's response to this demand. Training and consultation may prevent the loss of innocent lives in such a situation.

SUMMARY

Hostage negotiation is one of the most difficult situations any officer will have to face. It involves tact, understanding, and patience. More important, it requires all of the officer's communication skills. Every police officer should be familiar with the communication skills required in hostage negotiations. The officer on patrol may have to begin and carry out such negotiations while waiting for specially trained negotiators to arrive at the scene.

REVIEW QUESTIONS

1. What are the personal characteristics of a good negotiator?
2. Discuss the relationship between the hostage taker and the negotiator.
3. How much training should hostage negotiation teams receive?

PRACTICAL APPLICATIONS

1. Rank the following types of training in order of importance for members of a newly formed hostage negotiation team:

   Lecture on use of force

   Firearms training

Hand-to-hand combat training

Lecture on communication techniques

Lecture on the law of search and seizure

Sensitivity training

Introduction to psychology

2. List the equipment hostage negotiation team members should carry in their car when they are responding to a crisis. Assume they can carry a package no larger than what airlines allow passengers to carry onto a plane.

3. Circle the correctly spelled word in each of the following rows.

tempareture	tamperature	temperature	temperatuer
tranpese	trenspose	tranpose	transpose
traecherous	treacherous	treachous	trecaher
transeint	tranient	tranisent	transient
transquil	transquile	tranquil	tranquile
porngraphic	pronrographic	pronogaphic	pornographic
puntive	punetive	punitive	puniteve
quarantine	quaranetine	quarentive	quaranteve
quareled	quarrele	quarreled	quared
quato	quata	queta	quota

4. Rewrite the following sentences as needed.

a. Having a lot of work to do, he arrived earlier.

_____

b. The criminal left his fingerprints at the scene, this officer found several of them.

_____

_____

c. The defendant appeared in court and he acted nervously.

_____

d. This officer shot the pistol four times and cleaned it.

_____

e. The offender was finally booked and this officer went home.

_____

5. Define and explain the following words or terms.

a. hostage negotiation

_____

b. Critical Incident Negotiation Team

_____

c. Branch Davidian incident

_____

d. prison hostage situation

_____

e. terrorist hostage situation

_____

6. The following paragraph was taken from a police report. Make it a better paragraph.

When I arrived at the location of the victim's home, the victim, Bill Brown stated that he discovered that his television set was stolen from his home. Before leaving he locked all his doors and windows and returned only 20 minutes later. He claimed that person or persons unknown may have entered his home at some time during the last day and that he only missed the television set.

_____

_____

_____

_____

_____

_____

_____

_____

ENDNOTES

1. See G. Dwayne Fuselier and Gary W. Noesner, "Confronting the Terrorist Hostage Taker," *FBI Law Enforcement Bulletin* 59, no. 7 (July 1990): 6.
2. John L. Grey, "Keeping Crisis Negotiations Skills Sharp," *Law and Order* (September 1994): 177.
3. Authorities differ on the issue of negotiating face to face with the hostage taker. One of the FBI guidelines for negotiation listed in the focus box is to avoid negotiating face to face. The International Association of Chiefs of Police, however, in their Training Key Series no. 235 (Alexandria, Va.), indicate that the officer should maintain eye contact when meeting with the suspect.
4. G. Dwayne Fuselier and Gary W. Noesner, "Confronting the Terrorist Hostage Taker," 12–13.
5. Mitchell R. Hammer, Clinton R. Van Zandt, and Randall G. Rogan, "Crisis/Hostage Negotiation Team Profile," *FBI Law Enforcement Bulletin* 63, no. 3 (March 1994): 9.
6. J. M. Botting, F. J. Lanceley, and G. W. Noesner, "The FBI's Critical Incident Negotiation Team," *FBI Law Enforcement Bulletin* 64, no. 4 (April 1995): 12–15.

CHAPTER 13

Law Enforcement Records

LEARNING OBJECTIVES

After reading this chapter, you should understand the following concepts:

■ The objectives for any law enforcement records system

■ The areas within a police department that can be made more effective by using computers

■ The media's position on access to police records

INTRODUCTION

Any decision made in a law enforcement agency is, or should be, based on the evaluation of all available information. Information, or data, is located in several places: an individual's memory, written works, and electronic storage. The law enforcement agency's records division is the primary location for all related information on which police officers base their operational and administrative decisions. All authorities in the field of police report writing agree that an efficient and effective records section is an essential part of the planning and execution of operations.[1]

Law enforcement records systems vary from city to city and serve different purposes depending on the level or responsibility of the agency. Records for a local police department will differ from those maintained by a federal agency. Certain basic principles, however, should remain the same no matter where the agency is located or at what level it operates.

CRIMINAL JUSTICE RECORDS SYSTEMS

Any records system should have certain standard criteria incorporated into its operation. Scholars and authorities in the field recommend the following two standards as a minimum:

1. *Consolidation of all records into one division.* Such consolidation allows for centralization of authority and responsibility within the department. One administrator should be responsible for this division.
2. *Standardization of all records and reporting systems within an agency.* Such standardization provides for ease of administration and ensures the proper reporting of all necessary information.

Adoption of these standards will ensure that a records system is operational.

In addition, any valid police records system should allow the police administrator to carry out certain tasks. Any records system should fulfill the following 14 critical objectives:

1. Allow the police administrator to ascertain the nature and extent of crime within the agency's jurisdiction
2. Provide a means for updating the staffing level of the department
3. Provide a means for controlling the reporting and investigation of crimes
4. Allow police officers to arrest offenders by being able to analyze their modus operandi
5. Allow the police administrator to report and analyze traffic accidents with the objective of working with other city departments to correct dangerous intersections or roads
6. Allow the police to follow up on arrests and the disposition of cases
7. Permit the police administrator to predict trends in crime to maximize the use of law enforcement personnel by properly deploying them to the areas of greatest need

8. Allow the police administrator to detect unusual trends within the department and the community

9. Assist the police administrator in knowing how to assign and promote personnel

10. Provide information for use in criminal investigations

11. Help the police administrator ascertain the level and maintenance of police equipment

12. Allow the police administrator to predict future trends in criminal activity

13. Help the police administrator prepare the department's annual budget

14. Allow the police administrator to provide information to citizens and elected officials about matters of concern

Police records systems must ensure that any communication is clearly understandable. Most operational and administrative communication takes the final form of written documents. Written documents are preferable to oral statements because they allow less chance for misunderstanding if the document is properly drafted. In addition, written reports, orders, or policies allow members of the police force to refer to the document if any question arises concerning its application, effect, or content. Written documents may take many forms.

In some law enforcement agencies, oral statements are combined with written reports. For instance, patrol officers in the St. Louis County Police Department telephone headquarters and orally report to a trained specialist. The information is entered on a preformatted computer system that processes the report electronically.[2]

The mere collection of data or information without subsequent action, however, does not assist a department in carrying out its mission. In the following section, we examine how certain types of police records are processed.

REPORT PROCESSING

Processing police reports in a timely and accurate manner is one of the most important functions of the records division.[3] In this section, we provide a brief overview of using computers to process certain types of reports.

A police department, by its nature, generates numerous reports (Figures 13.1 and 13.2). These reports are normally stored in the records division. Without an efficient system of storage, retrieval, and analysis, any law enforcement agency can be overwhelmed by a sea of paper.

Computerization of certain records can save the department an immense amount of time. Some departments began to use computers in certain sections of their records divisions in the early 1970s. Even if those areas have been modernized within the last ten years, their status should be reviewed by technical experts to ensure that recent advances have not made them obsolete.[4]

Several areas of internal administration within a police department can be computer enhanced with little effort or expense.[5]

Training Records
Individual officer training records are maintained by the department. These records may be entered into a computer and updated with little effort. Many states require periodic

FIGURE 13-1 Vancouver Police Department General Occurrence Report: An Example of a Canadian Reporting Form: The Vancouver Police Department has direct entry into laptop computers. Soon, any police officer in British Columbia will have online access to any report entered into the system. *(Reproduced with permission of Chief Constable Jamie H. Graham, Vancouver Police Department)*

Instructions for Completing the General Occurrence Report (VPD1323A-G)

Effective 2001 Mar 21, this **General Occurrence Report (G.O.) (VPD1323A-G)** will replace the Investigation Report, the Form 19 and the VPD21 (Continuation Report). This report consists of 7 pages (A-G). Although the **G.O.** looks similar, there are some changes in format and additional information required. *Please take your time and read through the form carefully.* If you have any questions about how to complete this report, please call **717-3060** for assistance.

The following will assist you with the new format and information required. For all pages of this General Occurrence Report, either the **Original** or **Supplemental** box (top right corner) must be checked.

VPD1323A-Main (OCCURRENCE INFORMATION)

UCR – leave blank
Target Vehicle – was the vehicle the target of the offence
Violation M.O. – method of violation (this is a Stats. Can. requirement)
Injury - was anyone injured in this event
Property Stolen/Fraud Type/Fraud/Vehicle Count – leave blank

Role - PRIME allows for many role codes, however, the following will be the most commonly used. **There are changes in the meaning and usage of some of these terms so read carefully before selecting.**

Victim	• the subject of the person offence ie, assault, robbery, sexual assault
	• the business subject of a property offence ie, shoplifting, commercial BNE
Complainant	• the complainant is the victim of a property offense
	• ie, R.O. of stolen vehicle, owner of home BNE'd or stolen property.
	• Complainant does not mean the person who called 911
Witness	• anyone with evidence to support the investigation

> *Example:*   Armed Robbery – the bank is the victim and the teller is the victim, all others are witnesses
> Commercial BNE – the business premise is the victim, the business owner is the complainant, and the person who called in the alarm or who saw the suspect in the premise in is the witness.

Ethnicity - This field is mandatory. Use one of the following:
Aboriginal, Asian, Caucasian/White, Central American, East Indian, Negroid/Black, Other, South American, Unknown

Victim Offence (shaded boxes) - list the appropriate information as it relates to this particular person
   Level of injury – sustained by victim
   Wpn causing injury – handgun, knife, bodily force, etc.
   Rel of Acc – relationship of the accused to the victim
   Residence – was the person a resident of Canada at the time of the offence
   Officer – leave blank

VPD1323C-BNEMO (MODUS OPERANDI – BREAK AND ENTER)

This page is to be completed for every break and enter investigation. The number in brackets indicates how many entries can be made in that category.

Solvability factors - This is to be completed for all investigations.

VPD1323D-PersonMO (MODUS OPERANDI – PERSON OFFENCES)

This page is to be completed when investigating an incident involving violence towards an individual ie, assault, robbery, sexual assault, etc. The number in brackets indicates how many selections can be made in that category.

** PLEASE NOTE THAT THERE ARE TWO SUSPECT PAGES **
** ONE FOR KNOWN SUSPECT AND ONE FOR UNKNOWN SUSPECT **

VPD1323E-Suspect (SUSPECT INFORMATION)

Enter all pertinent description information. The number in brackets indicates how many entries can be made in that category.

VPD1323F-UnknownSuspect (UNKNOWN PERSON)

This is to be completed when the identity of the suspect in your investigation is not known. The number in brackets indicates how many entries can be made in that category.

VPD1323G-Text (TEXT PAGE)

A synopsis text page is mandatory for all General Occurrence reports.
The synopsis must be no more than 5 sentences in length.
A separate text page is required for each text type including property reports.

FIGURE 13-1 *(continued)*

VPD1323A-MAIN
(01/03)

VANCOUVER POLICE DEPARTMENT

GENERAL OCCURRENCE REPORT

☐ Original
☐ Supplemental

INTERNAL STATUS

OPEN

CLOSE

CJJS STATUS

Main

General Occurrence (G.O)

PAGE   OF

SECTION 1 - OCCURRENCE INFORMATION

LOCATION	LOCATION (Premise/Place of attack)	DATE OF OCCURRENCE	TIME
		FROM: ___/___/___ YY MM DD	
		TO: ___/___/___ YY MM DD	

INCIDENT OFFENCE TYPE	UCR	DATE REPORT TAKEN: ___/___/___ YY MM DD

STATISTICAL DATA

OCCUPANCY	TARGET VEHICLE	VIOLATION MO	WEAPON		INJURY
1. Joint	'Y' or Blank	1. Shoplifting	**Type**	**Status**	1. No Injury
2. Occupied by Vic		2. Purse Snatch	List Most Serious Weapon	0 - Unknown	2. Minor Injury
3. Occ by Acc		3. Pick Pocket		1 - Real	3. Major Injury
4. Occ by Vic, Acc maybe		4. Forced Entry		2 - Facsimile	4. Death
5. Not by Vic, Acc unknown		5. Unforced Entry			0. Unknown
6. Neither Vic or Acc					

PROPERTY STOLEN	FRAUD TYPE (Describe type: cheque, credit cards, etc, ..)	FRAUD/VEHICLE COUNT

ROLE	SURNAME	G1	G2	ETHNICITY	SEX	D.O.B. ___/___/___ YY MM DD	APPROX AGE

	ADDRESS			CITY	PROVINCE	POSTAL CODE

	HOME PHONE ( )	BUSIINESS PHONE ( )	EXTENSION	S.I.N. #	DL #	POI

VIC OFF	DRUG ☐ ALC. ☐	LEVEL OF INJURY	WPN CAUSING INJ	REL OF ACC	RESIDENCE	OFFICER	PLATE # OF VEHICLE INVOLVED

ROLE	SURNAME	G1	G2	ETHNICITY	SEX	D.O.B. ___/___/___ YY MM DD	APPROX AGE

	ADDRESS			CITY	PROVINCE	POSTAL CODE

	HOME PHONE ( )	BUSIINESS PHONE ( )	EXTENSION	S.I.N. #	DL #	POI

VIC OFF	DRUG ☐ ALC. ☐ ALC. ☐	LEVEL OF INJURY	WPN CAUSING INJ	REL OF ACC	RESIDENCE	OFFICER	PLATE # OF VEHICLE INVOLVED

SUDDEN DEATH

FOUND BY	LAST SEEN BY	DATE/TIME ___/___/___ YY MM DD HH:MM

IDENTIFIED BY	DATE/TIME	DATE/TIME OF DEATH	TYPE OF DEATH
			1. HOMICIDE 3. SUICIDE 5. UNDETERMINED
			2. ACCIDENT 4. NATURAL 6. OVERDOSE

ALC/DRUGS Y - YES N - NO	PRONOUNCED DEAD BY	DATE/TIME	CORONER INVOLVED (NAME AND PHONE #)

BODY REMOVED TO/BY	NEXT OF KIN (NAME, ADDRESS/PHONE #)

REPORTING OFFICER

1. NAME	2. RANK PIN	TEAM/SQ	3. ACCOMPANIED BY	4. RANK PIN	DATE:

COPIES TO
| 1 | 2 | 3 | 4 | 5 | 6 | 7 | 8 | 9 |

QUALITY CONTROL

DATA ENTRY

FIGURE 13-1 (continued)

VPD1323B-Entities
(01/03)

VANCOUVER POLICE DEPARTMENT
GENERAL OCCURRENCE REPORT
Entities

☐ Original
☐ Supplemental

General Occurrence (G.O) _____

PAGE _____ OF _____

ROLE CONTINUATION PAGE

ROLE	SURNAME	G1	G2	ETHNICITY	SEX	D.O.B. YY / MM / DD	APPROX AGE
	ADDRESS				CITY	PROVINCE	POSTAL CODE
	HOME PHONE ( )	BUSINESS PHONE ( )	EXTENSION	S.I.N. #	DL #	POI	
VIC OFF	DRUG ☐ ALC. ☐	LEVEL OF INJURY	WPN CAUSING INJ	REL TO ACC	RESIDENCE	OFFICER	PLATE # OF VEHICLE INVOLVED

ROLE	SURNAME	G1	G2	ETHNICITY	SEX	D.O.B. YY / MM / DD	APPROX AGE
	ADDRESS				CITY	PROVINCE	POSTAL CODE
	HOME PHONE ( )	BUSINESS PHONE ( )	EXTENSION	S.I.N. #	DL #	POI	
VIC OFF	DRUG ☐ ALC. ☐	LEVEL OF INJURY	WPN CAUSING INJ	REL TO ACC	RESIDENCE	OFFICER	PLATE # OF VEHICLE INVOLVED

ROLE	SURNAME	G1	G2	ETHNICITY	SEX	D.O.B. YY / MM / DD	APPROX AGE
	ADDRESS				CITY	PROVINCE	POSTAL CODE
	HOME PHONE ( )	BUSINESS PHONE ( )	EXTENSION	S.I.N. #	DL #	POI	
VIC OFF	DRUG ☐ ALC. ☐	LEVEL OF INJURY	WPN CAUSING INJ	REL TO ACC	RESIDENCE	OFFICER	PLATE # OF VEHICLE INVOLVED

ROLE	SURNAME	G1	G2	ETHNICITY	SEX	D.O.B. YY / MM / DD	APPROX AGE
VIC REP COMP	ADDRESS				CITY	PROVINCE	POSTAL CODE
	HOME PHONE ( )	BUSINESS PHONE ( )	EXTENSION	S.I.N. #	DL #	POI	
VIC OFF	DRUG ☐ ALC. ☐	LEVEL OF INJURY	WPN CAUSING INJ	REL TO ACC	RESIDENCE	OFFICER	PLATE # OF VEHICLE INVOLVED

ROLE	SURNAME	G1	G2	ETHNICITY	SEX	D.O.B. YY / MM / DD	APPROX AGE
	ADDRESS				CITY	PROVINCE	POSTAL CODE
	HOME PHONE ( )	BUSINESS PHONE ( )	EXTENSION	S.I.N. #	DL #	POI	
VIC OFF	DRUG ☐ ALC. ☐	LEVEL OF INJURY	WPN CAUSING INJ	REL TO ACC	RESIDENCE	OFFICER	PLATE # OF VEHICLE INVOLVED

ROLE	SURNAME	G1	G2	ETHNICITY	SEX	D.O.B. YY / MM / DD	APPROX AGE
	ADDRESS				CITY	PROVINCE	POSTAL CODE
	HOME PHONE ( )	BUSINESS PHONE ( )	EXTENSION	S.I.N. #	DL #	POI	
VIC OFF	DRUG ☐ ALC. ☐	LEVEL OF INJURY	WPN CAUSING INJ	REL TO ACC	RESIDENCE	OFFICER	PLATE # OF VEHICLE INVOLVED

REPORTING OFFICER

1. NAME	2. RANK PIN	TEAM/SQ	3. ACCOMPANIED BY	4. RANK PIN	DATE:

FIGURE 13-1 (continued)

VPD1323C-BNEMO
(01/03)

VANCOUVER POLICE DEPARTMENT
GENERAL OCCURRENCE REPORT
BNE MO

☐ Original
☐ Supplemental

General Occurrence (G.O)

PAGE ____ OF ____

MODUS OPERANDI - BREAK & ENTER (GO/DETAILS/IR (RESOLVE) OR IC (CON BNE)

1. WAY IN (1)
☐ D. DOOR
☐ W. WINDOW
☐ X. OTHER:_____
☐ Y. UNKNOWN

2. TARGET AREAS (5)
☐ B. ATTIC
☐ C. BASEMENT
☐ D. BEDROOM
☐ E. DEN/FAMILY ROOM
☐ F. BATHROOM
☐ G. GARAGE/CARPORT
☐ H. KITCHEN
☐ I. LIVING ROOM
☐ J. STORAGE AREA/LOCKERS
☐ K. RESIDENTIAL-OTHER
☐ L. BUSINESS TILL
☐ M. DISPLAY ITEMS
☐ N. SAFE BOX
☐ O. SECURE PARKING
☐ P. VENDING MACHINE
☐ Q. NON-RESIDENTIAL-OTHER

3. ACTION TAKEN (5)
☐ A. TURNED LIGHT OFF
☐ B. DEFACATED
☐ C. FAMILIAR W/PREMISE
☐ D. SET FIRE
☐ E. DEFEATED ALARM
☐ F. URINATED
☐ G. CANDLES/MATCHES
☐ H. FACILITIES/ATE
☐ I. USED FLASHLIGHT
☐ J. VANDALIZED
☐ K. WIPED PRINTS
☐ X. OTHER:_____
☐ Y. UNKNOWN

4. TYPE SECURITY (4)
☐ A. AUDIBLE ALARM
☐ B. SILENT ALARM
☐ C. BARS/GRATES
☐ D. DOG
☐ E. EXTERIOR LIGHTS
☐ F. GUARD/WATCHMAN
☐ G. INTERIOR LIGHTS
☐ H. LOCKED DOORS
☐ I. LOCKED WINDOWS
☐ J. NEIGHBOURHOOD WATCH
☐ K. OPERATION ID
☐ L. PHOTO CAMERA
☐ M. SECURITY FORCE
☐ N. FENCE
☐ X. OTHER:_____
☐ Y. UNKNOWN

5. WHY FOILED (3)
☐ A. ALARM TRIGGERED
☐ B. ALARM BYPASS/DEFEATED
☐ C. FAILED TO OPERATE
☐ D. INOPERATIVE AT TIME
☐ E. ENTRY UNPROTECTED
☐ F. BARS CUT
☐ G. CRAWLED BETWEEN
☐ X. OTHER:_____
☐ Y. UNKNOWN

6. TOOLS USED (3)
☐ A. VEHICLE
☐ B. BOLT/WIRE CUTTERS
☐ C. GRIPPING TOOL
☐ D. CHISEL
☐ E. DRILL
☐ F. GAS TORCH
☐ G. KEY
☐ H. LOCK PICK
☐ I. PRY BAR
☐ J. ROPE/CORD
☐ K. SCREWDRIVER
☐ L. SLAM HAMMER
☐ M. CHOPPING TOOL
☐ X. OTHER:_____
☐ Y. UNKNOWN

7. POINT OF EXIT (1)
☐ A. INTERIOR CONNECTING
☐ B. SAME AS P.O.E.
☐ C. GROUND
☐ D. UPPER
☐ E. FRONT
☐ F. GARAGE
☐ G. REAR
☐ I. A/C OPENING DUCT
☐ J. DOOR
☐ K. DOOR SLIDING GLASS
☐ L. FLOOR
☐ M. ROOF
☐ N. SKYLIGHT
☐ P. WALL
☐ Q. WINDOW
☐ S. OVERHEAD RETRACTABLE DOOR
☐ X. OTHER:_____

PROPERTY TAKEN (SUMMARIZE)

REMARKS

SOLVABILITY FACTORS (answer Y "yes" or N "no")

ARREST ____ SUSPECT ____ DESCRIPTION ____ LOCATABLE ____ VEHICLE ____ PLATE ____ WITNESS ____ MO ____

PHOTO ____ EVIDENCE ____ PROPERTY ____ SCENE ____ STATEMENTS ____ AREA ____ PROCEED ____ ACCOMPLICE ____

FIGURE 13-1   *(continued)*

VPD1323D-PersonMO
(01/03)

VANCOUVER POLICE DEPARTMENT
GENERAL OCCURRENCE REPORT
Person MO   General Occurrence (G.O)

☐ Original
☐ Supplemental

PAGE _____   OF _____

MODUS OPERANDI - PERSON OFFENCES   [PERSONS/DETAIL/PM]

RELATED PERSON: ROLE _____

ACTION (1)	VICTIM/ACTIVITY (3)	TYPE SECURITY (4)	ENTRY METHOD (5)
☐ A. ASSAULT	☐ B. ABOUT TO ENTER HOME	☐ A. AUDIBLE ALARM	☐ B. ADMITTED IN
☐ C. AGAINST CHILDREN	☐ C. ABOUT TO ENTER VEHICLE	☐ B. SILENT ALARM	☐ C. ATTEMPTED ONLY
☐ E. EXTORTION	☐ E. AT HOME - ASLEEP	☐ C. BARS/GATES	☐ D. FORCED ENTRY
☐ H. HARASSMENT/STALKING	☐ F. AT HOME - AWAKE	☐ D. DOG	☐ G. CUT
☐ K. ABDUCTION	☐ G. AT SCHOOL	☐ E. EXTERIOR LIGHTS	☐ H. KICKED/BROKEN OPEN
☐ M. MURDER	☐ H. AT WORK	☐ G. INTERIOR LIGHTS	
☐ R. ROBBERY	☐ I. DRIVING	☐ H. LOCKED DOORS	☐ I. LIFTED OFF TRACK
☐ S. SEXUAL	☐ Q. OPEN/CLOSE BUSINESS	☐ I. LOCKED WINDOWS	
☐ T. THREATENING	☐ R. OUT OF TOWN	☐ L. PHOTO CAMERA	☐ M. UNLOCKED/PICKED
☐ X. OTHER:	☐ S. SHOPPING	☐ X. OTHER:	☐ Q. LEFT OPEN
	☐ T. USING/LEAVING ATM		☐ S. PREVIOUSLY BROKEN
	☐ V. USE PUBLIC WASHROOM		☐ X. OTHER:
	☐ W. WAITING FOR BUS		
	☐ X. OTHER:		

TARGET AREA (5)	POINT OF EXIT (3)
☐ C. BASEMENT	☐ B. SAME AS P.O.E.
☐ D. BEDROOM	☐ C. GROUND
☐ E. DEN - FAMILY ROOM	☐ D. UPPER
☐ G. GARAGE/CARPORT	☐ E. FRONT
☐ H. KITCHEN	☐ F. GARAGE
☐ I. LIVING ROOM	☐ G. REAR
☐ J. STORAGE AREA/LOCKERS	☐ J. DOOR
☐ L. BUSINESS TILL	☐ K. SLIDING GLASS DOOR
☐ N. SAFE BOX	☐ N. SKYLIGHT
☐ O. SECURE PARKING	☐ X. OTHER:
☐ X. OTHER:	

RELATIONSHIP OF ACCUSED (Linkage of Accused)

☐ 0-UNKNOWN	☐ 8-BOYFRIEND/GIRLFRIEND
☐ 1-SPOUSE	☐ 9-EXBOYFRIEND/EXGIRLFRIEND
☐ 2-SEPERATED/DIVORCED	☐ 10-FRIEND
☐ 3-PARENT/GUARDIAN	☐ 11-BUSINESS RELATIONSHIP
☐ 4-CHILD	☐ 12-CRIMINAL RELATIONSHIP
☐ 5-OTH IMMEDIATE FAMILY	☐ 13-CASUAL AQUAINTANCE
☐ 6-EXTENDED FAMILY	☐ 14-STRANGER
☐ 7-AUTHORITY FIGURE	

RESIDENCE

VICTIM / ACCUSED COHABITATING -   Y OR N   (CIRCLE ONE)

SUSPECT

1. ACTIONS BEFORE (4)	2. VEHICLE ACTS (3)	3. IMPERSONATED (1)	4. APPAREL (5)
☐ B. ANSWERED AD	☐ C. CAUSED/FAKED ACCIDENT	☐ A. FUNDRAISER	☐ A. BALACLAVA
☐ D. FOLLOWED IN VEH	☐ E. FLAGGED DOWN VICTIM	☐ B. CUSTOMER/CLIENT	☐ B. CAP/HAT
☐ E. FOLLOWED ON FOOT	☐ F. FORCED VICTIM INTO VEH	☐ C. DELIVERY PERSON	☐ C. BANDANA
☐ G. PRESENT AT BUS STOP	☐ I. USED A CRIME VEHICLE	☐ D. DISABLED MOTORIST	☐ D. COAT/JACKET
☐ H. USED DRUGS/ALCOHOL	☐ X. OTHER:	☐ H. ILL/INJURED	☐ E. EARRINGS
☐ M. ASKED FOR AID		☐ I. POLICE OFFICER	☐ F. GLOVE(S)
☐ O. OFFERED CNDY/FD ETC.		☐ L. RENTER	☐ G. CHARACTER MASK
☐ R. REQUEST WSHRM/PHN		☐ M. REPAIRMAN	☐ H. STOCKING MASK
☐ OTHER:		☐ O. SEEKING SOMEONE	☐ I. WIG/TOUPEE
		☐ X. OTHER:	☐ X. OTHER:

5. ACTION DURING (8)	6. MADE (4)	7. DEMANDED (3)	8. DEMEANOR (1)
☐ C. BLIND FOLDED VICTIM	☐ A. DRIVE	☐ B. DRUGS	☐ B. APOLOGETIC/POLITE
☐ D. DEFEATED ALARM	☐ B. CONSUME LIQUOR/DRUG	☐ C. JEWELLERY	☐ C. VIOLENT/BRUTAL
☐ E. DEFECATED	☐ C. LIE ON FLOOR	☐ D. JUST BILLS	☐ D. CALM
☐ F. DISABLED PHONE	☐ D. OPEN REGISTER	☐ E. SEX	☐ E. NERVOUS/EXCITED
☐ G. FAMILIAR W/PREMISE	☐ E. OPEN SAFE	☐ X. OTHER:	☐ F. PROFESSIONAL/PLANNED
☐ H. GAGGED VICTIM	☐ F. PUT MONEY IN BAG		☐ X. OTHER:
☐ I. JUMPED COUNTER	☐ H. REMOVE CLOTHES		☐ Y. UNKNOWN
☐ J. LOCKED VIC IN ROOM	☐ I. TURN AROUND/NOT LOOK		
☐ K. LOCKED VIC IN TRUNK	☐ X. OTHER:		
☐ L. PROSTITUTION INVLD			
☐ M. RANSACKED			
☐ O. RESTRAINED/TIED VIC			
☐ U. URINATED			
☐ W. USED DEMAND NOTE			
☐ 2. WIPED PRINTS			
☐ 3. COVERED PEEP HOLE			
☐ 4. USED FACILITIES/ATE			
☐ X. OTHER:			

SOLVABILITY FACTORS (ANSWER Y "YES" OR N "NO")

ARREST ____	SUSPECT ____	DESCRIPTION ____	LOCATABLE ____	VEHICLE ____
PLATE ____	WITNESS ____	MO ____	PHOTO ____	EVIDENCE ____
PROPERTY ____	SCENE ____	STATEMENTS ____	AREA ____	PROCEED ____
ACCOMPLICE ____				

FIGURE 13-1 *(continued)*

VPD1323E-Suspect
(01/03)

VANCOUVER POLICE DEPARTMENT
GENERAL OCCURRENCE REPORT
Suspect

☐ Original
☐ Supplemental

General Occurrence (G.O) [   ]

PAGE _____ OF _____

SUSPECT

NAME (SNME, G1, G2) OR BUSINESS NAME

ALIAS | HEIGHT | WEIGHT

ETHNICITY | SEX | DOB/AGE | ADDRESS | CITY | PROVINCE | POSTAL CODE

HOME PHONE | BUSINESS PHONE | SIN # | PLACE OF BIRTH | **CAUTION**
(___) ____ - ____ | (___) ____ - ____ EXT. ____ | | | SEE BELOW

EMPLOYER | ADDRESS

OCCUPATION | DL # | POI

VEHICLE

LICENCE: PLATE _____ PROV _____ YEAR _____ PLATE TYPE _____

VEHICLE: VIN _____ TYPE _____ YEAR _____

MAKE _____ MODEL _____ STYLE _____ COLOUR _____

DESCRIPTION:

SUSPECT DESCRIPTION

1. CAUTION (6)
☐ A. ARMED & DANGEROUS
☐ C. CONTAGIOUS DISEASE
☐ E. ESCAPE
☐ M. MENTAL INSTABILITY
☐ S. SUICIDAL TENDENCIES
☐ V. VIOLENT

2. DEPENDENCY (1)
☐ A. PHYSICAL DISABILITY
☐ B. MENTAL DISABILITY-SENILE
☐ C. MEDICAL DEPENDANCY
☐ D. POSSIBLE SUICIDE
☐ E. DRUG/ALCOHOL DEPENDENCY
☐ F. COMBINATION OF ABOVE
☐ G. NONE KNOWN
☐ X. OTHER: _____

3. COMPLEXION (1)
☐ A. DARK
☐ B. LIGHT/FAIR
☐ C. SALLOW
☐ D. RUDDY
☐ E. FRECKLED
☐ G. ACNE
☐ M. MEDIUM
☐ O. OLIVE
☐ X. OTHER: _____

4. BUILD (1)
☐ A. SLIM
☐ B. MEDIUM
☐ C. HEAVY
☐ D. STOCKY
☐ E. ATHLETIC
☐ F. OBESE

5. HAIR COLOUR (5)
☐ A. BLACK
☐ B. BROWN
☐ C. LIGHT BROWN
☐ D. DARK BROWN
☐ E. SANDY
☐ F. BLONDE
☐ G. AUBURN
☐ H. RED
☐ I. DYED
☐ J. BALDING
☐ K. GRAYING
☐ X. OTHER: _____

6. HAIR STYLE (5)
☐ A. CURLY
☐ B. WAVY
☐ C. SHORT
☐ D. LONG
☐ E. DYED
☐ F. PONYTAIL
☐ G. BRUSH CUT
☐ H. TOUPEE/WIG
☐ X. OTHER: _____

7. FACIAL HAIR (4)
☐ A. MOUSTACHE
☐ B. FULL BEARD
☐ C. PARTIAL BEARD
☐ D. GOATEE
☐ E. SIDEBURNS
☐ F. MUTTON CHOPS
☐ X. OTHER: _____

8 EYE COLOUR (2)
☐ A. BLUE
☐ B. GREY
☐ C. HAZEL
☐ D. GREEN
☐ E. BLACK
☐ F. BROWN
☐ X. OTHER: _____

9. GANG (1)

SUSPECT

SUSPECT WORE

FIGURE 13-1 *(continued)*

VPD1323F-UnknownSuspect
(01/03)

VANCOUVER POLICE DEPARTMENT
GENERAL OCCURRENCE REPORT
Unknown Suspect

☐ Original
☐ Supplemental

General Occurrence (G.O) [_____]

PAGE ____ OF ____

UNKNOWN PERSON (Entities/Add/Person)

ROLE

SEX | ETHNICITY | LANGUAGE | HEIGHT | WEIGHT | AGE RANGE

1. COMPLEXION (1)
☐ A. FAIR
☐ B. MEDIUM
☐ C. RUDDY
☐ D. DARK
☐ E. FRECKLED
☐ F. POCK MARKED
☐ G. ACNE
☐ X. OTHER____

2. BUILD (1)
☐ A. SLIM
☐ B. MEDIUM
☐ C. HEAVY
☐ D. STOCKY
☐ E. ATHLETIC
☐ F. OBESE
☐ X. OTHER____

3. HAIR COLOUR (5)
☐ A. BLACK   ☐ G. AUBURN
☐ B. BROWN   ☐ H. RED
☐ C. LIGHT BROWN ☐ I. DYED
☐ D. DARK BROWN ☐ J. BALD
☐ E. SANDY   ☐ K. GRAYING
☐ F. BLONDE   ☐ X. OTHER:

4. HAIR STYLE (5)
☐ A. CURLY
☐ B. WAVY
☐ C. SHORT
☐ D. LONG
☐ E. DYED
☐ F. PONYTAIL
☐ G. BRUSH CUT
☐ H. TOUPEE/WIG
☐ X. OTHER:____

5. FACIAL HAIR (4)
☐ A. MOUSTACHE
☐ B. FULL BEARD
☐ C. PARTIAL BEARD
☐ D. GOATEE
☐ E. SIDE BURNS
☐ F. MUTTON CHOPS
☐ X. OTHER____

6. EYE COLOUR (2)
☐ A. BLUE
☐ B. GREY
☐ C. HAZEL
☐ D. GREEN
☐ E. BLACK
☐ F. BROWN
☐ X. OTHER:____

7. SCARS/TATOOS (Describe)

8. SPEECH (4)
☐ A. STUTTER
☐ B. RAPID
☐ C. LISP
☐ D. DUMB
☐ E. SMOOTH
☐ F. WELL-SPOKEN
☐ G. ACCENT
☐ H. FOREIGN LANGUAGE
☐ S. SLURRED
☐ X. OTHER:____

POSSIBLE NAMES

REMARKS

SUSPECT WORE

FIGURE 13-1 *(continued)*

VPD1323G-Text
(01/03)

VANCOUVER POLICE DEPARTMENT
GENERAL OCCURRENCE REPORT
Text

☐ Original
☐ Supplemental

General Occurrence (G.O)

PAGE _____ OF _____

OCCURRENCE INFORMATION

TYPE OF OCCURRENCE/OFFENCE	TEAM OCC.	SURNAME	GIVEN 1	GIVEN 2

TEXT

TYPE:

☐ SY – SYNOPSIS (maximum of 5 sentences)

☐ PR – PROPERTY REPORT

☐ OR - OCCURRENCE REPORT (NARRATIVE)

☐ VS - VICTIM STATEMENT

☐ WS - WITNESS STATEMENT

☐ AS - ACCUSED/SUSPECT STATEMENT

☐ PW - POLICE WITNESS – EVIDENCE OF _____ PIN _____

MEMBER INFORMATION

INVESTIGATOR	RANK	PIN	TM/SQD	ACCOMPANIED BY	RANK	PIN

FIGURE 13-2 Arizona Department of Public Safety Traffic Accident Report: An Example of a Large Agency's Reporting Form *(Courtesy of Director Dennis Garrett, Director of Public Safety, State of Arizona)*

ARIZONA DEPARTMENT OF PUBLIC SAFETY
CRIMINAL SUPPLEMENT TO TRAFFIC ACCIDENT INVESTIGATION

1. DR. NO.

2. DATE & TIME OCCURRED	3. LOCATION OF OCCURRENCE	4. TYPE OF OFFENSE/INCIDENT	5. COUNTY

6.   DUI ☐   HIT & RUN ☐   AGGRAVATED ASSAULT ☐   ENDANGERMENT ☐   HOMICIDE ☐   7. B A

SUSPECT

8. NAME				9. ADDRESS						
10. BUSINESS ADDRESS			11. OCCUPATION		12. SEX	13. RACE	14. WGT.	15. HGT.	16. EYES	17. HAIR
18. SOCIAL SECURITY NUMBER		19. DRIVERS LICENSE NUMBER		20. PLACE OF BIRTH				21. DATE OF BIRTH		
22. HOME PHONE		23. BUSINESS PHONE		24. ALIAS, MARKS SCARS, TATOOS, ETC.						
25. LOCATION OF ARREST				26. DATE AND TIME OF ARREST		27. LOC. BOOKED OR REF.		28. CITATION NO.(S)		

VEHICLE

29. SUSPECT	30. COLOR	31. YEAR	32. MAKE	33. BODY STY.	34. LIC. NO.	35. STATE	36. OTHER ID.	37. VEHICLE DISPOSITION
38. VICTIM	39. COLOR	40. YEAR	41. MAKE	42. BODY STY.	43. LIC. NO.	44. STATE	45. OTHER DI.	46. VEHICLE DISPOSITION

VICTIM

47. NAME				48. ADDRESS						
49. BUSINESS ADDRESS			50. OCCUPATION		51. SEX	52. RACE	53. WGT.	54. HGT.	55. EYES	56. HAIR
57. SOCIAL SECURITY NUMBER		58. DRIVERS LICENSE NUMBER		59. PLACE OF BIRTH				60. DATE OF BIRTH		
61. OTHER							62. HOME PHONE		63. BUSINESS PHONE	

64. LIST ALL OTHER SUSPECTS/WITNESSES/INVESTIGATIVE LEADS/EVIDENCE

65.	66. OFFICER(S)		I.D.	DISTRICT	67. REVIEWED BY:
☐ PENDING					68. DATE & TIME TYPED
☐ CLOSED BY ARREST					
☐ CLOSED, OTHER					69. CLERK NO.

DISTRIBUTION: WHITE: DEPT. RECORDS;   YELLOW: PROSECUTOR;   PINK: WORK COPY

802-04059 10/91

training for all officers or advanced training for officers when a certain number of years has elapsed after initial training. Computerized training records offer the department the ability to track the level and amount of training administered to each officer.

Personnel Records

Personnel records, like training records, require a large amount of time to maintain and update. By entering these records into a computer, the department can quickly update and cross-reference them to other files, such as training records.

Scheduling of Personnel

Scheduling was formerly a cumbersome task that had to be redone every time a change was made. Computers allow a department to insert personnel changes and modify scheduled hours with minimal effort. Numerous factors that go into scheduling a 24-hour-a-day patrol can be entered into a computer to assist in determination of the schedule.

Community Relations

The area of community relations is gaining more importance in police work. A computer may assist the department by allowing users to update speaking schedules and to maintain lists of community associations and citizens who work with the department to solve community issues.

Vehicle Maintenance

The ability to track vehicle maintenance schedules and repair costs is becoming more important in this era of tightening municipal and federal budgets. Tracking routine vehicle maintenance schedules and identifying the cost of upkeep is simplified with readily available software. Computerized systems allow immediate costing out of vehicle maintenance.

Purchasing

The ability to keep track of items purchased by the department is closely related to the next area—budgeting. Purchasing and inventory control of such items as agency-supplied uniforms, paper, pencils, and so forth is a task requiring attention to detail and subject to multiple accounting mistakes. Computers provide a method for updating constantly changing inventories and cross-checking figures.

Budgeting

Budgeting is becoming a most critical area for every law enforcement agency. The need to project expenses (and in some cases revenues) accurately is an ideal requirement for software spreadsheet programs. Even if the department relies on the city finance or treasury department for final figures, many administrators feel the need to have their own in-house method. A typical spreadsheet program costs $100 to $500 and is well worth the investment.

Payroll

Closely related to budgeting is preparation of the departmental payroll. In many departments, this service is carried out by a centralized office outside the agency. Typically, the finance or treasury department will prepare payrolls. Similar to using and preparing budgets, tracking payroll records to include sick time used, vacation taken, and other information of interest to administrators that typically appears only on paystubs may be desirable.

A computerized records system alone does not automatically ensure a more efficient records division. Computers do not think for humans. They process information that has been entered into the software program. Therefore, an effective records-processing system must be used in addition to putting information into computers. Many varieties of records processing exist within a police department. No matter what form or name they take, these records-processing systems should include the ability to cross-reference all criminal activities. Cross-referencing or cross-indexing criminal records requires that certain key information be indexed with other information so that anyone searching the database will find all other pertinent facts.

All crime indexing should include the following information:

1. The full name of the victim or complaining party
2. The full name of the person arrested or suspected of committing the offense
3. The name of the officer who took the offense report
4. The investigating officer's name
5. The full names of all witnesses
6. The crime classification

Cross-indexing of crimes is critical to properly using the *modus operandi concept*. Briefly stated, *modus operandi (MO)* is the method of operation. Certain people commit similar crimes using the same method each time, which leaves a "fingerprint" that assists the department in determining how many crimes have been committed by the same person and in some instances may lead to the criminal's capture. For example, a pattern or method of operation may be established showing that a rapist attacks young women and wears a stocking mask during the assault. In addition, he may utter the same words to each victim at the same time during the rape. This pattern becomes his MO. Even though some of the victims cannot identify his face, this MO may be sufficient for his arrest and conviction for all the rapes he committed using this method.

Whenever the department cross-indexes crimes according to MO, the method of operation should be further divided into the following seven areas:

1. Location—where the crime was committed
2. Person or property attacked
3. Time of the attack
4. How the attack was carried out
5. Method of attack
6. Object of the attack
7. Any special characteristics

Every crime should be indexed. Once the information is input, the computer can analyze the data and produce variations that may assist in the offender's capture.

Report processing is more than simply filling out forms correctly. It involves indexing the information and using computers to assist in the detection of criminal activity.

CONFIDENTIALITY OF RECORDS

The final aspect of law enforcement records that should be examined is the issue of confidentiality of police records. Many states have freedom-of-information laws that require all public records to be open for inspection by members of the public. Most of these statutes, however, set forth certain exceptions. Police records have traditionally been exempt from disclosure because if anyone could view investigative files, ongoing criminal investigations might be compromised.

Another area that causes friction between law enforcement officers and the media concerns the confidentiality of information about juveniles accused of committing crimes. Juvenile proceedings, as well as all the facts surrounding these cases, are confidential. This protection is established by various state statutes. The rationale behind keeping juveniles' names and criminal acts confidential is that publicizing these incidents could stigmatize the juveniles and possibly prevent rehabilitation. This topic continues to be debated and will undoubtedly continue to generate high public emotion.

The confidentiality of records is an area of high emotion when the department deals with members of the media. The media will argue that the public has a right to know, and that the police department does not have the right to refuse to release information, especially if the case has been referred to the district attorney for filing of criminal charges.

CONFIDENTIALITY AND POLICE INFORMANTS[6]

Informants expose crimes that otherwise may go undetected. When properly used and controlled, they provide information that improves police efficiency, assists in the apprehension and prosecution of criminals, and sometimes even prevents crimes from occurring. To use informants effectively, however, agencies must establish and maintain strict, written departmental policies on handling informants. Even when operating under tight controls, informants can quickly go bad or become unreliable. When they do, they create significant legal and public relations problems.

Only individuals with a *need to know* should be advised of an informant's identity. In practical terms, this means investigators and their alternates who work closely with the source. The squad supervisor or first-line manager should be encouraged to meet the informant so that the source knows people in authority support the program and so that the manager has a general "feel" for the informant. The person who controls the informant file room must also know an informant's identity in order to handle the filing and other paper-

work. These employees should be the only people who routinely handle informant information and who need to know the informant's identity.

As a way to ensure secrecy, informants should be assigned code numbers and code names. These codes replace the source's real name not only on all documents and reports, but also in personal conversations. Any information provided by the source must be documented and recorded with the code numbers and code names.

The files created must be maintained in secure rooms and access to them must be strictly controlled by an employee specifically assigned to control access. Only the informant's handler or alternate handler and the immediate supervisor should be allowed to examine these files routinely. A daily record that lists everyone who enters the secure room should also be maintained. This control is not implemented to create a bureaucratic roadblock, but to protect sources by limiting the number of people who know their identities. Institutionally, it also reinforces the importance of protecting informants' identities.

The department may be concerned that releasing the results of an investigation prior to a conviction may influence members of the public and have an impact on the prosecutor's ability to find an impartial jury. For the most part, this area of the law is controlled by statutes that govern the withholding of information and set forth specific guidelines for the release of police department files.

RULES FOR IMPROVEMENT

Problems with Verbs

Verbs cause more problems than any other part of speech because of the many forms they can take. Following are some of the common rules that are most often broken in crime reports.

Number

Verbs must agree with the subject in number. As a general rule, if the subject refers to a group as a whole, it is singular. If the subject refers to the individual members, it is plural.

> The majority was overruled.
>
> The government was formed.
>
> The audience rose to their feet.

If a verb relates to two or more nouns connected by a coordinate conjunction, the following three rules apply:

1. If it agrees with them conjointly, it takes a plural.
   The officer and her dog were reunited.
   Both the pilot and the copilot were at the controls of the airplane.
2. If the verb agrees with the nouns separately, it takes the number of the noun that stands next to it.
   Neither the suspect nor the victims were located.
   Neither the victims nor the suspect was located.
3. If the verb agrees with one noun and not the other, it takes the number of the one in the affirmative.
   The suspects and not the victim are responsible.
   The suspect and not the victims is responsible.

Certain pronouns—for example, *anybody, everybody, everyone, nobody, somebody, each, either, no one,* and *someone*—take singular verbs.

When singular and plural subjects are joined by constructions (e.g., *both . . . and, either . . . or, not only . . . but*), the verb takes on the number of the subject closest to it.

> Neither the victim nor the suspects were aware of the fire.
>
> Neither the victims nor the suspect was aware of the fire.

A clause or phrase that comes between the subject and the verb should not affect the number of the verb.

> The initial training, not to mention follow-up training, was substantial.

Voice

In Chapter 3, we discussed the use of the active voice and the passive voice. As noted previously, the active voice focuses attention on the doer and the passive voice focuses on what has been done. Your writing will be more forceful and concise if you use the active voice.

Active: Earthquakes have damaged parts of California.

Passive: Parts of the state have been damaged by earthquakes.

Mood

Verbs, like people, have various moods. The mood of a verb enables the verb to express attitudes and intentions.

1. The *indicative mood* is used in most statements and questions. This is the most common mood. It states a fact or asks a question.

   The victim left no writings.

2. The *imperative mood* is used in commands or requests.

   Read the words of Marvin Wolfgang.

3. The *subjunctive mood* is used when the writer is expressing a conditional statement that is dubious, doubtful, or contrary to known facts.

   If the officer were to read the statements, she would find that the facts are different.

SUMMARY

Basic law enforcement records may vary from jurisdiction to jurisdiction, but the principles behind their use will remain the same. Two basic types of reports are used: operational and administrative. Each serves a vital purpose, and to neglect one in favor of the other is to destroy the effectiveness of any records division—and ultimately the agency's operational capability.

Law enforcement, by its nature, involves access to or use of confidential information. Many times, this information is recorded in reports, which may cause a conflict with members of the media who want access to these records. Criminal justice professionals must keep such records confidential, however, if these professionals are to retain their credibility.

REVIEW QUESTIONS

1. What is the most important aspect of a police records system?
2. Should law enforcement agencies use computers and not maintain any paper records? Why? Why not?
3. This chapter contains examples of reports from a large law enforcement agency and an international law enforcement agency (Figures 13.1 and 13.2). What are the differences in the forms? What are the similarities?
4. List some reasons why police records should remain confidential even after the case has been sent to the prosecuting attorney.

PRACTICAL APPLICATIONS

1. Examine how you retain your personal records. Are they organized so that a stranger could find a specific item? How would you change your record-keeping system on the basis of your reading of this chapter?

2. Ask to review your college record. Inquire how it is maintained and updated. In your opinion, is this the most effective record-keeping system? What changes would you recommend?

3. Ask a classmate to describe the appearance of an instructor of another class at your university or college. Write a description of that instructor; however, do not write down the instructor's name. Then ask a different classmate to identify the instructor on the basis of your written report.

4. Circle the correctly spelled word in each of the following rows.

tranfer	trensfer	transfer	tranfere
translator	tranlator	translater	transletor
transfered	tranferred	transfar	transferred
treasuror	traesuror	treasurer	traesurror
trafficking	traficking	trafick	traffick
wounded	wounde	wuonde	woundlie
wather	waether	wheathar	whether
wittness	witness	wetiness	witeness
wristly	wristely	wriste	wrist
widthe	width	wedth	widthi

5. Rewrite the following sentences as needed.
   a. The datum were correct.

   _____

   b. Me and Tom was both correct.

   _____

   c. The accident was observed by me and my partner.

   _____

   d. The mob of looters were working in new city.

   _____

   e. An officer never forgets their first arrest.

   _____

6. Define and explain the following words or terms.
   a. law enforcement records system

   _____

   b. record division functions

   _____

   c. cross-indexing of crimes

   _____

   d. confidentiality of records

   _____

   e. active voice

   _____

7. The following paragraph was taken from a police report. Make it a better paragraph.

At which time, this officer dismounted from his police unit and upon arrival observed a male subject driving a blue car that appeared to be an old model Ford. The subject was hiding his face and refused to dismount from the vehicle. This officer order the subject to get out of the vehicle. The subject acted like he did not hear this officer. I then approached the subject car and noted that the individual had a gun in his hand. This officer immediately called for backup and when the car was surrounded by other police officers the subject threw out his weapon which on furhter examination revealed that the suspected weapon was a toy pistol.

_____

_____

_____

_____

_____

_____

_____

_____

ENDNOTES

1. See, for example, O. W. Wilson's classic work *Police Records: Their Installation and Use* (Chicago: Public Administration Service, 1942), 73–137.
2. Dennis George, "Computer-Assisted Report Entry: Toward a Paperless Police Department," *The Police Chief* 57, no. 3 (March 1990): 46.
3. For an excellent discussion of an effective system, see George J. Schmidt, "Computer System Improves Law Enforcement Operation," *The Police Chief* 61, no. 12 (December 1994): 20.
4. See "Information at Your Fingertips," *Law and Order* (February 1995): 54.
5. See "Focus on Communications," *Law and Order* (February 1995). (Special issue dealing with computers)
6. Source: Adapted from Harry A. Mount, Jr., "Criminal Informants, an Administrator's Dream or Nightmare," *FBI Law Enforcement Bulletin* 59, no. 12 (December 1990): 12.

Index